NOT THE
LIFE OF RILEY

A Deputy Prison Governor's whistle blowing
exposure of incompetence, corruption and
fraud in HM Prison Service and the wider
Criminal Justice System

Julia

The armed forces is just a
starting point in life,
we can all go on to
achieve wonderful things.
We first need to believe!

Michael Riley

M

Not the Life of Riley

Printed edition:
Also available in multiple e-book formats.

Published by:
The Endless Bookcase Ltd
Suite 14 STANTA Business Centre, 3 Soothouse Spring,
St Albans, Hertfordshire, AL3 6PF, UK.
More information can be found at:
www.theendlessbookcase.com

Pictures in Appendix C were taken by Michael Riley or
the author of a weapons board, courtesy of Darrell Dean
Antiques from the collection of Ray Ottenberg and
Margaret Johnson.

ISBN: 978-1-914151-82-8

Cover design: Friends of the author

Recommendations

1. A full review of sentencing guidelines for the Ministry of Justice.
2. Stop improper use of government D-Notices.
3. A separate investigatory body with a term of reference for the prison and probation service linked to the Independent Office for Police Conduct IOPC.
4. Relocate prison and probation service headquarters to the Midlands.
5. Explore A.I. technology to support prisons from headquarters.
6. Abolish area offices and all staff.
7. Invest in infrastructure to build 4 new 'Category B plus' prisons.
8. Reset the clock through diplomatic channels to return foreign national prisoners to their home countries.
9. Foreign nationals sign a contract on entry to the U.K which waives their rights to stay in the country if they break certain laws.
10. Standardise employer's human resource system specific to the recruitment of ex-prisoners in society.
11. Where complaints of corruption, fraud, incompetence, and bullying are raised proper use of policies must be used to investigate them.
12. A direct entry system from the armed forces into key work.

Contents

INTRODUCTION

I came out of the military, in my opinion, as a caring person who did my best to treat people from all sides of a bitter civil war as equals. The bomb and the bullet do not form the basis for winning the hearts and minds of the people. I can see that historically, there has been so much sorrow on all sides, affecting and touching everyone in some way, shape, or form.

I am nothing special as a person. I am what you would deem a council house kid, living in an area where many council house kids came from in the sixties and seventies. You could say there is a single-track road that we all start down at whatever level you are raised in our society. We all walk along it, from birth to death and at certain points in our lives we eventually see a fork in the road and choose which one to take.

Gangs are not a new thing; we had them around us as kids, neighbourhoods that stuck together, but we didn't know that's what they were at such a young age. Nothing seems to have changed much over time, has it? And I do wonder what's happened to people who I grew up with as a child.

I wouldn't say I was particularly gifted at school. Quite often most of us were left to our own devices during lessons, whilst the teacher concentrated on those they thought would do best to justify their teaching career and pay packet.

I suppose you could say we were quite poor, well, from a monetary point of view, but in terms of growing up, I was rich in terms of exploration and being allowed to live as a kid; playing football, exploring down the river, fishing, shooting air rifles, taking off into the countryside with our catapults and catching rabbits to supplement our family's diet.

As I grew up, I wouldn't say my mother was particularly maternal. My father left her when I was six months old, but my grandparents taught me a lot. I know that life started to change as kids just before our teen years. I wanted things like sweets, comics and a new football. We used to have a neighbourhood bobby who walked around our estate keeping an eye out on what was going on, maybe giving out the odd clip around the lughole if we were messing around too much. We started to make choices in life: people I knew as friends were in our gang, and no one outside of our area could join it. In my opinion, gangs have changed a lot over the years. When I was young, we used to run after the other ones who lived close to our patch, and they would do the same to us. It was more of a game back then. Nowadays, there is more malicious intent, where people are dying in different areas around the country, and the only clear driver that I can see for that is criminality in drugs, people trafficking, illegal economy and sweatshop manufacturing. Gangs will always protect their market share.

We always seem to have the same issues with the political parties discussing criminality and from what I can see first and foremost is that we have lost the whole infrastructure of families in place to deal with things effectively. Gangs are all around us, the most obvious being political parties, except they will use the law as their knife to take out other people or parties. Common sense when dealing with issues seems to go out of the window, and everything feels more dictatorial these days through messages that come down from Westminster under the guise of democracy through legislation. There are bloodsuckers on all sides trying to make money from the taxes the majority of people pay. Ultimately, it is those of us lower down the rich pecking order who suffer the worst, and the lower it goes, the worse it impacts people.

I started a paper round when I was nearly eleven years old, delivering newspapers to the local affluent estate near ours seven days a week. My God, it was character building - that's what they called it back then. Delivering the Sunday papers was hard work and the worst day of the week to do it, but I did it come all weathers – rain, sleet and snow.

Back then the cost-of-living prices were high:

A packet of twenty cigarettes cost 26 ½p which, when inflation is adjusted to 2022 prices, equates to approximately £2.50 in today's money (*Retrowow, 2023*). Memory lane prices below.

Prices adjusted with inflation from 1973 to 2022.

These are the prices of some items from 1973:

	1973 price	Inflation adjusted
Gallon of petrol	39p	£3.60
Bottle of whisky (Haig) (Co-op)	£2.45	£23
Bottle of sherry (Harvey's Bristol Cream) (Co-op)	£1.45	£14
Watneys Party 4 (Co-op)	45p	£4.20
Watneys Party 7 (Mac Markets)	78p	£7.30
Pint of beer	18½p	£1.70
20 cigarettes	26½p	£2.50
Pint of milk	5½p	51p
Large loaf of bread	11½p	£1.10
22" Pye colour TV (Currys)	£208.90	£1,900
24" Ferguson black & white TV (Currys)	£61.75	£580
The Daily Mirror newspaper	3p	28p
Average house price	£9,000.00	£84,000

½lb Lurpack Danish butter (Tesco)	10½p	98p
Nescafé 8oz coffee (Tesco)	54p	£5
Can of Coke (Mac Markets)	5½p	51p
Ford Cortina car	£1,075.00	£10,000
Polaris refrigerator (Currys)	£30.95	£290
Hotpoint Supermatic twin tub washing machine (Currys)	£73.36	£680
Bendix Autowasher Deluxe automatic washing machine (Currys)	£106.95	£1,000
Golden Wonder crisps	2½p	23p
One dozen large white eggs	32p	£3
1lb Stork Soft margarine (Tesco)	12½p	£1.20

Yes, I know we are generally all paying more these days, what does that tell you about companies today. Do we have greed inflation now? Prices paid in shops today suggest we do. Perhaps it's all the extra taxes we pay that make costs so high, with successive governments ripping us all off for years.

I used to push a lollypop stick up the out chute of the telephone boxes, first for tanners and thrupenny bits. Then when decimalisation changed our currency in 1971, I used to get ten pence pieces. They were returned coins from people who could not get through on their calls, but they always got stuck in the return chute. I just found a way of freeing them to enhance my pocket money. Back then, charity started at home (and probably still does today with the cost-of-living crisis we are all in).

I think my wage was around £1.20 a week for the paper round. I also tended my stepfather's vegetable patch in our back garden, receiving the princely sum of 50p a week. When I was fourteen, I managed to earn £5 on a milk round that took me from a 5 o'clock morning start until midday on Saturdays. As the dairy was situated near my Nan's house, I was allowed to take some milk, orange juice and six eggs up to her after the round was finished. I would then help her and my grandad with their shopping from Kwik Save. They were frail, and I felt good doing that.

Some of those I grew up with did not look on working as a viable option to buy things. Maybe schools should have values lessons taught in them. They wanted to get things easily. I must admit, it was tempting, but as I was getting older, I thought about where things would head if I followed that path too.

I used to go rabbiting with a lad from the travelling community who had a Jack Russell and ferrets. We used to go along the railway lines, things you probably can't do these days, but back then we took it all in our stride. I used to take a couple of dispatched rabbits home so my mum could roast them. The rest, after I had butchered them, cleaned them out and wrapped them in newspaper, I used to take down to Monkmoor pub to sell for 50p each to the pissed-up dads, who were going home after spending their wages on booze.

MONKMOOR PUBLIC HOUSE, SHREWSBURY

There was nothing around our neighbourhood for someone like me. My older brother joined the military after leaving school and was badged to the Royal Artillery, so when I was sixteen, I trotted off to the local army recruitment centre to take some tests. I was told I had passed them and did well enough to join the Royal Armoured Corps (RAC) as a junior leader.

I'm sure there were lots of agencies around back in the 1970s, but we only ever saw the police, no one else, and they gave the place a sense of law and order! I hear all the time these days that people don't see enough policing taking place in their communities. Everything these days is about spinning select figures to tell the public what they want us to hear. Where I live, we are told by the police and crime commissioner that there is less crime reported and that may be the case. What they fail to tell you is that the

101 number to report things on takes an hour to get through to when reporting non-urgent crime. I would guess that people get so pissed off waiting to get through to report a possible offence that they put the phone down, and even if they do manage to get through, by the time the police turn up to deal with it the perpetrator has long left the scene of the crime! We need a reset in society, not only in the police service but in all the other public sector areas too. People need to step out of their comfort zones and once again be proud of their civic duty to stop communities being taken over by those who want to commit crime and bring things down to their level, destroying many lives in the process.

Intervention is so important and vital for children at a young age and the communities in which we all live. If you don't intervene, you end up with children who don't know which way they are heading in life, and no one's around to make sure they don't progress into committing crimes, which costs us all more in the end.

When you see how much it costs to deal with law and order issues these days, if we primed services upfront when people are young, it could save a lot of money in the long run. Why can't different governments see that? They seem to tinker around the edges of everything except where it affects them or their friends directly, and only then will they throw our public money at it. Only people can vote for new changes, but lots don't, because they see the corruption up above and wonder what the point is. Maybe they just don't see how precious their voice is anymore, to change a two-party system that has bled us all dry over the years. I'm sure one day people will, and then it will make things better for everyone and not just the few.

Everyone I talk to say families have disintegrated; there is no cohesion anymore, we all live in our own silos, making our homes like little fortresses to keep others out. When I was a child, we just walked into our friends' houses and that's the way it was. That doesn't seem to be as common now.

There appears to be something so fundamentally wrong these days in the way society operates, something so big that it's ripping everything and everyone apart at the seams. Families cannot seem to exist without everyone within them of working age having to get involved in the struggle to survive. I certainly feel like a slave to those who are very high up in government and the civil service, many appear to live off the backs of others rather than be there to do what we voted them in for; to protect the interests of our country and the people who live within it.

My advice to politicians and civil servants is:

**"If it is not right do not do it;
if it is not true do not say it."**

Marcus Aurelius

I have included a glossary on page 321 of this memoir that I hope will give a better understanding of prison terminology. I think it is important for those who read this to be able to understand some of the information that may not be clear.

RECRUITMENT & RETENTION

As a serving soldier in Her Majesty's Queen Elizabeth II Army, I was badged to a cavalry regiment, 1st The Queens Dragoon Guards, a Welsh and border counties regiment. I had my first taste of Northern Ireland (NI) in 1980, aged eighteen years old, on a two-year tour of the province, stationed in Omagh, County Tyrone. That experience paved the way for me two and a half years later to train as an Arms Explosives Search (AES) dog handler.

My brilliant and absolutely trusted black Labrador was called Jason, or JC as I affectionately called him, and he was the closest I ever got to a true animal friend. He no doubt saved countless lives in his Army career and protected me from harm; he was an extension of my mind and body. You're such a close-knit team that you end up second guessing what the other may do. When we were on a shout, but specifically route clearances, looking for Improvised Explosive Devices (IEDs), he knew instinctively when I would give him the signal for crossing the road, and he would do it without me giving him any sort of command. Jason joined the Army in Melton Mowbray with the Royal Army Veterinary Corps (RAVC). He came from one of the estates where he was rejected as a retrieving gun dog. I was told Jason came from Sandringham of all places and was one of the Queen Mother's trainee gun dogs.

I was told he was moved on from Sandringham because he hated to enter the water to pick up game, not a good trait for a gun dog! All throughout his training in the Army, he was terrified of it, so I had to carry him over water obstacles as best as I could! He kept me and others alive with his super sensitive nose; our partnership was to last over four years and he was a true close friend.

After spending over six years serving in NI, I felt it was time for me to leave. Sometimes you can invite fate a little too close for comfort in your life. It was 1988, and I was nearing the end of my nine-year contractual service date in the military; it was due to end just before my twenty-seventh birthday in 1989. It was either leave the armed forces or sign up for the full twenty-two years and continue life as a professional soldier. A lot of handlers move on, and back then quite a lot rebadged over to the RAVC. I didn't fancy my chances of survival much in NI given the amount of time left to serve if I signed up for the full twenty-two and stayed in the province.

I have profound memories of Northern Ireland, a lot of good ones, but bad ones too, which included some friends that were killed as part of their duties. Dog handlers are a unique bunch of people, and though the job could be very routine, it was for the most part, very dangerous. I remember a saying that I believe came from a terrorist; "The Irish Republican Army (IRA) only has to get it right once, the British army have to get it right all the time."

In our down time we played hard. 8 Brigade, where I worked, along with other colleagues, meet up every year in Melton Mowbray, where some of us swing the lamp shade about our past trials and tribulations in the province, remembering our colleagues who were murdered. Leicestershire is where all our training took place. We were certainly a band of brothers in the real sense of the word, and I will never ever forget those times with those whom I have served alongside. God bless you all who are still alive, and to the colleagues we lost, rest in peace and party on in heaven. A small group of us paid for a memorial stone to be placed in the National Arboretum in Staffordshire for those killed in the line of duty, those who had paid the ultimate sacrifice for what essentially was a bloody civil war.

I eventually decided the best thing for me to do was sit the entrance exams for the English Prison Service. I travelled down to Belfast along with a friend of mine who was serving in 6 Ulster Defence Regiment (6 UDR) and also a serving dog handler. I passed the relevant parts of the papers they had set for candidates, and I was interviewed the same day by a panel of three; two men and one woman. I can only remember one of the scenario questions they asked me, which was about dealing with inmates who were watching a football match in a television room and who were predominantly black prisoners, and it was getting near to lock up time. Basically, they wanted to watch the end of the game and would not leave the television room until it finished. The question, I assumed was to test the way I approached and dealt with the situation, and because they had mentioned there were more black prisoners in the room than any other type, I thought maybe they had an issue with racism in the English and Welsh prison systems.

I asked them how long the match would overrun after the lock up was called, and I think that highlighting that mostly black prisoners were in the room was in fact a red herring question. They informed me there were ten minutes left until the end of the game. So I said, "Well, I would just report back to the officer in charge of the wing what was happening, but rather than cause a real problem that could arise if I tried to get them out there and then, I would let the match run its course. When it had finished, we could get them back into their cells for lock up and presumably there's some sort of action that could be taken after that." They basically said, "Yes, you can place them on report." I thought to myself, "I'm glad they didn't ask what happens if extra time is announced?" Common sense is something you need a lot of in the prison service, something which is sadly lacking with some of the senior managers.

I returned to my military base, which was at the time, in Derry or Londonderry depending on your own persuasion. The city's name is usually linked to the type of religion supported. Most soldiers I knew called it Derry, and even though I'm not the religious type, it just tripped off the tongue easily. Using the shorter version of the name wasn't an issue for me, but I guess it could be for some of my ex-colleagues.

Any jobs we used to do over the Catholic side, we referred

to as going into the city, or city side. A lot of us at the time didn't have those deep-rooted thoughts about the location, which the people of Northern Ireland had - a place for them that has had so much conflict and destruction in it over the years! We were there to do a job: to protect both sides of some deeply divisive communities from terrorism, whose views were absolute lines drawn in the sand. I hope things don't return to those times of the bomb and the bullet, which also impacted the lives of many others on the mainland, meaning England. We know over the years it became a target as an extension of the troubles, and I would be meeting the Brighton bomber, including one or two of their mates, close up and personal in HMP Whitemoor, some ten years in the future after their device blew up the Grand Hotel in Sussex.

Serving in the armed forces meant I had to rely on a cover man (we didn't have women providing cover in that role back then). Due to the type of work I was undertaking, I always had someone to keep an eye out for any terrorist activity. It didn't matter to me whether that person was black, white, or any other ethnic group; all I needed them to be was good at covering me and help keep me alive, just as I would be helping them stay alive as well as the backup team following us both.

All my concentration was needed to guide JC and to keep him alive! One of the biggest devices, if not the biggest, JC had to search for was an abandoned 800lb IRA culvert bomb. I must admit that one made my ass twitch from the start to the finish of the job. It took around twenty-three hours. There was lighting to help guide my way, and I guess my part took approximately six hours to complete the route clearance up to the device. After that part of the operation, we were then needed for any incident that may crop up which required the support of a dog team. My time was spent watching and guiding JC to see if the places we were searching were safe for everyone following us up the road. Being able to control his movements and make the right decision at the right time, to call him off a suspected Improvised Explosive Device (IED) or any other indications made by him was paramount. The IRA used to set secondary devices to catch out the unwary.

JC was an extension of me, and I was his guide. When everyone else was moving away from a device, we were moving towards it, getting as close as we dared, so a bomb disposal expert can then get on with what they are paid to do, dismantling it to make it safe or blowing it up. The IRA used several different ways to pack bombs up to murder people. This eight hundred pound device was made up of homemade explosives, something called Ammonium Nitrate and Fuel Oil (ANFO). They had packed it into aluminium beer barrels that had detonators wired into them, with a command wire running some distance away up a hill so the charge could be set off by the terrorist. The explosive device was placed in a culvert under the road to take out any patrols who used the route, either on foot or more likely in soft-skinned military land rovers. There would have been at least two terrorists on the end of the command wire to set off the charge, close to the border with Southern Ireland, so they could easily make good their escape. There was probably a good chance they would have had a few more killers there to put down some small arms machinegun fire during their murderous attack as well.

No dog handler likes to see their best friend blown up, but unfortunately, both handlers and dogs have been lost in the province over the years. JC did come close to being killed. After I had left the province, I was told JC had a close call with his new handler, he was very lucky not to have lost his life. The blast from an IED went up at forty-five degrees rather than straight into his body, but the force of the blast bowled him over, and although he was in shock, he managed to recover from the awful experience. JC and our times together in NI are another story, but he was a superb weapons and explosives search dog.

I was informed later the same day, in Belfast, that I had passed all that was required of me to become a prison officer in Her Majesty's Prison Service, but I would need a medical to make sure I was fit for the role that I had applied for. They said I would hear something in the post relating to the job, so that was it; I returned to my military base. When I speak to ex-colleagues who live out in NI these days, they say there is still a lot going wrong; you just never hear about it on mainland news. I'm led to believe terrorist groups have morphed into terrorist gangs delving into all sorts of other offending behaviour now, one of which is drugs!

Suddenly, out of the blue, a letter came through the post from the recruitment centre in Belfast inviting me to attend a medical at a local doctor's surgery. You will know by now my surname is Riley, so I guess some bright spark thought it would be a good idea for me, a serving soldier, to attend mine in a village not far from Londonderry, which just happened to be a strong supporting community of the IRA. Little did I know at the time how much of a part I would be playing in a prison, in terms of the Good Friday or Belfast Agreement years down the line!

On the day of my medical, it was decided by our intelligence service that it would be quite a low-key affair in terms of the visit. I needed to attend in the morning, so a colleague and I took a covert vehicle that we used over in NI for various operations. My mate who was driving and I were both carrying our standard issue Browning 9 mm handguns. Mine was held in an underarm holster, and my mates was in the side pocket of the vehicle for easy access in case things went tits up. Northern Ireland is a weird sort of place in terms of being part of the United Kingdom, and I certainly don't want to be discussing the issues that it has faced over the years and still faces with the current Brexit arrangements that are taking place.

The whole of Northern and Southern Ireland could be considered a terrorist's playground by the different factions; yes, I did say a playground. They don't really care about the damage they have caused in people's lives to achieve their goals. Over the years, it has been a sickening, bloody war zone with potential danger and death around every corner for everyone. Terrorist groups from different factions of their communities had all the time in the world to plan and execute their ideas to kill and maim civilians and security forces, which they did! Terrorists sometimes managed to score an own goal when trying to carry out their crimes, which ended up with them losing their lives after prematurely detonating their own explosive devices.

It never occurred to me that after leaving the armed forces and joining the Prison Service in 1989, I would be getting up close and personal in 1994 with some of those terrorists who may have wanted to kill me and my colleagues back in NI and later in Her Majesty's Prison (HMP) Whitemoor, in Cambridgeshire, and under the Good Friday or Belfast Agreement, I would also play a part in some of their repatriations to NI as well!

I can't remember the name of the doctors surgery, but we pulled up near the building and sat there for a while just taking in the surroundings. I then went and booked into the surgery, waiting to be called up by the quack. Once I was in their office, the doctor confirmed who I was, explaining that I needed a full medical on behalf of the employer whose employment I had applied for and that I would need to strip down to my underwear to be examined so that various tests could be conducted as part of that process. I explained to the doctor that I was a member of the security forces. I expected him to be somewhat nervous about that, but he quite nonchalantly said, "Don't worry, just slip off your stuff and let's get on with it." I said to him, "That's okay Doctor, but I'm actually carrying a gun, which I can't take off!"

Picture this: There I was, stripped down to my grollies (undies), with a shoulder holster on and my service handgun in the holster slung underneath my arm. I just thought to myself, "You couldn't make this up." Imagine the headlines: Soldier shot dead by IRA whilst having a medical in his boxer shorts!

A few weeks later I received the official letter. I had passed all elements of the recruitment process and should now wait to be called up as a prison officer in England or Wales for my official training. So that was it, nothing more, nothing less. It was all I needed to decide that my time in the Army had come to an end, and I was not going to carry on and sign up for the full twenty-two years and possibly end up as another statistic.

Life went on, and I was secure in the knowledge that, barring anything going drastically wrong after I was discharged from the military, at some point, I would be called up and once again serve Her Majesty Queen Elizabeth II, but this time in a different uniform.

I had the unhappy task of having to leave JC in the province. He was too young to demob with me, so I had to hand him back over to the RAVC staff at Ballykelly. It broke my heart, having been together for such a long period of time. I thought about the miles we had walked together through the years, all the experiences we had shared together, the finds he had detected and ultimately the lives we had saved as a team. It's one of the most dangerous jobs I have ever experienced, that could have cost us our lives. We knew that others in our type of work had indeed lost their lives. God bless them for their service to our country; we won't forget you.

As I said previously, JC was such a great AES dog. It hurt like hell to hand him back, but he was a dog who still had a lot of years to complete in terms of his career, now with another handler. Life goes on and I was sent back to the place where it had all begun for me, the Royal Armoured Corps (RAC) training camp at Bovington in Dorset. My military service came to an end and a few months later, the day before my twenty-seventh birthday, I was released from my contract after an exemplary military career under QEII, which was stamped on my discharge papers as I took my place, once again, back in Civvy Street, in Shrewsbury.

It was a strange feeling, being let loose after nearly eleven years in the armed forces and heading back to Shrewsbury, where I was born and bred. I didn't know what lay ahead or when I would be called up for my new job! There I was, unprepared for the life I needed to get my head around as a civilian. I attended an interview with an ex-Army Colonel to see what fitted in terms of my discharge papers. Basically, all I was fit for now was security officer type work. I thought to myself, "Now you know where you stand after all the shit you had to deal with over the years in NI."

I knew I was better than what this ex-officer was pigeonholing me into. I wondered whether people were getting kickbacks by pushing people into stereotypical employment back then, rather than looking at the person and working with them to better themselves and their future! Anyway, you need to get on with it, don't you, and I thought, well, I need to keep myself fit for the prison service.

I had previously helped on a milk round as a kid to earn money; I wouldn't go on the dole, I was too proud, so I walked into Shropshire Dairies in Frankwell, an area in my hometown of Shrewsbury. It was a stone's throw from where I was born. I asked them for a job, and they gave me one on the spot. It was fantastic in terms of exercise, I ran everywhere during the deliveries, from the milk float to the houses and back during the round, delivering all the usual stuff you find on an old electric shed on wheels at that time: milk, eggs, cheese, butter, orange juice, and yoghurt etc.

I enjoyed all the keep fit. It would have been easy to let myself go after all my military training and the regime you were used to after all the miles trogging around NI. It was quite funny ending up back in Shrewsbury when all I wanted to do was escape from there when I was sixteen.

I talk to a fair few serving and ex-military today, and even now they say the transition from the services is still difficult; everything has been contracted out to providers to help in the discharge process, and yet people still say it's a crap service. A lot of people would like a second career working in the prisons, police, NHS, etc, but there does not seem to be a proper system in place that can help them move on. The other thing is, services are bogged down with paperwork, and I hear that in places like the police service, people are expected to hold down a full-time job while probably having to take on lots of overtime and study towards a degree in policing. Where are people supposed to find the time for anything? A lot of pressure is being put on them; they need to get back to the basics first, master those to protect the public, do the job, and then later on, if they are of the mind, take on a degree. It's probably the same in the prison service. There is some hidden agenda at play in the services, and it needs to change to support workers better.

When I was in the prison service in my latter years, they were actively not recruiting ex-military personnel, but they are the people with good life experience and skills easily transferable to Civvy Street, working in prisons, and the police. Prisoners eat up and spit out someone straight out of university. The ones I saw on direct entry couldn't wait to get their twelve months of probation as an officer out of the way, so they could then disappear down to headquarters in London. They were going to be paid 60k a year, probably more now, and for what? They didn't actually contribute that much to a prison. I would think a two-year probationary period as a prison officer is much more sensible, split between a challenging environment and somewhere less stressful. They could then serve a further twenty-four months holding a lower management role in another prison nearby, moving to a more senior one for another twenty-four months before they could hightail it down to headquarters. This means people can see if they are up to the task of being an operational manager, or over promoted. In which case they can revert to a lower grade or leave the prison service. Six years on an initial contract is, in my opinion, fair to everyone, especially the taxpayer.

Medals from my military and operational prison service careers

HMP Shrewsbury. The Dana

After I had demobbed on 3rd February 1989, here I was keeping fit and getting plenty of fresh air working as a milkman when suddenly, at the end of November 1989 a letter dropped on the doormat. I opened it, low and behold it said I was to report to HMP Shrewsbury at the Dana 09.00hrs 18th December 1989 for a two week induction programme. Following that I was to report to Newbold Revel HM Prison Service College (PSC) Rugby for three months training as a New Entrant Prison Officer (NEPO). For those that don't know, the prison service, as I found out over the years, likes to reinvent itself by making up new names for old things, and this was a rebranding of a screw or warder! So now it was officer time. It amazed me how the prison service went about their recruitment programme. I don't hear anything for nine months since leaving Northern Ireland, and then, whammy, I'm called up.

Now I had my confirmation of a start date, it made me think of the inoculations that I had been given in the military; mind you, we never knew what half of them were for. But prisons have their own problems, with some prisoners more likely to have contracted various diseases due to their lifestyle, both inside and outside of the establishment. Hepatitis A, B, C, D and E are common ones as are human immunodeficiency virus (HIV), tuberculosis, scabies and flu. As I was joining the prison service, I could ask my general practitioner (GP) to provide me with the most recent jabs that could help protect me from contracting any diseases that may be around, but like everything else, you can still be unlucky and catch something. As you progress through your career, there are things like searching of cells, prisoners, visitors, areas, and courts which can also throw things up. One of the common ones was needle stick injuries, and if that happened to you, you needed to be tested at the GP surgery to see if you had contracted some disease or other. Thankfully in my case, I never caught anything over my long prison service career.

I discovered that HMP Shrewsbury's claim to fame was as an old Victorian gaol, built between 1788 and 1793 by John Hiram Haycock with Jonathan Scoltock and Thomas Telford as the surveyor. It ended up with the unenviable accolade of being the most overcrowded prison in the country. And here I was joining it two hundred and one years later. It was now classed as a Category B male local prison. Something I didn't realise at the time was how much closer to my heart this old gaol would become, and how this grey, dark prison could be so poignant to me. Maybe it was fate that had chosen HMP Shrewsbury for me as the place where I would be inducted into my career in the Prison Service (PS) at that moment in time.

I arrived fifteen minutes early, using a big metal knocker to bang on the massive wooden gate to alert someone inside. I had arrived, it reminded me of the part in the film Scrooge where Marley's apparition appeared on the door knocker. A smaller wooden gate built into the oversized one creaked open, and a face appeared from behind it. I waved my joining instructions at them, and I was told to go and show my papers to the elderly prison officer on the gate. I walked through to what looked like an office with bulletproof glass and shoved my papers into a small till so the officer inside could inspect them. I was signed into a big prison gate book so I could enter the prison, but even then, it gave me an opportunity to experience and get used to the sights, sounds, and smells of an environment that was totally alien to me.

Someone came to collect me from the Human Resources (HR) Department to take me through to another office. I noticed these gates to the inner sanctum were made of steel bars and formed part of the security perimeter of the establishment.

You never forget the sound of those gates opening and closing with the noise that they make, metal on metal, loudly clanging together. Once we passed through another gate we were inside the prison, and one of the first things I saw were names on a board of prisoners who had been executed at HMP Shrewsbury. I never knew or realised, and no one told me until 2015,

about the personal connections that this old gaol had in my ancestors' lives, and this was before I had even stepped foot on a landing to commence my career!

Most people who live in Shrewsbury and the public in general do not understand what happens in a prison. I suppose you could say it's out of sight, out of mind, for the local population and the many things that happened within its confines. It immediately struck me that the closest thing that I had ever seen that could come close to what I was experiencing was a re-run of a comedy programme on the television called Porridge with Ronnie Barker, Richard Beckinsale, Fulton Mackay and others. Documentaries on the real prison service show you what they want you to see, not the real problem areas and the gruesome stuff!

Most of our induction training meant that we were to undertake lots of physical education lessons, and I'm sure that the instructors really enjoyed giving us lots of physical pain, I'm laughing to myself now. Over the next five days of induction, we attended the wings as observers, where the main work with prisoners took place, visiting different parts of the gaol, including visits, healthcare and the gymnasium, where physical education instructors (PEIs) seemed to like beasting new prison officers, just as much as our military ones did. We did lots of cardio circuits and weights, which were like my old army workout, and after five days I was told I could have annual leave until the New Year. I was grateful to be off all over Christmas and New Year. I never expected to be sent home on annual leave and thought to myself, "Who recruits someone just before the holiday period and then sends them on annual leave." Maybe this was something typical that happened in the civil service. I wasn't complaining, but it felt odd! Suffice to say, I had a great time off and I was getting paid for it.

As part of any prison system, they have a control room which is basically in charge of the whole establishment, and it is they who control everything that happens, including the timing of it. Wings are given permission to unlock and lock up to open and close the regime for prisoners. Before unlocking, general alarm bells are tested by the night staff and each wing have radios linked to the control room. Radio procedure is something we all use and there is no messing around on the radio net. We operate using the phonetic alphabet system (*see Appendix E*), which uniform services like the police and military also do, although the actual callsigns used in each one can mean different things. A typical day in prison is scheduled to take place 08.00 to 20.00. Joining HMP Shrewsbury at Christmas time taught me that the prison service liked to waste public money.

PRISON SERVICE TRAINING COLLEGE NEWBOLD REVEL

HM Prison Service Training College, Newbold Revel

Arriving at PSC Newbold Revel was rather exciting. Meeting up with a whole load of new and different people with diverse backgrounds; all coming together to make an eclectic mix of personalities, cultures, and experiences to make a great cake over the next three months.

The first thing that struck me (especially being an ex-soldier) was we had to kind of march everywhere. I call it marching; it was more like a shuffle with a bit of arm swinging thrown in. There was an awful lot of classroom work. This meant looking at the different aspects of law, prison establishments, and learning all about the prison service rules and regulations covering them all in the careers we had now chosen.

We had to complete a first aid course, which was a pass or fail test to progress in training, and I would definitely need those first aid skills over the coming years with the amount of claret flying around. I don't mind seeing other people's blood, but I'm not particularly fond of seeing mine splattered everywhere. One other thing we had to pass was control and restraint. We spent lots and lots of time covering something called Aikido, a modern Japanese martial art developed by Morihei Ueshiba designed to protect oneself and the person who is attacking you. The primary goal in the practise of Aikido is to overcome oneself instead of cultivating violence or aggressiveness. It made me think of the interview I had sat in Belfast and the questions that were asked of me back then.

Aikido formed the basis of control and restraint, which every member of staff must pass at its basic level in training at the college so they can operate as part of an effective team when they join their prison. If you were unable to complete the course, you could be back squadded. What this meant was, instead of passing out and receiving a posting, you would have to take the three-month training course again. Some staff like me were then chosen to take that further when they reached their establishment, to a higher level called control and restraint three, which is used primarily for riot control, either at your establishment, with other teams in your area, or further afield if the need arises.

The art of Aikido is practised in a dojo, a Japanese place for meditation and training. There were also different mock-up cells, exactly like the ones found in prisons around the country. As part of our training, we were told that we would be acting as staff and prisoners and that as part of any exercise we were not to hold back anything as prisoners when it came to our turn to fight in a cell. The reason for that, some prisoners in a real prison are not there because they play tiddlywinks; they are there because they are extremely dangerous and could kill you, so it has to be full on.

It's always a fair fight when using Aikido in a controlled manner. There are three to four uniformed officers to remove a violent prisoner from a cell to achieve the desired result when relocating them to a safe area in a segregation unit. Prisoners know this when they want to fight them, and for the most part, they know that staff will use approved techniques to get them from their cell down to the segregation unit. Prisoners will also play up to an audience, it increases their status amongst their peers and shows they are fighting against the system. That is not to say that over thousands of removals that improper use of force was ever used, but I hope that those incidents would be few and far between and those caught doing so would be charged and action taken in line with policy requirements.

In training, everyone took turns to act as a prisoner. One situation I was involved in sticks in my mind when it was my turn to act as the aggressor. I was in a normal type of cell with a few items of furniture. I'm not a small guy by any means, and I was just thinking, right, come and get it you fuckers. So I was winding myself up before the fight

to come, knowing that I had to give it my all to make it realistic for the officers, and broke a leg off a table to use as a weapon.

When a team goes in, they are instructed by an SO outside the cell. They advise you to surrender and you are given a few opportunities to give up peacefully. After that time, regardless, it's game on. The door opens and in rush three officers dressed in protective clothing consisting of fireproof coveralls, helmet, night stick, strengthened gloves, elbow and knee pads. The first person in the cell holds a short shield to hit the prisoner with. I start smashing the hell out of it with the table leg, but with the combined weight of three staff pushing me towards the back wall of the cell, I let go of the weapon and I'm slammed into the wall hard. The team had made a mistake. They had pinned me lower down on my body with the shield, so I was able to reach over it, managing to get hold of someone's helmet. I pulled it as hard as I could, and for some reason it came away from their head. Moral of the story: make sure your helmet is tightly and correctly fitted. I then began to batter the two other staff with it, just like using a bowling ball, that's when the fourth member of staff came in to support the other three. I knew enough not to smack the officer without a helmet as that would probably have done some serious damage. The fourth person in took over from them, so I gave them a few whacks with the helmet as well for good measure. The person without a helmet then became the fourth member of staff and withdrew back to the cell door.

In all the melee that ensued someone managed to throw the shield away and they all went for the different parts of my body to try and subdue me. All I wanted to do was fight, but eventually three on one was too much and they managed to get me down on the floor. A head person, one on my left and one on my right arm, and number four moved in from the cell door onto my legs. The officer who manages to hold the head is then the person who takes charge of the whole removal and directs what happens next. It never changes; the head person is always in charge once control is established. I was wound up and struggling so hard that they had to handcuff me in the cell, hands behind my back, meaning they were able to relocate me safely to the segregation cell. People looking in said it was a good scrap, but the result is still the same; the successful removal of a prisoner, namely me. The other thing is, they can also double up teams and send in another one to help. So no matter how hard you try to win, you will always lose in the end, and the same happens in any prison!

Another thing that was right up there in terms of good times at Newbold was that the training college had its own recreational areas and bar. We were in there most nights, and it could get a little rowdy, but no trouble was caused by anyone. Ex-forces guys would play a game called claptrap, but that is far too disgusting to explain in this book.

We lived at the college and partying until the wee hours in the morning was normal. The beds in the rooms were single and small, as was the accommodation, but we managed to have some small parties even in there! They used to say prison officers were trained at Newbold Revel and screws at Wakefield!

As we progressed through our basic training, you began to get a feel for the type of work that we would be expected to do. I always remember a principal officer at the college saying to me, "Be firm, but fair, and treat people as you would wish to be treated yourself." That stuck in my mind and stayed with me throughout my career and beyond, along with another piece of advice, "Never promise anything, and don't lie like a hairy egg."

Respect and reputation are earned by what and how you do things when working in a prison with your colleagues and prisoners, but it is a great feeling when people trust your judgement to get the job done, whatever it may be. What I didn't expect was how, the higher I managed to get up the promotional ladder, the dynamics of the job with other managers changed things. Whose coattails you hung on to was vitally important in the clique that operates within the operational and non-operational governor grades, whether working in a prison, area office, or headquarters in London. All I ever wanted to do in the prison service was do a good job for the Queen, not have to choose between a bunch of prima donnas so full of their own self-importance that the job suffers.

I didn't know this at the time, but when I joined Her Majesty's Prison Service, quite a few governor grades, especially governing governors can be quite narcissistic. Not all, but there are more of them than not! They seem to detach themselves from what is going on, and those who balls things up and can't manage in a prison get moved to London with their mates. They then resurface in another gaol somewhere else after a few years, having gained more promotion through failure; instead of someone (the clique) applying poor performance procedures and then dismissing them from the prison service, they are only in the job for themselves and what they can get out of it. They soon get rid of people in the uniform grades when they mess up, but even that takes a long time. That's what I don't like about the civil service. In my opinion it appears to have double standards in the way it treats its staff. Someone having a degree in "crap" for instance does not make them a good governor or anything else. Life skills and experience should count for a lot, but if you are not linked to the clique, you may as well forget about getting on in the very senior grades and beyond in the civil service; friends only promote friends. Thinking about that, I'm actually amazed I reached deputy governor level!

When bullies are in charge, they like similar people around them so they can protect their interests, as I found to my cost later on down the line. They also promote into all the other parts in the public sector, and people wonder why our country is in such a mess.

They also like to play games with people's feelings and minds by playing them off against each other, maybe to deflect attention from their own development needs as a person. What is that all about? The clique seems to operate like a group of Masons! People always wonder why prisons sometimes kick off, here's a tip: try looking at the senior managers who run them! I have worked in prisons where some governing and other governors are afraid to manage properly and deal with poor performing staff appropriately because they either do not want to upset them or some union reps feelings. That is not to say there aren't good staff or union reps, there are some outstanding ones. You may also find there are those who for some reason, will not support whatever you say or do because it's not right or good enough for them. I used to say about one union rep, they could disagree with what you are trying to do regardless of what it may be, but if you then said, "Well okay then, let's do it your way," they would then disagree with that as well. As I said, there are some good ones, but some are stuck up their own jacksies, and forget the real reason why they are there. Thankfully, they are few and far between.

The clique which operates right up to the highest levels of

the prison service and beyond, need to understand that they are part of the problem that exists. The games people play in prisons detract from the real reason why we all should be working there: to rehabilitate and guide prisoners who, for whatever reason, are there because their peers and courts put them there, and even those who will never be released are still part of the community in an establishment. With the types of terrorism that seem to be around in society these days, where people are willing to sacrifice themselves to reach their ideological goals as part of a bigger picture, it makes me wonder what the general public now thinks about the death penalty, linked to certain offence types, and what the results would be if there were a public referendum on that today?

About a week before the end of training we found out which prisons we were to be allocated to as part of the shortfalls in staffing numbers throughout the various establishments in England and Wales. There were one hundred and twenty-six prisons in the England and Wales estate when I commenced my service. There was some sort of weird, unusual process that prison service headquarters must have had to follow in deciding where to allocate prison officers as part of their process. We all had to choose three prisons that would suit our preferences to work in. Mine being Shrewsbury and two others close by in the West Midlands. Remember, I lived in Shrewsbury. Towards the end of our three months training when we had our pass out parade, we all, except any staff back squadded, received our letters in an A5 brown envelope. I think there was a clerk somewhere, or it may have been a governor, in the depths of some cellar who never got out much and took revenge on us by throwing darts at a prison service map on a wall that had all the different prisons named on it in England and Wales.

The reason I say this is because I opened my envelope and I had not been allocated any of my three choices. Someone in that dark cellar room, in their not-so-infinite wisdom, had decided to send me to HMP Lewes. I thought to myself, "Where the fucking hell is Lewes prison?" It may have been on the frickin' moon for all I knew! I went over to the main board, which displayed the establishments and worked out how far it was from where I was currently residing. It was 224.71 miles from Shrewsbury to East Sussex, 224.71 fucking miles. I just thought to myself, "Someone is taking the piss!" After I had received my letter and found out where it was I was heading to, I had the option of submitting an appeal in relation to the process, but the senior officer in our classroom sprouted out merrily that I would be wasting my time, as I had chosen to work in the prison service; so would get a "tough shit" response back. I suppose it could have been worse, although not bloody much. It could have been a London posting, where properties were expensive to buy on a prison officers wages, so it was a case of "suck it up, buttercup" and get on with it.

That's another thing about the prison service: they don't like anyone complaining, or you end up in their little black book. Yes, out there, we know it happens! I didn't get into the little black book until I reached deputy governor level, the highest grade I managed to achieve due to the clique. They don't like people who don't fit into their little boxes. Lots of them take good ideas you come up with and then submit them as their own. They are ruthless, as I was going to find out dearly, later on, when they would try and bully me into submission under the guise of management rules.

The clique which operates right up to the highest levels of the prison service and beyond, needs to understand they are part of the problem that exists, and why things keep failing. I wonder how the public will feel when they hear that failure and incompetence is well rewarded in the prison service and beyond, including all the other services in the public sector as well. We need to be more honest in the civil service and understand that people can hide within it, and if they belong to a clique, they can get away with so many things. Of course, the civil service will deny that, but the reality of it all is that the taxpayer should not be funding inadequate services and deserves better with the money that is being wasted on people who, quite frankly, should not be in the role of a civil servant!

FIRST POSTING HMP LEWES 1990-1992
CATEGORY B LOCAL

INTERNAL PHOTOGRAPH OF A VICTORIAN PRISON

Well, my three months of training were nearly up, and it all ends with a pass out parade. A bit of arm swinging and marching here and there, a quick salute to QEII, and then we were issued with a start date for our new establishments. Some five days later I would be commencing duties at my new place of work, and a mixture of excitement and trepidation coursed through my veins. I was on an adrenaline high.

Joining a prison for the first time is a unique experience for any individual officer to do. The Army had provided me with lots of skills, experience and knowledge which were easily transferable to a prison setting, but nothing ultimately prepares you for it. I phoned up the prison training principal officer (PO) who sourced me some temporary accommodation until I could find something more suitable, and they would meet me at the prison gates when I turned up for work.

Five days later, I was knocking on the very large wooden front gate of HMP Lewes. After about ten minutes, I was met by the training PO. He shook my hand and said, "Welcome to another old prison." What everyone out there needs to know is that there is always something going on every day in a prison. A lot is so repetitive, like arguments, drugs, and threats, that to mention them all the time would bore you to death, so I have picked out ones that have stuck in my mind, which hopefully will give you more of an idea of the operational side of working in a prison.

HMP Lewes is also known as Lewes Prison or Lewes County Gaol. It was built on Brighton Road in Lewes between 1850 and 1853. Using designs by the architect, Daniel Rowlinson Hill, the prison followed the model of Pentonville prison with four wings (one each for males, females, juveniles, and debtors). Now it held local prisoners for trial, there was also a young offender landing and a separate lifer wing.

I was shown around the various areas in the prison, and I would spend two weeks undertaking a local induction programme to familiarise myself with the regime, which basically meant working in all the different parts of the prison with the regular staff. Once this was completed, my first area of duty there would be to work alongside regular officers on the young offenders (YOIs) landing. After twelve months, I would move over to the remand wing, which also housed the segregation unit below the main accommodation; however, if there were shortfalls of staff in the establishment, you could end up working anywhere.

The first thing you do in any prison is have an induction

interview with the governing governor, followed by the deputy governor. Those who operate in prisons will know the governing governor does all the nice stuff and the deputy governor runs the establishment, but only if the accountant agrees with it! I'm chuckling to myself again.

I also had to meet the union representative; typically, this was a prison officers association (POA) rep, who is a uniform officer grade, but I have seen some senior officers in the role as well. I have met some good and bad reps over the years. Their primary job is to look after the interests of their members, which revolve around the agreed staffing levels in any prison, linked to their contractual work hours. Prisons also employ officer support grades (OSGs), who are typically not in direct contact with prisoners but could be drivers, for instance, to take a prisoner escort to a court hearing. (Roles have changed significantly over the years.) An escort usually consisted of a senior officer and two officers back then.

The people I have mentioned apart from the accountant are known as operational staff, including PEI's and providing valuable support to them are the non-operational staff, which include but are not exclusive to accountancy, human resources, catering, administration, NHS healthcare, religion and education. Another important group within any prison is the works department, which carries out any necessary maintenance within the establishment.

The two induction weeks are important to try and sort your domestic life out, in and outside your workplace, getting paid, and settling into a unique prison environment with a very diverse group of people.

CELLS TYPICALLY HAD TWO OR EVEN THREE BEDS IN THEM

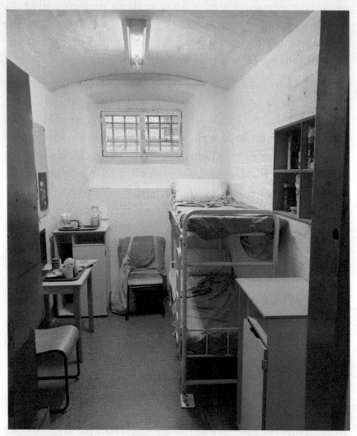

You need your wits about you when joining as an operational officer grade dealing with prisoners face-to-face. After my service in the Army, I would say I was pretty streetwise. People who joined without some sort of background like mine have had a rough time of things with inmates. Prison is a dog-eat-dog world, the sooner you realise that the sooner you will understand the working environment and the dangers that you may face. No matter which prison you commence work in, it's a steep learning curve. They are like mini cities that must operate in harmony, and most of the time they do, but with the types of clientele you are dealing with, it means that at some point, someone will kick off and you may get hurt. Over my operational years I have been seriously assaulted once, have been on the receiving end of lots of minor assaults, and have witnessed countless assaults on others! It is part and parcel of the job. You need to factor that in when you weigh up the risks of anything you do in life. You hope it won't happen, but it can, so you need to face that fact when working in such an environment. The other thing you may be unfortunate enough to witness are suicides. They happen along with numerous other forms of self-harm, and no matter how hard you try, you may not be able to save everyone, but when you do, saving someone's life makes the job worthwhile.

I joined the prison service to make a difference, and over the years, I hope I have set a positive mental attitude (PMA) to influence prisoners through the staff who worked with me to leave prison after their incarceration to lead good, productive lives back out in the community.

Back in the day, when I worked in prisons, operational statistics highlighted that 80% of inmates were committing 20% of the crime in England and Wales, so when they leave after serving their prison sentence, they do not reoffend. 20% were recidivist offenders who caused most of society's problems, causing 80% of the crime in our local communities, which means they keep returning to prison as career criminals. The latter types are mostly in it for the money, but there are also the habitual sex offenders.

I would have been labelled as a "care bear" officer at that time, but when you want to make a positive difference, it can be a powerful motivator to continue doing that same thing for others. I didn't have an easy life, I will always be a council house kid, but what I did have was the determination and drive to improve my life. Don't get me wrong about being a "care bear" though. I could be just as tough as other staff if the need arose, but it must be done in a right and proper way.

There are all sorts of things that you will see happening in prisons. They can be quite complex places to work in with some of the most disturbed people you can imagine, but what you must do is leave it all behind you once your shift ends and you walk out the gate. Don't take your work home, and don't take home into work. Some staff used to sit in their cars for half an hour or drive around to clear their heads. Work and home life are two completely different things and should be kept separate to keep one's sanity. The other important thing is when you enter the prison, you are the new entrant; you are at the bottom of any pecking order, so whatever background you had before starting work with HMP goes out of the window, and you must prove yourself to earn your stripes all over again. Everyone, especially prisoners, are well savvy; you just have to be savvier. The hierarchal structure in a prison is very regimented, and everything comes down and you must learn to deal with it, nothing goes back up, although the prison service would disagree. Governors don't like things sticking to their expensive suits and are well versed in the art of Teflon management in the clique, nothing sticks unless they make a mistake, but even then, they will protect the clique to avoid public scrutiny.

Typical prison management grade structure:

Governing Governor 1; 2; 3; 4 / Manager A; B; C; D
Deputy Governor 3; 4 / Manager D; E
Governors 5 / Manager F; G
Principal Officer PO / Senior Officer SO / Officer O/
Officer Support Grade OSG

To win your spurs with staff in a prison you have to step up to the plate when things kick off. You need to have all your senses in tune with the environment and as the new officer, you are the person staff push into a situation first. They do this to see whether you have the bottle to be a part of the team. This was done as a quick take out, for instance, when a prisoner refused to attend court. In a prison, you may have to enter a cell to take someone out. What this means in reality is that you take the first punch so colleagues can pile in to take control of the situation, and they did! You don't wait to plan control and restraint; the regime in a local prison would just grind to a halt. Straight in and get the job done, and put them on the bus for court, which we ran back then in terms of security. I think more staff got injured because of piling in than taking the prisoner out using Aikido, and I think control and restraint, which was operating in prisons could only be a good thing to help us all when it is planned appropriately as an intervention. The smooth dynamics of a working prison are important to keep the lid on it. You could argue, to a degree, who runs the prison; after all, there are far more prisoners than staff when it comes to locking up at any time. There must be mutual disciplined respect, once again, it reminded me of the interview I had back in Belfast some time ago.

The other thing about the remand side of HMP Lewes was that prisoners were locked up for long periods of time each day, nothing new in any remand prison. It could be up to twenty-three hours a day depending on what the scheduled staffing levels were on any given day. If we were asked to work extra hours to help keep the regime running, these were known as time off in lieu (TOIL). Paid overtime had been stopped the year before I started working in the prison service, but staff at the time who voted for the new contract of work said, "They sold all of us new staff down the river." It's probably the same in any new contract where it pays them better money overall. "So, it's look after number one," I thought to myself.

Understanding and knowing what prisoners and staff are like in the working environment is extremely important, so the establishment operates effectively, but adding to the mix the smuggling of drugs into the prison by people livens things up, and it can make for a fireworks sort of day.

The personality of an individual can make or break a situation. Mine was calmness and being able to have a laugh, but if the shit hit the fan, training took over and I could deal with things effectively enough, but sometimes the way some colleagues acted could get us into a whole load of shit, which can develop very quickly into riots with the destruction of wings and the ever-present life-threatening situations. You knew when some staff were on duty, things could get out of hand. It's almost as if they took great pleasure in winding prisoners up to get a reaction from them, but in my opinion, thankfully that type of member of staff is few and far between. They are out there in many different sectors; it's hard, but they need calling out as well.

To get to the point of a riot means an awful lot of pointers have been missed. A catalogue of errors which have resulted in a catastrophe, normally because people at the top have not listened to staff about what is happening on the ground floor, especially the security department. Staff from every area in the prison can submit a security information report (SIR), which allows us to bring to the attention of someone that something is not right. The security department then collates all the information for the security governor, who can develop plans of action to provide solutions to whatever may be happening in the establishment.

It may be that you provide a piece of information that is the last piece of a jigsaw puzzle. You won't know it, but it could be the difference between life and death or keeping everyone safe. The other thing that was good practise, although it didn't happen all the time, was to send an acknowledgement back to the person who wrote the SIR. It shows you took notice of it, and they feel better about the fact they may have been going off duty; it makes them feel good when they are next on duty. Although not everyone used to write back to people, I did when I worked in security a few years down the line.

Before in cell sanitation was introduced, prisoners had buckets to use overnight in their cells if they wanted to use the toilet. As a new officer, I was at the bottom of the staff ladder and a daily task for prisoners in the morning was to slop out. One officer, i.e. me, had to be stationed near the sluice room door. Smelling the crap and piss of sixty prisoners slopping out from their nightly purges daily on your landing is not a joy to behold; it really was foul and stank to high heaven! You never get the smell out of your nose or the air for ages; you can literally taste it in your mouth. We used to open the roof vents to try and get rid of it, but you could only do that if it wasn't raining or snowing.

ROOF VENTS

The sluice room was also a place where scores could be settled between rival gangs or two individuals who had a beef with each other! I have to say it was a degrading practice, and thankfully, over the years prisons have been modernised with in cell sanitation and a lot of other things to raise standards. This, I am sure is a debatable subject, but being found guilty of an offence and incarcerated for it is the punishment for a crime set by their peers and the courts. What you are trying to do is give prisoners the ability to have some self-respect and decency in their lives by keeping them in touch with events outside, and television is a powerful tool to be able to do that.

Listening to the news, etc. I do understand it when people shout about prisoners having better care than a lot of people who live in our communities, and to that, I say, the government needs to make sure life is of a good standard for everyone, that's what we pay all our taxes to them for, don't we? Sustainability for all is paramount, but if you can't get off your backside to work or can't be bothered, then you shouldn't think you are automatically entitled to benefits that are better than anything else out there in other countries.

When prisoners mess up and if the rules dictate, they can be placed in a segregation unit or Rule 45 prior to being seen the next day by an adjudicating governor. It keeps them away from the main population and from causing more trouble and problems for staff and prisoners. The segregation unit can also be used for a prisoner's own protection (Rule 45 OP); due to them being under threat, you try to move the perpetrator, but sometimes you can only move the victim. It's not great or perfect, but that's the reality of life in prison. Normally, the type of offence they have committed means the pressure for them to stay on a landing or wing is too great and they must be relocated to the segregation unit under Prison Rule 45.

The other thing that may happen to you is not very pleasant; thankfully, it's one of those things that never happened to me, but when a prisoner has a grudge against an officer or anyone else, they may "pot them". This means that the churned-up contents of a bucket of shit and piss, which is meant to be emptied in the sluice room drain, ends up over a member of staff or two. This could happen for many reasons. For instance, they may have been placed on report for something the night before or been refused canteen. Invariably you may end up rolling around on the floor with the person who perpetrated the offence. If that happened, your uniform was bagged for incineration and you were issued with a new one.

"Slopping out" was and is a pretty degrading thing, harking back to Victorian prison days, but the dangers are also more acute when a prisoner has hepatitis, HIV, etc. When we were in scuffles with prisoners, quite often you would end up on the floor rolling around and it was quite usual that your watch could be smashed as a result. Luckily, you could claim for the damage to it and purchase a new one. I had two watches broken over the years, and I used to wear cheap ones. What's the point of taking a Rolex to work if it gets smashed up, or worse, if it gets nicked off you by prisoners. That's one thing prisoners did all the time: ask, "What time is it, Gov?"

Lots of prisoners do not like using buckets to defecate in. I don't think I would either to be honest. Crapping in front of another cellmate or mates, watching the other person's end game from their previous meal the next morning. The only other thing for them to do is form a shit parcel with newspaper as the wrapping. You would be amazed at how much faeces humans can produce, but when it is squeezed through the metal security meshing and pushed out of the windows up to four stories high, someone has to pick it up. And in 1990 this happened to me overseeing something called the "chiefs party". It meant taking some young offenders out with shovels and a trolley so they could pick it all up from the gullies and windowsills so it could be taken to the incinerator and burnt. Not so bad a job in winter apart from the cold; but in the summer turds tend to ferment! HALLELUJYA for toilets in the modern prison service! Slopping out was meant to end in 1996 but persisted in Gloucester Prison a lot longer for some reason.

There is something you don't automatically get when working anywhere in a prison and that's respect. You gain your own reputation as a prison officer by what and how you do things and common sense is way up there, above everything else. The first three months is the time when people make judgements about you. The first thing I did when I was posted to each prison (bar 1) was shut my gob and listen to what was going on and read up on staff and clientele. Prisoners make judgements about you within the first two weeks! There are some very nasty prisoners in terms of their reputation and violence, you ignore that and them at your peril. You must gain brownie points with your peers and higher managers in the way you work. Get on with it without whinging, don't go sick, and you agree to extra duties through TOIL when asked.

I sometimes think that governor grades, especially those who are direct entrants into the prison service and don't have a criminology or relevant degree (even then I'm not so sure), except for something obscure, don't realise the intricate game that you must play in a prison and that's what it all boils down to, especially with prisoners: a game; like cat and mouse, some people forget that as they climb the greasy pole of the management ladder. I think I will ask Monopoly with my help to make up a game that reflects a prison and court environment; instead of "go directly to jail," it would be to spend an hour in the slop house or a spell in the segregation unit.

Prisoners will try and make illicit alcohol in prison, which we called hooch. Generally, it's made from whatever they can find to mix with it, oranges, potatoes, sugar, all kinds of fruit, mixed with bread or yeast from the kitchens, and then they need somewhere warm to hide it so it can ferment. It's all part of the game of seeing who can stay one step ahead of the other.

Batteries were the only way a prisoner could get their radios to work, and often they were battered and left on radiators in their cells to try and charge them up some more until their next canteen day came around. They also have an alternate use; batteries in a sock can make a very handy weapon when swung around the head and then smashed into someone else's skull, face, or other sensitive parts of the body.

The other thing they liked to do was heat up a plastic toothbrush, then take a blade from a razor and embed it into the plastic which then sets rock hard. They can use the tool to slash someone's face. It can cause some seriously deep wounds and bad injuries. They also used to set multiple blades in the plastic as well. Prisoners used to call an injury made by a blade "striping" and cutting someone's face, body, etc. with multiple blades close together meant it was difficult for the healthcare staff to stitch it up, so they kept bleeding out. If they couldn't seal up the wound, then we had to take the injured prisoner to hospital for further treatment.

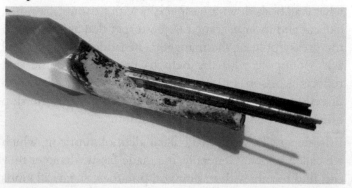

Slashing someone's face usually had some meaning in prison. It's normally used to stripe prisoners who were in rival drug gangs or who had told staff or police things in relation to ongoing crimes as an informer. Having the scar on a prisoner's face meant everyone would know what it meant, so prisoners who could not hack normal location were usually allocated Rule 45 for their own protection.

The 20% of prisoners who keep reoffending see bird as an occupational hazard. In any environment where there are inmates who fit into this category, they usually stay in the area where they live to commit further offences. We know who they are, so when they end up back in prison, it's almost like they never left. There tends to be some mutual respect between most prisoners and staff. The majority of prisoners don't want to rock the boat. They want to do their bird and get out to commit further offences; time is money, as they say. Another group of people who used to end up in prison were the homeless, normally around Christmas time. They would offend, so they could be sent to prison. They had somewhere warm to kip and three meals a day; it was like a short holiday for them.

When prisoners are locked up for long periods during the day, the way they move things around is by using string lines to swing from cell to cell or by asking the cleaners to do it on the quiet. Normally, it would be things like tobacco, matches, drugs, and newspapers. When control room staff see it happening on the cameras or staff outside let you know which cell windows things are being swung from, we had to surprise them quickly to try and retrieve the contraband. Prisoners are placed on a report if drugs are found and placed before a governor grade the next morning to answer the charges that have been laid against them the night before. They are issued just after lock up, just in case the prisoner kicks off.

It is then up to the adjudicating governor to hear all the evidence from all parties and decide if any rules have been breached or not and to find the case proven or dismiss it. I would get a lot of practice involved in that process as a governor grade myself ten years down the line! The thing is, as with any process of that nature, it really is all about common sense and weighing things up to come up with a reasoned decision using natural justice. You can't go through your whole operational adjudicating career without being involved in some sort of violent incident; those types are usually referred through the prison liaison officer for a police investigation. It's just an occupational hazard. You deal with it and move on to the next thing.

There are three things that prisoners see as sacrosanct in their lives inside prison: visits, canteen and scran (food). The other thing that has stuck for hundreds of years is that they call everyone in uniform Guv. They don't like the whole Sir bit, but Guv is something everyone understands. I didn't like being called Sir. I am an ordinary person doing an extraordinary job. It's just different moments in time, which can make it a difficult and stressful job sometimes!

I don't advocate violence in any way, but having lived with it since I was a teenager and throughout both my military and prison service careers, you become numb to it all in the end. The fight or flight feeling, the adrenaline that courses through your body and brain as you evaluate things to make decisions many, many times faster than normal. In those 1.5 seconds, you can see more clearly and with more frames per second. Your brain is calculating five hundred different decisions in that time and when your body reacts, you are expected to make the right decision. If you don't, sometimes it could mean the difference between life and death. I believe it when people say it felt like time had slowed down. I had this sort of experience before when I was in an army vehicle and we were involved in a serious collision with an artic lorry where one of my colleagues died. For me, this is because time basically did slow down. The blood pumping around your body at around 12,000 miles or 19,000 kilometres a day plays a big part as well.

In the military dealing with dangerous situations gave me a massive buzz. That indication by my dog, which helped hone my skills, a bit like the sixth sense - that Spidey tingle, that warned Spider Man of impending danger. Things eventually become second nature to you, and you hope as time goes on, you mature and become someone that everyone can rely on to make the right decision at the right time to avert a disaster. If I could bottle that stuff, it would make a great wow drink instead of all the drugs some kids chuck into themselves to get the same effect these days.

As I previously mentioned, visits play an important part of a prisoner's life. Most just want to see their loved ones, catch up on what is going on and keep that extra connection with the outside world. The drug dealers just see it as another way to smuggle illicit substances into prisons and over the years, they have tried many ways to circumnavigate prison security to ply their trade. In 1990 this meant it was plugged (wrapped in cling film or a condom) somewhere on the visitor coming into the establishment, so it wasn't found on the initial entry search.

Plugged means it is either held in the vagina or rectum of the visitor coming into the building. They will sit with it until the time is right to pass the item over. Visitors would purchase things from the canteen and try and slip it into an item to pass it over, whether that be a packet of crisps, a chocolate bar or a cup of tea. The secret is trying to unplug the item without being seen by staff and do the business. Depending on the size of a visits hall there is normally a senior officer and around six staff on duty to play the game of cat and mouse. I used to wonder for every item we found or stopped being passed, how many got through, so the recipient had happy days in someone's cell. If we managed to catch someone with a substance, we normally used C&R to get it off them. They just don't like handing it over to you; "Quelle surprise" there then.

Drugs cost a lot more to purchase in a prison environment than on the street. A heroin wrap outside the prison was worth ten pounds, but inside that jumps to three times the price, so it's a lucrative business. The dealers don't take any risks, and why would they when they have minions to do the dirty work for them. They were taking the hit when they got caught, so the dealer stays safe. A lot of people get into debt with the dealers, so they don't have much of a choice when they are manipulated and a member of their family or a friend has to try and bring drugs into the prison, so their loved one inside doesn't get hurt. Drug dealers are very good at manipulation and getting others to do their dirty work.

Prisoners would try to swallow or plug the items that were being passed over. If C&R was used, it meant we had to take the individual down to the segregation unit to be stripped searched and placed on report for adjudication the next morning. The visitor would be arrested and handed over to the police. The visits room also had cameras which the control room operated to help us identify and nab people.

Prisoners loved to 'chase the dragon', which is burning heroin on foil. We used to find loads of it around!

When prisoners ended their visit, we also had to strip search a certain percentage of them to find illicit items. This meant they had to strip off the top half of their body. Staff would look at and search all of their clothes, feeling and patting them down to try and find stuff. They would then put them back on and take off their lower garments, but not their grollies. It all ended with a "Drop 'em for the Queen." This meant them pulling down their grollies, squatting, bending over and spreading their arse cheeks with their hands, so staff could see if anything was secreted inside them. A pretty crap job if you'll excuse the pun, but as the junior screw; you were always allocated that particular task.

There is also an illegal market for NHS medication in prison, where prisoners who are prescribed medication sell it to other inmates. Although prisoners are meant to be observed swallowing their allocation at dispensing time, they somehow manage to hide it to sell on. It would be so much better from a security point of view if everything came in liquid form.

Sometimes prisoners would try to slip past staff and run back to their wing. When this happened, you pressed an alarm bell to get other staff to respond and chase them before they handed over any contraband to someone else or plugged it themselves. It could be like the Keystone Cops chasing them around, but it made for an active day.

Our visits hall was also used for official business, where prisoners met up with solicitors and other agencies. They had large, windowed rooms to conduct their discussions in, out of earshot of staff, but we could still see into the spaces in case of trouble.

Well, one day, two police officers came to see one of our inmates. As prison officers, quite a lot of the time we had to use the gift of the gab to talk prisoners around when they were angry and de-escalate situations. I have seen quite a few police officers over the years come into prison for a visit who don't seem to be able to deal with prisoners like that. I think it's because they are always taught to take control of situations and quite rightly so outside in the community when the need arises, but when they step into a prison the rules of the game change dramatically for them.

The two police officers sat in one of the rooms, all of which contained alarm bells. Anyway, they sat with their backs to the wall, with a table located between them and the prisoner, who sat by the entrance to the room with the door closed. Everything seemed to be okay at first, but then all we heard was shouting coming from the prisoner in the room. The prisoner had pushed the table into the two police officers, jamming them into the back wall, and then proceeded to assault them over the table. We managed to get into the room, get hold of the inmate and drag them out into the visit's hall and back to the wing. It doesn't normally take long to put the individual into locks and relocate them back to the wing. We would let them go just before they went back into their living area, and they would be fine with that; although we would issue them with a nicking sheet later, and this was done at 20.00hrs after lock up. Prisoners in the visits area found this sort of thing highly amusing as there is usually no love lost between the police and prisoners. To be fair to the police, they were usually issuing more charges or interviewing them about further unsolved crimes that they were trying to mop up. This was also a good time for visitors to hand over their contraband whilst staff were distracted trying to deal with the incident. So the police stunt could have been a setup, maybe!

Drugs in prisons have always been a problem. It seems to be a forever changing beast, and sticking a plaster on a wound that is gaping and gushing blood will not fix the root cause of the problem. The balance has never been on the side of security due to the way prisons are run. You can put things in place like closed visits, but when one smuggler is caught and placed on it, another twenty take their place to bring contraband into prisons, just because of the profits in drugs alone.

Prisoners will try to protect their market share, and there are normally around two to four main drug dealers vying for position in a prison and because of the money involved, they will use violence and intimidation to carry on with their trade. We can move them on to other establishments as part of security and safety, but we have to have good cause to do that due to all the nice solicitors letters we receive after they have been transferred, normally sprouting human rights, away from family, closer to home, etc. as a reason to move them back. I would think solicitors make a lot of money at the taxpayers' expense to send us letters, but my advice is, if you want to kick off, then don't expect to stay in your local home area! We normally exchange them for another prison's problem child, and the whole thing starts again. Hardcore prisoners tend to know each other, so it continues like a carousel; it all keeps going around and around. Drug dealers are smart, intelligent, resourceful people (unless they take the goods themselves) and use force with muscle to get the job done. They intimidate and cajole within the environment they operate in; violence to them is part of the game.

Gangs operate in the same way when they pursue their lives outside, but if they have grudges to settle, they can do it inside prison. When I was on duty one day, it happened on the wing I worked on. I was on the 2s, which is on the ground floor. The segregation unit was below ground floor level and located on the 1s. The alarm bell was activated. It is quite loud, ringing continuously, and only the most senior officer on duty on that wing could call up the control room for it to be switched off, so the prison can switch back to a normal regime.

The shout came up from the main office that it was up on the 3s. All the alarm bells on the wing are linked to the central office and to a separate control room, which informs you in which part of the prison and the location the bell is coming from. Staff are also informed via the radio net for key people to respond to the alarm bell. If it comes up as "all available staff" to the troubled wing or area, then it means we are in deep shit and it will take everyone and the prison cat to deal with whatever confronts them. The first response staff attend, if it's dealt with, the control room and SO informs everyone that is the case and we go back to a normal routine. If not, then the rest of the staff lock up the wings and go to help colleagues where the trouble is. Between the gaps on the landings are metal safety nets, just in case someone goes over the railings.

Falling from the 4s or 3s to the ground if there was no netting will likely kill you. Better a broken bone by landing on the netting than a broken neck. When an alarm bell is activated and you have an idea of the location, you go as quickly as you can just in case one of your colleagues is getting hammered. On this occasion, I was the first member of staff to get up to the 3s. You just follow the noise, and I could hear staff behind me as we thundered down the landing towards the cleaner's cell which has three beds located in it. Prisoners who were around outside on the 3s were just staring at where the commotion was coming from.

I reached the cell door first, it belonged to the wing cleaners. It could only have been ten to fifteen seconds after the shout had been raised. As my eyes adjusted to the light in there, I could see the prone shape of a person laying on the floor. They appeared unconscious and there was a load of claret around the head area where they had fallen on the floor. The cleaners were at the back of the cell, swinging metal bed ends around like maces from the medieval times trying to keep another three prisoners at bay. Another officer who had managed to get inside the cell just after me came to my right-hand side.

We stepped over the lifeless body on the floor to grab at the prisoners in front of us, risk assessing as we went along. It was really, really slippery where I was, with blood everywhere, but between us, we managed to manhandle the three prisoners out of the cell, one by one, with staff behind us dragging them out onto the landing. When the cleaners saw us, they stopped waving around the metal weapons. I basically shouted at them to drop them, they obeyed the order, dropping them on a bed and cell floor with a loud thud. I would say the metal bed ends weighed between two and four kilos each, nothing like the prison service providing the items to cause the damage with metal on bone. We then handed them over to other staff. I guess there must have been around fifteen to twenty staff on the wing, more than enough to deal with all the prisoners. I then had to deal with the lifeless looking person on the floor. Jesus, you never forget the sight of things like that. I called up on the radio for healthcare assistance and to get an ambulance. Everything happens at once, but it all comes out naturally and in a calm, controlled manner.

I bent down to pull the person over onto their back because they were face down on the floor, and I could tell straight away they had likely been hit with one of the metal bed ends. They were unconscious but still alive. I always remember the way all the blood had congealed in the time it had taken to deal with the incident. It moved with the person in front of me in a great congealed lump. The side of their face had a big indentation around the cheek and eye socket, which was now empty with what I guessed was the optic nerve hanging from it, and what was left of the eyeball looked as if it had been squashed during the fight and battle to regain control in the cell. It looked a right mess and thankfully, healthcare arrived not long after to take over and get them into a stable position so we could take the prisoner to an outside hospital. I am so glad that I had asked for an ambulance straight away because it didn't seem overly long before it arrived at our location, unlike the time it takes these days.

As the prisoner was located on our wing, a quick risk assessment was conducted, and then before you knew it, I was in the back of the ambulance with another member of staff, whizzing off to the local A&E where our uncuffed, unconscious prisoner would be assessed for emergency surgery to fix up the injuries they had sustained. It would be a few days later when I was tasked to be a part of the bed watch staff again to help ensure the escort was still in place. Prisoners require a level of escort appropriate to the risk required to keep them and the public safe.

The risk assessed escort depends on what the security department in any prison decides is appropriate and all reports are signed off by the duty, deputy, or governing governor, who checks that everything falls within the guidelines and policies of that prison and the notoriety of the individual. Looking at the person again made me think they were lucky to be alive. Their face was bandaged up quite heavily, but they were awake and talking to people. They couldn't remember anything about the incident, you don't tell them anything either about what had happened in case it may prejudice any police investigation.

There is an unwritten rule in prison with prisoners, well, most of them and I don't know where it came from or when it happened, but if you tell the authorities about who did what to you, you become a grass, a snitch, a rat.

I found out that this prisoner would not press any charges against anyone in the cell where the incident occurred, and as staff had not actually witnessed who had assaulted them, the police would take no further action. Case closed. I do know that the hospital could not save the prisoner's sight because of the damaged eye socket, so whatever the argument was about (it was most likely involving drugs), well, they had paid a price for it, and I suppose it would make a good story for their grandkids in the future!

Working in a prison, there's really nothing quite like it. As you will appreciate the clientele for the most part, don't want to be there. However, they understand that they have lost their freedom and there is an old saying, "You can't beat the system." Prison rules and regulations cover pretty much everything and if it doesn't, then there is a catch-all rule that covers anything else that may crop up linked to recklessness!

The first time I saw the aftereffects of a hanging, not on me as such but on colleagues around me, it made me realise the vulnerability of prisoners, staff and their families. I think this is why I always said leave everything at the gate, don't take it home with you. When I worked in the military and the prison service in the early days, there was no such thing as help with the trauma of whatever you may be feeling about certain situations, but the other thing is, the image of what has happened is then imprinted into your mind like a photograph, but you have to lock it away. I used to be able to block out those images in both occupations, and you dealt with it, rightly or wrongly, with "dark humour." The ability to use a joke, even if it might be the most distasteful thing at the time, can help you deal with what is in front of you.

In the early 1990s, whilst serving at Lewes, we could see the riots unfolding at Strangeways up in Manchester. These were hard times for a lot of people. Being a part of a control and restraint team in our prison, we were on standby to respond but were never called up to help deal with that riot. We thought, "There but for the grace of God go I." One prisoner killed one hundred and forty-seven officers, and forty-seven prisoners were injured. You become numb after a while to things that happen, but it's also the extra pressure put on all who work on the front line to make sure things get done within a complex and often dangerous prison environment.

Hanging oneself is obviously a catastrophic event, and who knows what is going on in someone's life where they have made that decision to end it all. Sometimes you get snippets of information that, in themselves, don't make up the whole picture to complete a jigsaw puzzle, and sometimes a blame culture can exist. You do have to learn from a process. That should be plainly obvious in any job, but when governors and others do not, then we should not be afraid to tell them that they need to move on from the prison service, but it appears to me those people don't seem to learn from previous mistakes that well. The magic roundabout kicks in and people get promoted and moved to headquarters or some other civil service job to keep them safe in the clique.

As I have said, this was the first time I had been involved with a hanging in a prison setting and it happened during a period of night duty. Every so often, you had a scheduled set of night duties to complete and then you had a week off. Normally, I added some annual leave onto the end of them to get a couple of weeks off. I used to quite like doing a set of nights, and you also had some staff who didn't like doing them at all, so you could change a two-week set of shift work and swap duties. Great in the summer when you could add two weeks on and get three weeks off to go on holiday somewhere.

All prisons have a pegging system which meant you had some sort of object built into the fabric of the walls in various places around your wing and on each landing. You had to either touch a button or press a handheld device up to a reader, which then sent a signal to a main panel in the administration block to show that you were going around the wing doing your job properly and these were set by the night manager. It meant you had accessed all areas within your area of responsibility. However, pegging systems can be vandalised, so they don't work effectively.

The pegging signal was sent back to a central point, which logged the action and meant you had not fallen asleep. It also meant if you had prisoners on a self-harm watch, you could check up on them. Those individuals who were on a self-harm watch had elevated risk assessments dictating how often they needed to be observed. You had to get a response from them, so you knew they were okay at the time of the check. This is then logged in their main self-harm folder. Prisoners on a constant watch were kept in the healthcare centre.

I was conducting my checks during the night, and it is a boring job going around the wing. It is usually quiet after around 22.30hrs at night when the inmates settle down and you have not been distracted by them trying to get you to pass newspapers, baccy (tobacco), and skins. Once you naff them off a few times, they soon get the message. You hope that the set of nights you have is a good one and no incidents occur. It was quiet during the night, but that was about to change. It must have been around five in the morning when a call came over the radio system (we had open call radios on nights to listen to each other) that a code blue had been called in the segregation unit, which was below the remand wing I was working on, and the senior officer on duty came through the wing with a healthcare officer and another member of staff.

We all went down some steps to the lower ground floor entrance (the 1s) into the segregation unit, where the member of staff there said they could see a prisoner in cell three standing on the radiator pipe and they were not answering when they were calling them. On nights you cannot open a prisoner up on your own, as you don't have a set of keys except a leather pouch with a cell key in it for emergencies. You make the call whether it's an emergency or not, unless you obviously know that they are dead, as it could be a ruse to overpower the member of staff and take

your key to unlock other prisoners. We looked in through the observation panel and the senior officer opened the cell door which meant there were five of us to deal with the incident unfolding before us.

Once we were inside and close to the prisoner, we could see what looked like a shoelace around their neck, which was also tied to the inside bars and mesh. I always remember thinking it looked like they were just standing on the heating pipes which ran through the cells and staring out of the window. I lifted the person up to try and alleviate the pressure of the noose from around their neck and support the dead weight whilst one of the other officers cut the ligature from around the prisoner's neck.

Other staff also took the weight of the individual, and we laid them on the bed in the cell. Their lower body clothing was wet, which I assumed was urine, and the bladder had released any liquid in it at some point. Before the senior officer had arrived, the control room had phoned the emergency services to dispatch an ambulance to the prison. The healthcare officer was administering CPR, and we had a re-sus-e-aid (first aid device) on their mouth to breathe air into their lungs. It creates a barrier between the officer's and the person's mouth to stop any liquids from coming into contact with each other, such as HIV, hepatitis, etc.

I guess we must have been going at it for around fifteen to twenty minutes before the ambulance service arrived to take over. Although it was clear that the prisoner was dead, you keep trying to resuscitate the individual, and you hope that the professionals who deal with that area of work can then bring them back. Unfortunately, in this case, it was too late, and they were, as far as I can remember pronounced dead at the scene. The ambulance service then took away the deceased, and a member of staff went with them to the hospital morgue so a post-mortem could take place at some time in the future, and the deceased person's cell was sealed for further investigation. Initially, it becomes a police issue in case there are any suspicious circumstances surrounding the death and they need to take any further action. The death is automatically referred to the prison ombudsman's office for further investigation. This is to ensure that the cause of death does not have any issues in relation to misfeasance in a public office and that further action in the prison service needs to take place.

In the case of the prisoner who died that night, nothing untoward was found, and the coroner's office held an inquiry into the death. We all had to attend to give evidence and be questioned on anything the coroner decided was appropriate. Everything was fine in terms of staff going about their duties, and the final verdict was suicide. The prisoner then became another statistic in the death in custody numbers in the prisons of England and Wales.

Deaths in prisons are evaluated at prison service headquarters by psychologists to learn any relevant lessons, and any information is disseminated to area offices and establishments for implementation. Politicians don't really understand prisons. They don't go in them very much, and as long as they are ticking along nicely, they haven't really got time for them. So rather than being on top of things over the years, they and their predecessors have cut spending in one way, shape, or form, increasing the risks for everyone working in a prison environment. Not that there aren't savings to be made. Coupled with some of their clique promoted friends in the civil service and running some establishments, area offices and senior civil service positions, it's been a recipe for disaster, and the prison service has and is suffering badly.

In my opinion, when corruption, fiddled promotions and pension gains are rife in the senior management and civil service grades, they put their interests and themselves above everything else that should be important when managing in the public sector. Radical changes need to take place to stem the flow of drugs in prison and a far better strategy is needed than the ones that have been played out so far between the relevant services of the police, prison, probation, social services, NHS and other support services. They are all precious about the way they conduct their own business, which is usually top heavy in management, where there are again, "too many chiefs and not enough Indians", where many jobs for the "friendly" cliques operate. The whole shebang needs a root-and-branch shakeup to change the culture of the senior civil service and the fat cat attitude towards managing our precious resources, so taxpayers' money is spent wisely and appropriately. There are too many people who receive large pay packets who are only in it for themselves and not for the real reason of wanting to make effective change, except with a target. Maybe I should try and get elected to become an MP to effect change from within the prison and civil service.

I would certainly love to be in the Ministry of Justice and Minister of Prisons to see what better strategies I could put in place for prisons and to go back and deal with the corruption with people still in the service and with those who have left and moved on to higher positions within other areas of the civil service. Is the whole of the prison service institutionally corrupt? My opinion, I don't honestly know, but I would say a lot of senior people may be from my experience of working in the prison and civil service.

No two days are the same working in a prison environment. Generally, you do have more good days than bad ones, but you must be prepared for the latter because they can sometimes mean a decision you make could mean the difference between life and death. There must be a theme there, I have mentioned that a few times throughout this memoir. There was one time when I and another prison officer had to take a prisoner to go and meet someone in an office. No one told us what it was for, so we couldn't tell the inmate. When we arrived, the person gave them a letter and said, "Papers served." Apparently, it had something to do with them losing their children. The prisoner immediately started to wind themselves up, so when we got them back to the wing, they went back to their cell, but five minutes later, they came out and started shouting at staff, and when I say staff, I mean me and the other officer. The prisoner came striding up the landing, swearing and threatening us. This was one of those fight or flight situations.

I stood my ground and turned side on to make myself less of a target (part of Aikido), waiting for them to attack me, but the other officer started backing away along the landing and then started running. The prisoner just walked past me and started to go after the other member of staff. They didn't catch the officer, but during this time, someone activated the alarm bell, so other staff could react and help out. I learnt a lesson that day about working in a prison and facing up to a prisoner in front of others. They saw me as someone who would stand up to aggressive behaviour and not back down, so they would not try it on with me, but the other officer was seen as a soft touch, and from that day on, I noticed how they had a harder time as a member of staff with prisoners. I had drawn a line in the sand, and they had not, and prisoners capitalise on that. They test you to see how far they can go, but the prisoner who was kicking off that day was dealt with just by calming them down and explaining that we did not know what was going to happen to them when we took them to see the person who gave them the letter. We can all see red mist, but de-escalation is the name of the game.

The thing is you must still deal with the aggressive outburst. In this case, the prisoner was placed on report by the other officer for their threatening behaviour, and they were dealt with on adjudication the next morning. If found guilty under a prison rule, there are a range of punishments that can be awarded to the prisoner by the adjudicating governor. Which would you choose, and what punishment would you award under those identified in the glossary?

Remembering different things from your work environment that stick out from similar incidents or days that are usually quiet are obviously relevant in your own mind. One prisoner who was on remand had an unfortunate experience whilst trying to commit an armed robbery. There are some very intelligent criminals out there, but I guess this person wasn't one of them. When committing the offence, they had taken a shotgun with them on the job to achieve a desired outcome, but for some reason, they had shot themselves through their own foot. I guess they were pretty inexperienced in dealing with guns, and one would think after that happened, they would not have got far trying to escape from the police because they wouldn't have been in prison now if they had! Well, they used to wear a bandage around their foot, which incidentally stank when walking around on the wing. The wound would try to heal up, but then it would just open up again. They had to receive treatment every day, and I don't know what eventually happened to them, but I do remember the smell, and it was rotten. Maybe they will remember it if they read my book. I did wonder in the end whether they kept their foot or had it amputated.

When we used to escort prisoners to court, I was the unlucky sod that had to be cuffed to a potential Category

A remand prisoner who belonged to a biker gang. The Crown Court was just down the road from the prison, but the police were not taking any chances with them; bearing in mind it was just down the road, we had an armed double police escort to get them there.

It's the only time I have ever done that sort of escort with sirens blaring out and all the traffic having to move out of the way to let us through. Now I know what prime ministers and other so-called people of importance receive all the time, rather than us poor sods who have to sit in traffic jams every day!

Prison food isn't that bad considering how much the prison catering staff were given to cover three meals a day, although it does contain plenty of rice, potatoes and chips. That's why prisoners spend a fair bit of time attending the gymnasium, pushing weights to become big and strong to fight staff (I'm laughing at myself again). The gymnasium is one of those things that is a good tool to use if a prisoner is found guilty on an adjudication. Although again, it can be a fine balance between good order or a riot in a prison.

When I worked on the young offenders landing and something was going wrong, things happening that we couldn't figure out, the officer leading the landing would just inform the cleaners that if people didn't stop piss assing around, then the whole landing could lose their gym time. Now the cleaners were the ones who used the gym a lot, and a young offender in a man's body can be a challenge when using control and restraint, especially when the experienced officers were for the most part in their fifties. Rolling around on the floor with a young offender isn't much fun.

The lead officer said things would get sorted, and sure enough, by the next day, things were back to normal, and you would know who the culprit was when they were walking around with a black eye. As a new officer, you learnt how to play the game from experienced staff because that's what it's all about: thinking smart and thinking well to get the job done in the easiest way possible without having a brawl with prisoners. The thing is, learning in a prison environment doesn't necessarily mean doing as others do.

During my time at Lewes, I must have had a shout about five times as part of a control and restraint three team to attend other prisons. For those, you get dressed up in riot gear and wait for the nod to attend another establishment, but then things get resolved, and you have that come down from psyching yourself up.

We were dispatched to attend a HMP prison that held foreign nationals who were refusing to come off an exercise yard. We had some transport to take us to the location where we disembarked along with other control and restraint teams. We must have hung about for around two to three hours; our commander told us that in our case we were going in and we had to clear the prison exercise yard where foreign national prisoners were refusing to leave it and return to their accommodation. We were located in a prison workshop before we were due to deal with the problem. The workshop of all things made cuddly toys, so I grabbed a bunny rabbit to take with me. We were dispatched to the yard, and as we were advancing towards the prisoners, I had the rabbit sitting on the top of the long shield I was carrying. To cut to the chase though, the prisoners decided they didn't want to fight with us and surrendered. The prisons that responded to the call all took some prisoners back to their respective establishments to break up any troublemakers. We took six, they were double cuffed so they couldn't fight against us. They were processed in our prison reception, split up, and integrated into our establishment's general population.

Sometimes, no matter how good things may seem to be going with lots of male prisoners being together in different parts of the prison, there comes a time when no matter what you do, a tussle has your name on it, and when I was allocated a day's shift down the segregation unit, you had to be on your toes. Some prisoners just don't want to conform, and they spend a lot of time in the seg unit doing their bird, happy to be isolated from the rest of the establishment. Down there on the 1s, we had three officers and a senior officer on duty; prisoners were let out one at a time, so when trying to get things done, it made for a time-consuming job. At lunchtime, the staff set out the hotplate with all the food for prisoners, and there would be a range of food depending on what each person's dietary requirements were. Each prisoner was given five minutes to pick up their meal, served by staff, and hot water was given at the cell door when they were banged up. When you were a day tripper anywhere in the prison because the prisoners didn't know you, if they had a beef, ninety-nine times out of a hundred, it would be the unfamiliar member of staff who copped it! This time, it was me. We served the food, and as the prisoner got closer to me, they basically said, "What the fuck are you looking at?" and threw the plate of food at me. As I stepped back, they pushed the small urn of gravy off the side of the hotplate where they were standing; it landed on the floor with a loud clang, gravy splashing out all over the place. We had to get around the hotplate and grab the prisoner, but we all ended up taking a tumble as we slipped over on the gravy, landing in a big pile of bodies on the floor.

We partially restrained the prisoner, but we literally had to drag them back to their cell and put them in it because of how slippery things had become. Once we managed to get them in the cell, we ended up placing them in a front, face down control and restraint position. We held them in a set of arm locks and a figure four leg lock. In this position, the arms go behind the prisoner's back high up, bent at forty-five degrees, and the officer who ended up as leg person pushed down and up on the arms, whilst their body also pushed down on the prisoner's legs. A combination of those positions meant the prisoner could not move with the weight of the officer on their back.

The two staff proceeded to exit the cell, shouting out, "Cell or door clear." As they got clear of the room, the leg officer pushed down hard on the prisoner's body, then sprang back to exit the cell at speed, and then an officer by the door pulled it hard to slam it shut. We were in a right mess. The problem was we still had to finish serving the meal, but one quick call and staff came down to help finish off. However, the next procedure is that whichever prisoners require lunch will have it delivered to their cell door and staff will take hot water for them too. The new staff will also give the prisoner who kicked off a new set of clothes, but for that to happen, the inmate must go to the back of the cell wall and face out the window. That way they don't have enough time to turn and attack the officers. Clean clothes are put just inside the cell door, and then it's locked shut. Unfortunately for them, they end up with a sandwich and a cup of water. As the day unfolds, they talk to the prisoner to try and get them back on a level playing field, but they will be placed on report by me for what they did. Can you see which prison rule fits the type of adjudication they sit, and what punishment you would give if they were found guilty by an adjudicating governor?

Staff keep a spare set of clothes in their personal lockers, so it was a case of us getting a quick wash and changed, and then off for our own lunch. You never know what's around the corner when working in a prison setting. We had healthcare officers in our prison, and I remember one set of nights when one prisoner was really playing up. They were allegedly mentally ill, and the healthcare officer said they would need to administer a liquid cosh to stop them from playing up. We all had to enter the prisoner's cell to restrain them whilst the officer administered the injection. I can still hear the screeching howl and the look on the prisoner's face as the healthcare office struck home with the needle in their backside. The liquid cosh quickly made the prisoner succumb to its power and they went limp, but they were frothing at the mouth, and their eyes were just staring blankly as if there was nobody home. I have no idea what was in that injection, but the terminology of liquid cosh was very apt.

When I responded in the daytime to another alarm bell in the healthcare ward, a prisoner was trying to take a female member of staff hostage; that's what it looked like as we piled into the area. I remember a PO taking out their stave and whacking the prisoner on the arm just before we dived on them. Once things were resolved, I noticed that the prisoner's arm was quite swollen, so they had to be taken for an X-ray, and it transpired that the blow from the stave had actually broken their arm, but due to the circumstances of the event, it would have been seen as using minimum force to subdue the individual from taking a member of staff hostage and the problems that may have caused in terms of their wellbeing.

Another officer and I saw an advert asking staff if they would like to apply for accelerated promotion. The first part of the application meant we had to attend a selection centre and take some different written and psychological tests. The long and short of it was, I failed, and they passed it, so my route to getting up the ladder had to be through the normal channels. "C'est la vie," as they say. Life goes on; you brush yourself down and carry on.

In HMP Lewes, we had a lifer wing; it's one place I didn't work very often, but it was usually in the evening if I did, and the staff there were normally the most experienced in the prison because of the clientele. It's fascinating to watch prisoners going about their business; security is paramount and everything else comes after that, but as a new officer, we had one prisoner who people may know out there. They did a fair bit of bird, can you guess who yet?

Well, they looked quite unassuming going about their business that evening: grey hair, small in terms of height; I'm 6 feet 1, or 1.85cms tall, but they were around 5 feet 7, or 170cms tall. They were part of the London gangster scene way back when they and their brother were known as "the firm" in the sixties. I'm sure you may have guessed it by now. Yes, it was Reggie Kray. I guess that was HMP Lewes's claim to fame, with their brother Ronnie locked away in Broadmoor doing their bird. I think it's rather weird that our royal family are also known as "the firm!" I wonder what Reggie and Ronnie were thinking when they came up with the same title.

What made this evening for me was, prisoners just got on and did what they normally do: watch television, play pool, cards, dominos or other games. The lifer wing was more laid back for them all, so they liked it to be relaxed with no hot shots on there. They just wanted to get on and do their bird without any hassle. The strange thing I noticed was that when the evening association was ending, near to bang up 20.00hrs, after the ten-minute call came to lock away at 19.50hrs, prisoners finished off for the evening and stood, waiting outside their cell doors.

When Reggie Kray was ready to go away at 20.00hrs, it

was almost like a respect thing amongst prisoners. It looked to me as if they gave a nod to all the other prisoners; it certainly seemed to me like they were top dog on the lifer wing, and after doing that, they all went behind their doors and banged up. It's the only time in my career I have ever seen something like that, so even though they were now getting on in years, they still commanded the respect of the other prisoners, who appeared to give it freely. Criminal loyalty, I guess! The important thing for me as a member of staff was another day shift had finished without anyone suffering any injuries.

As time went on and I was accepted as a new officer, I was thinking, "Well, is this what being a prison officer is all about?" That's when I saw a national advert asking for staff to volunteer to join a new prison that was being built. A place called HMP Whitemoor up in the fens of Cambridgeshire. I asked my colleagues what they thought, and all they said was, "Every seg unit in the country will empty when that place opens." So I volunteered to head northwards, and governors were instructed to release staff to move there! Within a month, I was heading up to Cambridgeshire from East Sussex and commencing duties at my new place of work. Fuck was I going to be in for a shock when Whitemoor opened properly, way different from Lewes, that's for sure.

What I did learn at Lewes Prison was that manipulation can be used to prevent any problems from occurring, but you can be sucked into a way of working that, after evaluation, means you will have to make hard decisions about whether you will go with the flow or challenge things in an appropriate manner. The only real way of doing that is by climbing up the promotion ladder, applying to sit the SOs paper at the appropriate time and getting promoted! It's funny how the paper pegging system used to break down on a regular basis on night duty. I always pegged, but then you would find out that things had clogged up the next morning, so what you had done as part of your duties during the night had not been logged anyway. I accept machinery can break down, but not to the extent that it appeared to do in Lewes Prison on nights. I have found some people can be the weakest link in any procedure, so when I was trying to produce something new, I had to start with the weakest link and do the "what if" scenario as part of any risk assessment, which is something I learnt very quickly as well. It's probably something that happens everywhere in business. I learnt the six P's: Perfect Planning Prevents Piss Poor Performance but supported by Keep It Simple Stupid (KISS).

One last anecdote of my time at Lewes. There was a prisoner who was really fit, they were always up and down from the main prison to the seg unit. It was always a pain in the ass trying to move them as they used to oil themselves up all over their body, so they were as slippery as an eel. We quickly found a new way of using a long riot shield which measures around six feet, or 1. 8 metres long and a couple of feet, 0.61 metres wide. It was difficult trying to move the prisoner from their cell to the block. What we used to do was strap them to the shield and physically carry them down to the block, unorthodox maybe, but it bloody worked!

HMP WHITEMOOR: TOP SECURITY CATEGORY A DISPERSAL PRISON. 1992-1998

I arrived at Whitemoor in early summer, and there were no prisoners located there then. Staff were allocated to start training to change up from the different category prisons around the country. This was like the Starship Enterprise compared to the two Victorian gaols I had worked in previously – a different, brand-new prison. What a difference to someone new like me who had only been in service for approximately two years and served in two old nicks, although you could argue less than two weeks at HMP Shrewsbury wasn't really working. The government wanted Whitemoor to be a flagship prison, so all the staff were given a public expense paid move from their current establishments to this prison, located just outside a very small sleepy town called March in Cambridgeshire.

The local town's population were extremely angry though. They were originally told that the prison was going to be a Category C male training prison, but then the government of the day changed it to a top security establishment. Such a large influx of staff though would have had a dramatic effect on the local economy, as March was in the back and beyond. This was one of those times where the Conservative government of the day had an open cheque book and were just throwing money at the place. From my recollection, when we all met with one of the governors down in the visits hall for briefings, the one question that stuck in my mind from someone in the audience was, "If we place prisoners on report will they actually receive a punishment?" I don't know if they had worked in a dispersal prison before, but the governor grade was not best pleased when they were asked that question and basically said, "That will be down to the adjudicating governor." It did make me wonder whether the question was asked because governor grades may not support the security requirements for a new top security dispersal prison, and maybe some more experienced staff knew something I didn't know.

Joining a new prison was a unique experience for me because we were a whole bunch of new people who had to get used to each other. The one thing people did, though, was share experiences from where they had previously worked. We did lots of control and restraint training over the coming weeks. That went by, and in handing over a prison to the public sector meant we had to search the prison cell-by-cell, wing-by-wing, area-by-area. They were zoned off as being complete until the whole place was sterile. The searching took around a week to complete. We literally did it how you see police doing it sometimes when there has been a serious incident. Side by side, on your knees in some cases, making sure the place was spotless of anything that could be used as escape tools or weapons to use against any member of staff. Little did I know at the time that things would go pear shaped not too far into the future; maybe that governor in the visit's hall knew something and wasn't passing it on!

All the new furniture was delivered to kit out each cell, including televisions. To most people, seeing all this new stuff when there are lots in our communities who don't have anything and would probably like access to the same facilities is confusing. I often hear people say, "If I can't have things to keep me alive, I may as well commit a crime, go to jail, get three square meals a day, a roof over my head, and a place to stay warm." It sometimes makes you wonder about things when all we get with the two main political or coalition parties is the same shit, but on a different day. No wonder so many people don't vote in England and Wales, but they only have themselves to blame when things keep going wrong. However, I can understand why they don't vote when all they see are self-serving politicians these days.

In Whitemoor, there were four main prison wings: gymnasium, hospital, chaplaincy, workshops, segregation, and a special secure unit. There is one main wing of sex offenders who were held on Alpha (A) wing, Bravo (B) wing was directly opposite to A wing and held a mixed combination of offenders who could not survive on main wings and who would not participate in offending behaviour courses. Some were housed awaiting allocation to go on to A wing for a course. Further up the long indoor walkway, through a few security gates, was Charlie (C) and Delta (D) wings. The Special Secure Unit (SSU), segregation unit and healthcare centre were set on their own, away from the large housing areas of the main house blocks.

The SSU was a prison within a prison. It had its own perimeter wall, security cameras, and staffing. It was there to house the most dangerous prisoners who presented the most serious risk to our country, which meant IRA terrorists in the main but some prisoners who had access to large sums of money and who, if escaping, may leave the country, so serious gangsters who could undermine the law and order of our country from abroad. Apart from this new SSU at Whitemoor, there were more dotted around the UK. A separate segregation unit to house disruptive prisoners, prisoners awarded cellular confinement from adjudications, and Rule 45s.

Our healthcare centre was located above the main seg unit, and there was a whole workshop area at the bottom of the secure corridor down from A and B wings. Mainstream C and D prisoners moved separately from A and B wings due to the nature of offence types. There was no love lost between the prisoners from A, B and C, D wings. There was a library and church facility set between the mainstream and vulnerable prisoner wings.

After a few months had passed, we were informed which wings we would be working on, some staff were allocated to the SSU. I was sent to Bravo wing. We had one governor V, two POs, four SOs, and forty-two officers, along with officer support grades (OSG), chaplaincy, probation, psychology, physical education instructors (PEI) who were prison officers, workshop instructors, control room, visits room and healthcare staff. It meant we could operate 24/7 to maintain a regime that allows prisoners to live full, productive, and active lives, even in a top security prison.

First, we were told that C and D wings would be the first to accept prisoners, gradually filling them up. Once they were nearing full capacity, we then commenced filling A and B wings. I just want to say that the staff at my old prison were dead right: "Yes, you were right." Segregation units around the country did start to bloody well empty, very quickly in fact, as problem children in other establishments were shoved onto escort vehicles all heading to Whitemoor. Those staff must have been laughing their heads off, and to the governors who authorised the movements, bloody well cheers, yer bastards. I think we must have only been open less than a week before the first alarm bells started going off. We certainly got plenty of exercise running all over the place, and it wasn't long before the seg unit started filling up. The early days of Whitemoor will be a time I will never, ever forget. There were so many fights, prisoner on prisoner for the most part, but also assaults on staff. But what it did do was bond staff, knitted us closer together. Having left one band of brothers in the military, here I was forming with another band of a more diverse nature in a dispersal prison. We had a common theme here: to make sure none of us were killed working for the prison service.

As things were progressing, at some point the SSU started to fill up, but we never heard a peep from over there, but that doesn't mean to say nothing was going on, as I would personally find out in 1994! It did seem like nonstop action every time I was on duty. A and B wings were fairly quiet, but as staff, we did talk to each other, and it seemed that there was a lack of control over prisoners, which is directly managed by the governing governor and their subordinates. After months of running around, we were certainly raising things with our union. It was fucking dangerous, but things didn't seem to improve, even after we had made our feelings known. I felt really sorry for all the officers up on the main wings; we were responding to their alarm bells, and they were working on C and D wings, day in, day out. I have a lot of respect for those staff, B wing was a mixture of mainstream prisoners with Cat A and those who would not participate in courses to help lower their offending behaviour risk.

One day the alarm bell sounded, and over the radio came, "All available staff to C wing." I was very fit in those days. An all available staff call means something is going south pretty quickly, and in a dangerous way. The SO on duty in our wing let four of us respond. Those with radios stayed behind in case something happened on our wing, so we went hurtling up the secure corridor to C wing.

The gates between the wings were already open, thanks to the staff working in the chapel. Piling into C wing, it was obvious that staff had withdrawn from one of the spurs, which was on the right-hand side (Green Spur), as we headed towards the centre office. There are three spurs on each wing (Red, Blue and Green) and three double sets of landings (1s, 2s and 3s) on each spur, with landings being opposite each other. The riot had already started without us!

The spurs were locked off, so prisoners could not attack the centre office and access the other landings and spurs. It was evident that a major problem was developing, and the SO was quick thinking on duty that day. They had got their staff to lock away prisoners on the other two spurs, so we only had to contend with the one that was playing up. There must have been sixty to seventy prisoners on the spur. The SO called out over the Tannoy for the wing to bang up, but that fell on deaf ears. Some prisoners were just standing around, and a lot had disappeared into cells and wanted no part of what was unfolding in front of us. Some inmates just sat out on the landings, watching what was going on like a cinema show, but they would bang up when the C&R teams arrived. There were around twelve prisoners who were hell-bent on causing as much trouble as they could. A few prisoners on the 1s landing started throwing pool balls at us, who were located just outside the centre office on the 2s. Thankfully, they were shit shots, and I would have loved to whang some of those pool balls back at them, but we are there to take control in a proper and coordinated way. This was going south very quickly. They had started building a barricade with wooden furniture down there and shoving it against the centre spur gate on the 1s setting fire to it. It didn't take long and only seemed like minutes had passed before the fire started taking a hold and flames started licking up around the 2s landing, where the centre office was located. I was thinking we were going to lose the whole wing at this point, as we would have to start evacuating the other spurs. Dodging pool balls was easy enough, so I grabbed a hold of another officer and told the SO we were going up to the centre 3s to try and fight the fire. There was a central barred gate, which we could access next to Red Spur, which runs from top to bottom on the wing. We sprinted, two steps at a time, up the stairs. Unlocking the gate on the 3s landing, we went over to a fire hose box; by now the flames must have been fifteen to twenty feet high. You don't have time to get nervous, training takes over. I unlocked the red fire hose located by Red 3s and dragged it out towards the Green 3s landing. Thankfully, those who were causing all the problems had stayed on the 1s. The other officer switched on the water in the hose box as I pulled the hose out, dragging it towards where the fire was burning and the smoke, which now started to drift up to where we were on the 3s. I pushed the hose through the bars holding the nozzle downwards, so all the water just gushed out and fell like a waterfall on the burning furniture below. It seemed to have little effect, and prisoners were still chucking furniture on it stoking up the flames. After around five minutes of doing this, there must have been a good surface layer of water starting to build up on the ground floor.

It didn't stop the prisoners from playing up further. One had made their way up to the 3s; they were stood right at the end of the Green Spur landing, probably around one hundred and twenty feet away from me. The prisoner had a weapon, the broken thick end of half a pool cue in their right hand, and what looked like the sleeve of a jumper pulled over their head with a couple of eye holes and a mouth cut in it. It looked like someone wearing a gnome's hat but covering their face as well. I nicknamed him the Smurf, but I couldn't actually identify them. Anyway, they started advancing up the landing towards me, I kept pointing the fire hose downwards. When they were approximately twenty feet away, I just shouted at the top of my voice for them to stop and not to come any further, but they kept advancing. As far as I could see, they only had the pool cue on them as their only weapon, but when they got to around twelve feet away, I thought, "Fuck this." They were getting way too close to me for comfort, so I did the only thing I could think of and turned the fire hose on them. That had the desired effect in terms of stopping them in their tracks, but I never expected what they would do next. They laid the broken pool cue down on the landing floor, stood up, and just started washing, as if they were taking a shower, except fully clothed. This was prisoner mentality for you at its best, and remember, it's all a game to them, common sense goes out the window!

I thought to myself, "Yes, you carry on doing that, mate. If you are doing that, then at least you are not fighting against me." He kept washing no longer than a minute, and they then picked up the broken pool cue, disappearing into a communal kitchen. Each landing on each spur has a kitchen in a dispersal prison, as prisoners are allowed to cook their own meals if they wish. I turned the fire hose back down on the flames below. The prisoner reappeared around ten seconds later. They must have known what would happen at some point soon because they held a bottle of washing up liquid and commenced squirting it all over the landing before backing up along the Green 3s. The fire was still raging. Prisoners who did not want to pack in causing trouble and wanted to continue fighting had broken up anything that had wood in it and thrown it on the bonfire. The prisoner that had come up towards me started making their way back down towards the 1s. It could only have been a few minutes after that when someone grabbed me from behind and told me I was needed to help make up a Control and Restraint 3 team, which consists of twelve staff and one commander. I knew at this point our silver command suite would be swinging into action and communication links would be set up to directly chat with our gold command suite in London, who could support the governor grade in command of the incident unfolding in our establishment.

Everybody and their uncle would be contacted to ensure this riot was contained and extra resources supplied to ensure the riot was brought under control and to a safe, successful conclusion.

Looking back, once prisoners started to play up in a group, the whole riot thing must fuel itself from an adrenaline point of view for them to just carry on causing problems. Maybe that's indicative of the problems we face in society today, and we are too liberal in dealing with the problems in our communities in a robust, straightforward way. We seem to bounce between Conservative and Labour governments, who both seem to drag our country down rather than support all the people within it. We need change, which I know is hard to do sometimes, but it seems to me as if successive governments just want to feather their own nests and pockets whilst lying to the electorate.

I disappeared off the landing once the other officer took the hose from me. I headed to our staff locker rooms to get changed into my riot C&R gear, which comprises of an all-in-one fire-retardant overall, helmet, reinforced arm and knee pads, and combat boots. Completing the dress was a nightstick, which was attached to a belt. In bringing this riot to an end, we were going to be clearing the landings of prisoners with long shields, with one full team on each landing, split into two so each of the landings were covered on the same floor, thus ensuring all three landings were covered. Two full C&R teams were needed on the 1s, and they would enter the spur from a gate at the far end where there was no fire. So in total, there were four teams and four commanders. We would all enter together to overwhelm the area and the prisoners. There were still two staff on the fire hose, and as it happened, the team I was in had to clear the left side of the Green

3s. All teams entered the spur at the same time. I could see that the fire was starting to diminish and was not as fierce as it had been, but the fire brigade could not attend the wing whilst the prisoners were still damaging the spur and fighting against staff. I knew that they, along with the police and ambulance services, would be waiting outside the prison.

We all had to move down each landing on the Green Spur at the same time, checking communal rooms and cells as we went along and locking them shut as we did so. When we reached a cell, it didn't matter who was in it; the idea is to take back control first, so if there were five prisoners in a cell, we just locked the steel cell door shut and proved it to make sure it was properly locked, so they could not get out and attack us from behind. Once control of the spur had been re-established, we could sort out which prisoners belonged in which cells and relocate them back to their own accommodation. It probably only took about ten to fifteen minutes to complete the task, even though it was very slippery on the landing with water and washing up liquid.

As soon as the spur was clear, we headed down to the 1s, and the fire brigade could attend the wing to finish extinguishing what was left of the bonfire and make it safe. It was noted where the perpetrators of the riot had disappeared to, which was pretty much any cell they could find open after the teams moved onto the landings. After something as damaging as a riot takes place, once control has been taken back by staff, commanders were able to assess what needed to be done next. There appeared to be around an inch of water on the floor, so it was still quite slippery and unsteady underfoot. Some of the staff were chosen to take down what was left of the barricade, whilst others were kept back to relocate prisoners who may have been banged up in different cells. I was one of those chosen to help take out and relocate some of the perpetrators involved in the riot. The segregation unit was on standby to receive the violent individuals, along with our healthcare staff to ensure there were no injuries to those who were relocated. There were six main antagonists who were now located in cells on the 1s who had to be escorted down to the block and were in locked cells, which meant if there were two prisoners in a cell, it would require six staff to take them out of each cell, plus two leg staff if they were needed. Some of the rioters immediately gave up and were walked to the block and placed in a secure cell. At that point, they are seen by healthcare and given new clothing to wear. The kit they had on was bagged and tagged for police investigation, just in case the prisoners are charged with a criminal offence and the evidence is needed for the courts.

There were only three prisoners who decided they wanted to continue the fight. In the cell we were allocated, there were two inmates. After looking through the observation panel, we picked out and confirmed our target with the other team that was following us in, so they knew who they had to hit, and we wouldn't mess things up. You hope the other team are quick enough to follow you into the cell and disable the other target, so we don't get jumped on, but all this is done without hesitation, a bit like shock and awe tactics.

Time to go in with the short shield to use in combined spaces.

I used my short shield to enter a cell and hit our target hard with it. As quickly as that is done, the short shield is then chucked back towards the leg officers to grab and take out of the cell. We managed to grab hold of our prisoner. I held them by their clothes near the head, the other staff had their arms, and we dragged them straight out of the cell, subduing them by taking them to the floor so we could all get proper locks on, while the other staff had also taken their prisoner down in the cell. Our prisoner was face down, thrashing around like a goldfish out of water, but it didn't take long for them to be wrapped up and asked by healthcare on the spur if they "were okay," which they said they were. It's a long walk down to the block from the wing. We cuffed our prisoner, hands behind their back, walking them in locks down a secure corridor on the ground floor that staff use exclusively for things like this.

It probably took about eight minutes to take them from the wing to the block but seemed longer. Once inside the seg unit, we relocated the prisoner in a cell designated by the staff who worked there, and another healthcare nurse double checked our prisoner to make sure they had no further injuries. We then conducted a strip search for weapons, passing the clothes taken off them to the block staff, who then bagged and tagged the items. We give the prisoner new clothes that are passed to us at the same time, so they maintain their decency. Once relocated and banged up, the staff involved in the incident need to get changed back into normal uniform and back on duty.

The prisoners who we took out and down to the block were not having any of it. Straight away they started smashing up their clean cells in the seg unit, so we just switched off the water. There is an access door to either the right or left of a cell door, so staff can reach the stopcock. We also switch the electrics off, but only when life is endangered. We didn't have endless numbers of cells to place them in, so now it was a case of letting them stew in the damaged ones they were now in. The duty governor of the day asked our team if we could stay on to cover a night shift in the segregation unit, which we always do at times like these. It's all for one, and one for all. I was pretty knackered at this point, but we took some comfy chairs out of the staff rest room, sat down, and listened to the racket that was now reverberating all around the unit.

A team took over from us for a short period of time, so we could fill in lots of forms about use of force, and any injuries to the prisoners, as well as write a witness statement for the police. We needed food, which the kitchens provided us with, and changed into new riot gear for the night shift. We ended up back in the block as the only contingency team in case the prisoners wanted to cause even more problems than they were doing, and yes, they did throughout the night. The biggest fear was that the cell doors would not stand up to their relentless onslaught, but there was nothing to worry about. They think they can actually break out of the cell, but they have two hopes: Bob Hope and no hope. Some of the prisoners eventually did not want to play up anymore and went quiet, but there were two who decided they just wanted to continue kicking up and causing as much disruption as they could. It was going to be a long night, especially for all of the other prisoners trying to get their heads down.

Whilst the disturbance was taking place, staff in our security department would be working overnight contacting other establishments so they could take some of those from us who had participated in the riot, as well as securing escorts with secure cellular vehicles to transport them. Prisoners playing up normally try to smash the observation panel in the cell doors so that they can push things through to attack and injure staff. I do have to admire their tenacity though, going at it for hours and keeping everyone awake in the block - guaranteed to make you friends with other prisoners, not!

When approaching cells, you must have your wits about you in relation to a prisoner trying to blind you with a weapon or stuff being thrown at you, normally urine, but it could also have a bit of number two mixed in as well. Having the short shield helps as you push it against the door, just to the side of the observation panel, and slide it along to flick the metal door flap open, which covers the reinforced Perspex window set into the steel cell door, so you can observe what is going on in safety. When a prisoner puts the cell call bell on, we go through a procedure to find out what they want. It's funny, you forget a lot of things over time, but I remember the prisoners' names. You never know; they may even be reading this book and recognise themselves from this anecdote without me naming them here.

Well, after opening up the observation panel by slide and flick, I looked in, and the cell had been destroyed. The bed was still in place. They are bolted to the floor in the block, but the sink had gone, along with the pipes and taps. They shouted to me, "Hey, Guv, what do you call this?" They are dancing around, doing some sort of shindig like a Scottish dancer. On the floor are the metal pipes with the taps still attached; they had ripped them from the wall and the toilet. They had placed them on the floor, jumping and dancing over them. I said, "I don't know," and they just said, "Tap dancing."

I laughed at that comment and closed the observation panel again. The noise quietened down around four o'clock in the morning. Those that had smashed things up were left where they were. There was no point in moving them to clean cells, and anyway, there were none to spare. Around six in the morning, transport started arriving at our prison, and one at a time, our team made sure individually that the perpetrators were handcuffed in their cells, processed in reception, and then loaded onto different secure vehicles to be taken to different establishments. After all the problems the prisoners had caused, none of them fought against us when we took them to reception. I'm not sure if they had breakfast before they left, but I'm sure the receiving prison could rustle something up for them when they arrived. The spur where everything took place on C wing would be under a controlled unlock for a few days as it was cleaned up and new furniture provided to bring it back on stream. It's surprising how quickly things settle down once something like a riot has ended. Well, until the next time!

It will, I'm sure surprise some people about the lengths some prisoners will go to, to make things work for them whilst incarcerated in a prison. There is, as I have said previously, a pecking order and some prisoners sell their bodies to make ends meet. You can't see it happening, but it does occur. Being locked up for long periods of time means even the toughest prisoners crave something that others may sell. I'm sure you have guessed it by now: sexual favours. Some younger prisoners sell themselves so they can buy extra canteen to supplement their workshop earnings. For them, it's playing it off so they can get an easier life, even with the risks of catching some disease or other. It can also be taken from them as well, by those who do not wish to pay for sex. Getting raped, for want of a better word, they are too afraid to inform staff for fear of the repercussions against them. One younger prisoner who was around their mid-twenties came up with their own solution on how to prevent things from happening to themselves if they didn't want them to.

Picture this: a plastic roll on deodorant bottle. Hopefully, people will remember the old style "Mum" type ones? They were fairly small, but they had quite a large cap on them. Prisoners are allowed to exchange razors for new ones with staff, but for some reason, they still manage to get hold of used ones to take out the blades, whether they are used as part of a weapon or, in this prisoner's case, to defend themselves. They broke two full blades in half, then melted them into the inside of the white cap from the bottle and pushed the cap inside their anus. It meant if any prisoner decided to rape them, they would be in for a very nasty surprise, which would end in their genitalia being shredded as they forced their way into the prisoner's orifice. The only problem for them was that at some point, it ended up deep inside the colon, and eventually, they had to be taken to an outside hospital to have it surgically removed.

Dispersals can be very dangerous places for prisoners, and equally so for staff. Hostage taking can happen at any place, at any time, and with anyone. C wing had two prisoners who managed to get into where the inmates canteen was being distributed.

They took the OSG hostage so they could just eat food and throw tobacco out through the windows to prisoners in an exercise yard. That is the way some prisoners live their prison sentences, and for me, that's where we need some really basic prisons because those small minorities need closer supervision so they cannot damage anyone or anything. Maybe they cannot be rehabilitated! The same goes for drug dealers, who ply their trade on the streets or in prisons. We need a few new prisons built, which I would call Category B Plus, a cross between top security and a local but with a stricter regime. A place where those who want to abuse the normal functioning of a prison are moved because of the damage they are doing. These should be built away from urban areas; that way, telephone blocking could be more effective, and some could not undermine the security of normally run establishments.

Violence tends to be more extreme when prisoners are serving long sentences, especially if they feel as if they have nothing to lose. There was an officer who, for whatever reason, appeared to have upset some prisoners, and in particular a certain one, or maybe some other prisoners paid them a contract to seriously injure the member of staff. I don't know over what period of time things had built up, but I was told the officer was tight on prison rules when dealing with prisoners, and it would appear resentment had built up within the mainstream wing they worked on. It came up on the radio net that an officer was down as the alarm bell was activated and healthcare needed to respond. The prisoner had been apprehended by staff, but I can't even begin to imagine the pain that the officer must have gone through. It transpired that the prisoner had boiled up a saucepan full of hot chip oil. The officer was on the 1s going about their business when the prisoner, who was on the 2s above them, poured the scalding hot cooking oil over the top of them. I'm told that the screams from the officer could be heard over the whole wing. It makes me feel sick just thinking about that incident, and it shows that some prisoners do not care whether staff get injured or even killed, and some are willing to display extreme violence towards others.

I would say it probably takes a good eighteen to twenty-four months for a new prison like Whitemoor to settle down, and staff certainly kept fit with all the problems we had to endure on the coalface. You could say that may have been the fault of governors because it is they who ultimately run the establishment. I think staff generally felt unsupported in trying to operate the different regimes in the prison. The governor decided to set up something called a prisoner development spur (PDS) on C wing. You may as well have called it the prisoners free for all to assault staff spur. Prisoners on there were subject to an unlock by three staff for everything. Staff were required to work up there on an ad hoc basis, and one day it was my turn. The prisoner who was to seriously assault me had put three staff off duty the previous week. One of them had lost a few teeth as a result. Well, it was my turn to be there on a shift, for the most part unlocking with three staff works okay. It was lunchtime, and we were going through a long, laborious task of prisoners individually coming out of their cells to get their lunch. We were on Blue 3s, and the two main members of that wings staff informed me that this particular prisoner had been seeing dragons flying around in their cell during the last few days. What they didn't tell me was that this prisoner had been the one who had put three staff off sick last week.

I have been involved in a fair few fracases over the years, whether that was in the military or the prison service. I know there's always a risk in any job; you understand that. However, this time, the two members of staff stood by the side of this prisoner's cell door, and I was to unlock them for lunch. I opened the cell door, pushed it open, and stepped back a couple of paces.

I spoke to the prisoner just to say, "You can go and get your lunch now." I looked away for a split second, bad move, to almost nod for them to go to their right, and in that time, I felt the hardest punch I had ever received off anyone. They must have round-housed me, as I spun around completely and ended up facing them again, but I had gone down on one knee. The other two staff pounced on the prisoner quickly, whilst I launched myself directly up and into the prisoner. I hit their body with the full force of mine, with all the strength I could muster, and with my full weight going forward. As a result, we all hit the wall at an angle, and I can remember the alarm bell going off. After I had hit the prisoner hard with my body into the landing wall, I went over the top of them as we all went over onto the landing. I quickly managed to get back around and grab their head as the other two staff were on the prisoner too, grabbing their arms. There was a fair bit of my claret around. Yes, this time it was mine; my mouth was full of sweet tasting blood, and all I could do was keep spitting it out everywhere. My teeth must have split the inside of my cheek from the force of the blow. I was the head person, and I remember an officer arriving and belting the prisoner a few times in the face, although I had no idea who they were. The next part is all hazy, as I can't remember helping to take them from the wing to the block. I must have been well concussed, but they were relocated to a block cell. In the seg, unit staff told me to get up to healthcare. I don't remember anyone helping me, but they may have. Once there, you would not believe what someone said, "It's lunchtime, you will have to come back in an hour." It was so weird, but all I could think about was getting back to Bravo wing and having a hot, sweet cup of tea. Not that it would have helped me. I'm sure someone must have helped me. I can still remember sitting in the staff room on Bravo wing, my white shirt covered in my blood. I do know I went back to healthcare, and a doctor saw me and immediately had staff call an ambulance, who came and transported me to Peterborough Hospital. I ended up in A&E, where I spent the afternoon. My face was pretty sore by then, and the right side had swelled up like a balloon, and my right leg was killing me around my knee. I think I was exceptionally lucky to keep my teeth after what had happened to the other staff the week before. After a thorough check up in A&E, the prison paid for a taxi for me to get home from hospital. By this time, the inside of my mouth was blistering up, and that was hurting more than the punch did. It meant I couldn't have anything apart from cold water or milk to drink. I was on training the next day, so the prison paid for a taxi the following morning for me to get back to the training department, as I also had to pick my car up. I remember a governor grade being there, saying, "Bloody hell, you shouldn't be here," but I just said, "I swore that a prisoner would never put me off work." Thinking back, I must have been a mug, as I could probably have had a week or two off after being assaulted like that. A few months later, I was having surgery on my knee for soft tissue damage because it had aggravated an old injury from my military days.

I never got away Scot free from injury, although I'm sure there are some staff who have gone their whole career without a scratch. Lucky bastards. There will always be assaults on staff; it's the nature of the beast in a prison environment, and there are probably assaults happening frequently these days. What I have noticed is that when they get rid of lots of experienced staff at the same time, trouble always follows in prisons after they have left the service.

One night on Bravo wing in October 1993, another A shift for me of twelve hours would throw up another of those times during the evening. I was one of the centre officers who helped control the core day. Prisoners, as part of that regime, are allowed association time during weekday evenings. When prisoners come back from workshops after a day's labour, they return to their respective wings, are served their T meal at 17.00hrs, and then locked away so staff can have their break and get their scran over a half-hour period. We unlock after that; prisoners can associate on the wing or go to the gym until lock up which is called at 19.50hrs. It gives them ten minutes to sort themselves out before being banged up for the night. We called, "All away," and as staff started locking up, a member of staff put out a code blue, which meant someone had been found unresponsive and healthcare staff were required on Bravo wing. Staff had found a prisoner in a cell on Green Spur 2s. Colleagues from other landings were coming in to sign their prisoner numbers as correct in their area.

Looking over towards Green 2s landing from a centre office.

I went over to the cell on Green 2s where the unresponsive prisoner was, and when I looked in, I could see a prisoner laying on the bed with an officer giving them the kiss of life. I noticed they were not using a re-sus-i-aid, and giving anyone mouth-to-mouth, especially in prison, is high risk. I got mine out and told the officer to place it over the prisoner's mouth. The device is there to form a barrier between people when someone is trying to revive an individual, but it's also to protect the member of staff from foreign bodies, like sick etc. When I looked at the body on the bed, I could see that their feet were a bluey black colour, and their toes were curled back. I asked where the prisoner had been found and was told, as we saw them now. Something didn't ring right, and my gut instinct kicked in, telling me something was wrong. There also appeared to be some sort of ligature in the cell, and it would have been impossible to kill yourself and get into the position of lying on the bed the way they were positioned.

Healthcare staff arrived and carried on with trying to revive the prisoner. From my viewpoint, after looking at his feet, he had been dead a short while, and I mean an hour or so rather than minutes. When the ambulance crew arrived, they basically said nothing more could be done, which is always their call to make from a prison point of view. I went to the centre office to ask the senior officer to notify the police. I grabbed a device that allows us to seal the cell door. As far as I was concerned, this was now an unexplained incident, and I went back to the cell and locked it off. The wing was banged up by now, so as a staff group, we were able to chat about what had happened. The night staff were coming on duty, but some of the day staff would need to stay behind to write witness statements and see if we could figure out what had occurred. The police arrived to look at the cell and conduct forensics. Soon after, the coroner's staff arrived to take away the body, as it would need an autopsy done to establish the cause of death.

After some discussion, the staff who worked on Green Spur identified two prisoners who had been associating with the deceased prisoner that evening. Sometimes you take in more than you think when just going about your job. As we thought this may be a case for the police, it was decided that the two prisoners should be escorted down the block. Their clothing bagged and tagged, so we may have evidence to support a police investigation. Their cells would be locked off as well in case there were things in them that could support a prosecution.

There was a quick discussion. From that, we found out that one of the prisoners had a wing knife still signed out to them. I am one of those people who will not put other people in a situation that I would not be prepared to go into myself. I volunteered to go to the prisoner who had the utensil to retrieve it and escort them down the block. They were located on Green 3s, so as a team of three, we went to the prisoner's cell. I opened them up and asked for the wing knife back, as it should have been handed in on locking up. They handed it over, and I told the prisoner that we would be escorting them off of the wing to the segregation unit. They asked me what the problem was, so I said that would be explained to them when we reached the seg unit. They walked with us to the block. Once located, they were told an incident had occurred on Green Spur and that their name had been mentioned as being a part of that. As a result, they were to be placed on Rule 45, good order and discipline, and removed from normal association until such time as an investigation is concluded in relation to the incident. The other prisoner was located on Green 2s, the same landing as the deceased, and some of our other staff relocated them to the block as well. Both prisoners had to be placed on report, clothing bagged and tagged so that a continuity of evidence process could take place in case of further court action. As time went on and the police investigated the incident, after a post-mortem had been conducted, they decided that a possible murder had been committed. The information about the two inmates our staff had identified and escorted to the block was fundamental in taking them to court. The information that I heard later down the line was that the two perpetrators who were incarcerated for murder had gone to the prisoner's cell wanting to show them how to escape from being held by someone. It sounds ridiculous, but apparently, the victim had let one prisoner hold them from behind in a bear hug, and the other prisoner simply strangled the individual. I can imagine a struggle would have ensued, but the two prisoners had duped them into that situation. They were younger and fitter than the person they had murdered. The case went to court, and the two alleged perpetrators were eventually found guilty by a jury for murdering the prisoner that staff had found unresponsive.

Whitemoor was and probably is still a dangerous place to operate in, and little did I know that in 1994 how that would come to the fore again. I was still an officer on Bravo wing, and I was one of those designated to respond to alarm bells if they went off in the evening. Staff had radios to listen out for any problems around the prison. I was one of the Bravo wing call signs. It had been an uneventful day so far, but just around bang-up time, an "all-available staff" came out over the radio net, "alarm bell SSU." All electronic secure gates are controlled by the control room staff.

This is my account of what happened on that night in September 1994. Attached to the end of my statement is part of the public enquiry report by Woodcock and two other articles. Compare them all; what do you think about it all?

It was a hell of a run for me to reach the SSU from Bravo wing. I set off running along the top secure corridor, leaving the metal gates open as I went through them, knowing other staff would be following up after me. We never had any alarm bell activations from the SSU, so I knew it was going to be a real incident. To reach the SSU from B wing was a pain in the ass, going through the top secure corridor and then having to be buzzed through an electronic gate, dropping down a secure staircase, through another electronic gate, and out into a sterile area. It opened out into a big courtyard, which held secure vehicles that brought in or took out escorted prisoners from the prison and linked to the establishment's reception area. I legged it across the sterile area carpark. My heart was starting to pound after sprinting all the way from Bravo wing.

Instead of heading towards the main gate, I had to head towards another electronic gate over to the far side of that compound. Once I managed to get through that, I proceeded to sprint towards the SSU. As I was making my way along the road leading down to it, I noticed a senior officer standing outside of the SSU's front gate. I was first there, which surprised me as B wing was the furthest part away from the SSU in terms of getting there. The SO shouted at me, "There's an escape in progress," and told me to head around the back of the SSU as there were prisoners going over the wall. Unfortunately, they FORGOT to inform me that the escaping prisoners had firearms, so there I go, belting around the corner, heading off towards the back of the SSU. In the distance, I could see a figure standing by the inner meshed security fence of the main prison, a bit farther on from the outside wall of the SSU. I kept on running towards the person by the fence, and they dropped down onto one knee, raising their arms up into a firing position. I saw the tell-tale signs of smoke coming from a weapon, and before I could hear the noise of the discharging weapon, I was thinking to myself, "This fucker just fired something at me." With that in mind, I started to veer off from directly running towards the individual and took off to my left, the only

107

other place to run, which led over to another part of the prison's inner fence. I just kept running and followed it down towards the person who had fired a gun at me. They could see I wasn't stopping, so they backed themselves through what appeared to be a hole in the fence into the sterile area between it and the domed outer prison wall. As this was happening, I could see there were other people in the sterile area: one at the bottom of the makeshift ladder and the one with the gun. It shocked me to see that there were two prisoners already sitting on the dome of the outer prison wall. I can only guess that it must have only taken them around ten minutes or so to get where they were now. It was incredible and quite shocking to see how far they'd managed to get since the 'all stations alarm' was raised by the control room staff. Obviously, these were prisoners from the SSU, and there were questions going around in my head, "How did they get out so fast? How did they manage to get their hands on any sort of firearm?" And I was fucking angry that this toe-rag in front of me was trying to shoot and possibly kill me.

The prisoner who had tried to shoot me had managed to get back through the inner prison security fence, and as I ran down towards them, they pushed the fencing closed, making it very difficult for me to try and gain entry. It had been cut out in a large rectangle shape. As I got near the individual, I slowed down to risk assess in my mind what was going on and what I could do. I could see a firearm in one of the prisoner's hands in front of me, and I could see one of the prisoners on top of the dome had a weapon as well. One prisoner was standing at the bottom of some sort of makeshift ladder, which looked like it was made up of two sets of badminton poles that the group had somehow slung together to make two long poles.

There was a metal hook that passed through the inner wire

fence, around six feet off the ground. It had some bedding and rope intertwined through it and made into some sort of rope that I guessed must have been approximately twenty-five metres in length and disappeared over the top of the dome. As I was taking all this in, a dog handler and a senior officer appeared by my side. The prisoner located just inside the fence said, "Stay where you are, or I will shoot you." I made a remark to him, saying, "Yea, right, it's a blank starting pistol." I assumed the prisoners sitting on the dome could hear the conversation. However, as all this was happening, the prisoner at the bottom of the makeshift ladder climbed up it onto the top of the dome. At the same time, one of those who were perched on it exited over the other side, using the homemade rope to help lower themselves down. I found out later that six prisoners had escaped from the SSU, but when I arrived, I only spotted four of them. Two must have already gone over the prison dome and escaped before I had actually arrived, which meant they had executed their plan without fault.

The mouthpiece balancing on top of the dome, who was stabilising the poles and ladder, appeared to have another gun and was shouting down to his mate nearest to us by the fence (the same one who had previously tried to shoot me), telling them to shoot one of us who were now standing outside the inner security fence. Thankfully, from my point of view, they didn't follow that order, but what they did do was cock the gun they held in their hand and eject a bullet out of the chamber onto the ground. They quickly picked it up, pulling the fence back slightly with their free hand, and threw the bullet onto the floor in front of me. I radioed through to the control room, saying that the weapons the prisoners had were real and not blank guns, as I had initially thought. The weapons had real ammunition in them, which looked to me like .22 calibre bullets. The prisoner had scaled up the makeshift ladder quite quickly, and as the one disappeared over the dome, the other one was already halfway up it. The senior officer knew the prisoner in front of me and started engaging in conversation with them, informing them that we needed to come through the fence and would put the guard dog through to get them. The dog handler, for some reason, basically said, "Don't shoot my dog." I just said, "Fuck that. Get the dog through the fence." But the handler would not commit the dog. Once two of the prisoners I saw had gone over the top of the dome, this left just two. One on top of the dome, and the other guarding the hole by the fence with a gun. The latter said, "Don't come through the fence." They then made their way over to the makeshift ladder. The one on top of the dome was pointing their gun down at us, covering the escape of the last prisoner, who quickly started to make their way up the ladder. They managed to get about halfway up, but for some reason lost their grip and fell back down. Luckily for them, they landed on their feet. They immediately went up again, and this time they managed to reach the top, quickly disappearing over the other side of the dome to lower themselves to the ground on the other side. The prisoner, who I thought must have been the first up on the dome, ended up being the last one to go over the prison wall and the dome on top of it.

They grabbed the rope, taking the strain of it in both of their hands, and I thought to myself, "Right, you ass wipe, I'll fucking stop you." I pushed the inner fence open and quickly darted through the gap. I jumped up, grabbed hold of the makeshift rope, and pulled it as hard as I could, with all my weight and strength, downwards and towards me. I managed to pull it just enough so that a small amount of slack appeared. I then simply let go of it, and the rope snapped away from me due to the weight of the prisoner holding on to it. That was enough for the homemade rope to break, and it whipped away from me and the metal hook linking it to the fence. The last thing I saw was the person disappearing with the rope that made a noise like the sound of a whip as it snaked over the top of the dome after them. I thought to myself, "They are going to be in for a rough landing when they hit the concrete floor on the other side." I guess a fall from that height could kill them, but they seemed to want me dead not long ago, so I didn't pay too much thought to what may have happened to them after they were no longer visible to me. I was just using minimum force as I saw it to try and stop a terrorist escaping from lawful custody. The next thing I did was run over to the makeshift ladder and just push it to the left, so it came crashing down. The senior officer and dog handler were still standing by the fence. I informed them I would head towards the main gate so I could get out of the prison and help give chase. It took me a few minutes to get back to the main gate through the sterile area. I threw my keys into the main gate's key shoot, and the staff let me through the various sterile electronic gates to exit the establishment.

I turned to my right and ran about one hundred and fifty metres towards the officers' mess. There were quite a few people in there. I shouted that an escape from the SSU was in progress, and there were a number of prisoners who had managed to breach the prison wall and were now on the run, and they should keep the officers' mess doors locked. I then hightailed it down to where the prisoners had managed to get over the wall. I thought to myself, "The prisoner who had fallen must have landed very heavily on the concrete." However, there was no one there now, no prisoners, nor staff. I was wondering what to do next. I was thinking, "Where would they have escaped to?", "Where would I go?"

If anyone has visited March in Cambridgeshire, you will know that it is so flat in that area, with no hills, some rivers, and lots of very big water dykes that are probably twenty to thirty metres across. An officer came around the corner. I didn't know who they were, but I told them there was no sign of anyone and that we should follow a path leading towards a road past the officers' mess. We headed off towards an open field that eventually led to either a river or dyke. Once we reached it, we turned right, as it was obvious by then the prisoners had not headed towards the town of March. We started to walk along the edge of the dyke or riverbank as the ground in the field was quite uneven, and it was also quite dark. The farther we walked, the more we eventually left the lights of the prison behind us, which shone in the distant background along with the mess and road streetlights. We could see flashing lights further on and over to the left in the distance towards the main road, which I assumed must be some sort of police response teams. The prison control room must have told them that an escape was in progress. They were probably tactical support units, which meant they would have firearms, and not long after that, a helicopter appeared. I have no idea where they had been tasked from.

They had something that I call "night sun" from my days in Northern Ireland, which lit up areas on the ground. They also had thermal imaging, which can detect people on the ground who may be hiding. We must have walked a fair bit, but we eventually reached a track that may have been a public right of way. I suggested we make our way along it and head towards the police lights that were flashing away in the distance. As we made our way along the track, we spotted some clothes and some homemade weapons (*see Appendix C for examples*), along with some scalpels, so we now knew we were heading in the right direction, although I didn't understand why those items were just lying there on the ground. We left the items where they were, as they would become police evidence in any court case later, and we didn't know if anyone else had either found or touched them. The prison control room came on the radio, saying that four prisoners had been apprehended and were being taken back to the prison. The time passed very quickly, and it wasn't long before the thermal imaging camera picked up where the other two prisoners were. As far as I was aware, they were picked up and taken back to the prison, as it came across the radio for all staff to return to the establishment. We went back along the track and picked up the items that had been discarded, we assumed, by the prisoners. Once we arrived back, we were sent to the block to help relocate the captured prisoners into cells and put them into sterile clothes, so any items they had on them were bagged and tagged along with the items that had been picked up by us.

The prisoners were seen by healthcare to see if they had any injuries. They may have received a few cuts and bruises whilst being recaptured. I identified the prisoner who had tried to shoot me and the other one, who had been the mouthpiece on top of the wall. Once things had settled down, we were required to head to the visits hall, where we were met by a governor grade. It was getting late, but we were told we had to write our witness statements there and then before we could go off duty. I wrote my statement as I had witnessed how things had unfolded in front of me, and I did not talk to other staff about what I had written down. It had been a long day, and I was knackered after completing an A shift (twelve hours) and then responding to the alarm. It must have been about half one in the morning when I eventually left the prison, but I was just glad everything turned out alright. But you can imagine, in the morning, the media were going to be all over this story like a rash, but that wasn't my problem; that's what governors are paid for. I bet the prime minister would have known about the events of the night before when they were tucking into their full English breakfast the following morning.

I lived around ten to fifteen minutes from the prison, but when I eventually got home, the first thing I did was run a hot bath, pour myself a large brandy, put it at the top of the stairs and soak in the bath for a while. It was really hot, but after that, I got out and sat at the top of the stairs, drank the brandy, and then burst into tears. I think there must have been so many emotions flashing around in my head, and the steaming hot bath must have been the thing I needed to push the unwind button. But I also think about the fact that someone had tried to shoot me. It was better to get it out of the system than let it fester and eat away at the mind. The "what ifs" always run through your mind, and I didn't find out until later in the night before I left the prison for home that one prison officer had been hit directly or by a ricochet bullet that had been fired in the SSU whilst the prisoners were escaping.

It's disappointing that the control room never told us that an officer had been wounded by use of a firearm, especially when I initially thought it was a blank gun being fired at me! What I am almost certain about is that the first prisoner on top of the dome must have been the last person off it, as they were the one supporting the makeshift ladder. Although I only saw four prisoners at the time, two must have gone over the dome whilst I was running to get to the SSU. The two prisoners that were on the top of the dome when I got there must have made their way up the makeshift ladder one by one, and when they went over the top, as soon as one of them started to go over, then the third prisoner by the ladder must have started to climb, and so on, until they all disappeared from my view. The first prisoner up onto the dome must have been an anchor point for the top of the badminton poles and ladder. As far as I could tell, they were helping the other climbers as they reached their position on top of the dome. That made sense to me because, with the person on the top securing things, they could all exit the prison in a timely manner. If more than one prisoner had tried to get up the ladder and over the top, then there was a good chance the poles would have collapsed, and then they would be in a right state trying to put everything back up, and it would have given us the opportunity to tackle them in the sterile area, or those that were left anyway. I have never seen anyone else's witness statements, so I have no idea what others may have seen from their perspective, but I know my observations are the truth as I see them.

The thing about the Whitemoor escape was that from the staff's ground floor perspective, it looked like appeasement towards the prisoners in the SSU by junior governors, senior governors, civil servants, and the John Major government of the day were at play, in this case, because of the negotiations towards the Good Friday or

Belfast Agreement, as it is known, which was then ratified under the Blair government in 1998. Many staff believed that security of the prison and staff were sold out to ensure terrorists were kept sweet with the process, as it was being discussed in diplomatic offices in the background, so they could eventually be repatriated to Northern Ireland. The only question I would ask those people who escaped is, "With the Good Friday or Belfast Agreement going forward, why try to break out of a prison when the likelihood would be soon that they would be repatriated to Northern Ireland?" The only one I do understand who would want to escape from lawful custody at that time would be the armed blagger.

I did see some camera footage a little while after the escape that showed the after-effects of my snapping the homemade rope away from the inner security fence. It showed the prisoner falling from height. It also showed prisoners trying to run away from staff and the guard dogs and the discharge of a gun whilst the dogs were running after and close to the escapees. I worked with military guard dogs in the army, and they would not have acted in the same way prison guard dogs did; they attack you, hold you down, and will continue to attack until called off by the handler. There could be a flaw in the way prison guard dogs are trained.

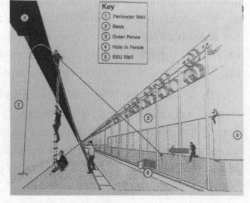

PUBLIC DOCUMENT, PARTIAL WOODCOCK REPORT OF
THE ENQUIRY INTO THE ESCAPE OF SIX PRISONERS FROM
THE SPECIAL SECURITY UNIT AT WHITEMOOR PRISON,
CAMBRIDGESHIRE.

Section 3: The events of Friday 9th September 1994

3.1   Until 8.10 p.m., Friday 9th September had been a very normal shift within Whitemoor SSU. The full complement of 7 staff were on duty. The two officers allocated to the control room were monitoring an outgoing telephone call and the security cameras, respectively. The Senior Officer and three of those on General Duties were playing a game of scrabble and the fourth officer was reading a book; all five were located in the general association area of the Unit.

3.2   In the preparatory period and early stages of the escape, the majority of the self-made escape equipment, consisting of a wooden-runged rope ladder, other lengths of rope, metal poles and a clamping device, was probably passed out via the windows of the hobbies room, into the area called the sterile area which is located between the SSU building and the SSU security wall. This area was devoid of CCTV camera coverage.

3.3   The six escapees had each donned suitable clothing, with three of them wearing double sets of clothes thought to be in anticipation of a night on the Fens. They moved into the exercise yard, passing through the general association area unchallenged by staff. It was not the practice in the SSU for staff to supervise inmates in the exercise yard. Concealed within the escapees' possession were a pair of bolt croppers, a screwdriver, a stanley knife and a pair of pliers. They cut a hole in the exercise yard fence, which was not alarmed, bent back the cut area allowing entry into the sterile area and access to the SSU security wall.

3.4   They collected the rest of the escape equipment and, using the metal poles to provide support, the metal clamp, with a rope attached, was pushed up the face of the wall and lodged astride the top. The escapees then climbed the rope in turn, some descending the other side unobserved by SSU staff.

3.5   Whilst the tail-enders were still negotiating the first wall, the other escapees cut a section out of the next fence and forcefully bent back the resultant flap to gain access to the sterile area which is inside the outer wall. This action set off the fence alarm which alerted the Emergency Control Room (ECR) in the main prison.

3.6   Control staff watched incredulously as the CCTV screens revealed escaping inmates methodically climbing the outer wall, apparently unhurried by fear of challenge or recapture.

3.7   The ECR staff telephoned the SSU and alerted them of the escape in progress, by which time there was already an escapee at the outer wall. It was all happening in slow motion but everyone seemed powerless to stop it.

3.8   Jolted into action by the emergency telephone call, several SSU officers ran out into the exercise yard and one dived through the hole in the fence, into the sterile area. Although most of the escapees and equipment were by that time over the SSU wall, the officer saw the last two still climbing a rope and another one sitting astride the wall. He ran towards the rope, intending to tackle the last two inmates when he was hit by a bullet fired by the escapee sitting on top of the wall. Other officers assisted their injured colleague back into the exercise yard but this did not deter a number of other officers who had arrived from the segregation unit from entering the sterile area, under threat of being fired upon.

3.9   The other escapees had, meanwhile, passed through the second fence and set up the rope ladder at the outer prison wall to give access onto the beak. The ladder was attached to the top of the two sets of volleyball and badminton poles, adapted to fix end to end, and was supported by at least one guy rope. They put a further rope down the outside of the outer wall. This last rope was attached to the second fence, utilising a 'U' bolt clamp, and the end dropped over the top of the wall, to the ground below.

3.10   Whilst the ladder was being set up at the outer wall, one of the last escapees stood guard at the hole in the second fence, brandishing a pistol. Prison officers and a dog handler arrived at the area of the breach in the second fence; the gunman challenged them and fired at least one shot.

3.11   As the response progressed, staff were deployed both from within the prison and from the shift arriving for the start of their duty. At one stage there were four of the escapees perched on the top of the outer wall. As one of the escapees descended the outer wall, a dog handler approached him but was threatened with a pistol and backed away without releasing his dog. A group of officers gathered at the corner of the outer wall, outside the prison boundary and about 15 metres south of the escapees location.

3.12   Further officers stood near the inner fence, held at bay until the last man climbed the ladder. As the last escapee descended from the wall, however, a prison officer inside the establishment released the anchor point of the rope and the escapee fell heavily to the ground.

3.13   With all escapees down from the wall, they turned and ran northwards along the perimeter road, pursued at a short distance by the group of prison officers, including a number of dog handlers with dogs, some of which had been released from their leads. During the early stages of the pursuit one escapee fired one shot and then attempted to fire again at the officers but the gun appeared to jam. A substance, believed pepper, was thrown at the dogs.

3.14   Within a short distance of the prison, one escapee became isolated from the rest and was arrested by pursuing officers. The remaining five ran off towards the nearby nature trail, along the route of a disused railway line. About three-quarters of a mile along the trail the fleeing inmates were challenged by unarmed police officers with high powered torches, located on a railway bridge. Three of the escapees responded to a shouted instruction from the pursuing prison staff to lay down, perhaps believing the police to be armed.

3.15 The remaining two escapees branched off across surrounding fenland and went to ground. They were located some ninety minutes later by the use of a thermal imager operated from a police helicopter. They had hidden in vegetation at the base of a bank near the edge of a field, only a few feet from a main road. Officers on the ground were then directed to their location and the recapture was completed.

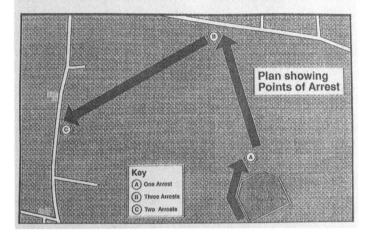

Plan showing Points of Arrest

Key
(A) One Arrest
(B) Three Arrests
(C) Two Arrests

ARTICLE FROM THE PUBLICATION AN PHOBLACHT 23 JANUARY 1997.

In what is fast becoming a sensational trial into the breakout from Whitemoor Prison in September 1994, the prison governor has given evidence in court, under oath, that he misled the Woodcock Inquiry into the escape.

The trial of six men - Republican prisoners Liam O'Duibhir, Peter Sherry, Liam McCotter and Paul 'Dingus' Magee, miscarriage of justice victim Danny McNamee and English prisoner Andy Russell - began on Monday 13 January at Woolwich Crown Court in London.

Prison Governor Brodie Clarke has provided the most controversial evidence. A 22-year veteran of the prison service, Clarke was appointed Governor of Whitemoor in May 1994. The prosecution case is that the items used in the escape were all smuggled in by visitors, including the guns and a bulky bolt cutters. Clarke gave evidence that the security procedures for searching visitors were inadequate, that there was no X-Ray machine, no metal-detecting portal and no use of hand-held metal-detecting wands. Later this evidence was directly contradicted by a junior governor at the prison, Governor Vert, while visitors to Whitemoor who have spoken to An Phoblacht recall stringent security measures, including metal detecting equipment.

Clarke also gave evidence that the men, all High Risk Category A prisoners, had no Category A books during their time in Whitemoor SSU. He later retracted this evidence and said that the books had been there but were not used. A prisoner who is 'on the book' routinely has his every move recorded in that book by prison staff, his photo is in the book and any disciplinary actions recorded. The book always travels with the prisoner. Michael

Mansfield, appearing for Liam McCotter, quoted prison rules to the governor, showing that not to have filled in the books was a complete flouting of those rules. Andrew Russell, who is defending himself, put it to the governor that the books were not available to the court because they would show that he was having a shower in the SSU at the time the fence was cut and that none of the other men were in the yard. The judge ordered Clarke, who is in line for a promotion, to produce the books.

Michael Mansfield then asked Clarke how many visits he had made while governor to the SSU. Clarke was adamant that he had made between six and a dozen visits. Mansfield than produced the security gatebook for the SSU which showed that Clarke had not been in the SSU between July and December 1994. Clarke said there must have been an error. Mansfield than referred Clarke to his statement to the Woodcock Inquiry into the September 1994 escape. In that statement he said he had visited the SSU at most three times. "Did you lie to this court or did you lie to Sir John Woodcock?" asked Mansfield. Clarke then said that if that was what was written down then he must have misled Woodcock.

It also emerged during cross examination that prison staff had been invited by the Prison Service to a training session in September 1996 to cover a briefing and role play for staff giving evidence at the trial. Clarke claimed that the role play had prepared the staff for the trial in a manner that would not obstruct the course of justice. He rejected a suggestion by Tony Jennings, counsel for Danny McNamee, that the purpose of the session had been to 'all get together and sort it out'.

The six men are charged with breaking from the prison, possession of two guns with intent and with intent to commit a felony. Magee is also charged with causing grevious bodily harm. All have pleaded not guilty. Magee has chosen not to attend the trial.

The breaking charge is significant as it differs from the more usual charge of escaping. 'Breaking' is an archaic charge going back to Fenian times, when dynamite was often used in escape attempts. The maximum sentence under English law for escape is seven years. For breaking it is life. However, for the prosecution to prove the breaking charge they have to prove that the men caused physical damage to prison property while making their exit from the prison.

This task is proving difficult. Although two perimeter wire fences were cut, the prison authorities claim to have no surveillance tape pictures of the fence being cut, nor of the men firing any shots despite all the sophisticated surveillance equipment around the prison.

Crown Counsel Waters told the court in his opening address that the fence had been cut at a 'blind spot' for the cameras, that the first fence was not alarmed, that the alarm only sounded in the prison's control booth after the men scaled the SSU wall and reached the second fence. He also asked the jury to believe that there was no camera cover for the cutting of the second fence and that the surveillance camera system had no automatic recording facility. He claimed that it was more than four minutes after the men reached the second fence, in the process setting off a trembler alarm, before an inexperienced prison officer finally remembered to push a manual record button.

The prosecution case also includes evidence that a security camera which should have rotated to sweep the SSU exercise yard had been fixed in one direction when a prisoner complained of paranoid feelings that the camera was following him. The first sight of the men on the surveillance tape that has been made available to the court begins just inside the outer prison wall.

Michael Mansfield QC has this week suggested to various prison officers that the men did not cut the fences but that this task had been carried out by prison officers. Already there are indications that the prosecution may ask the court to drop the breaking charge and replace it with a charge of escape. The case continues.

NICKI JAMESON FOLLOWS THE STORY OF THE
WHITEMOOR ESCAPE 3 JANUARY 2017.

The second trial of the six would-be escapers from Whitemoor prison came to an abrupt end on 23 January 1997 when Judge Maurice Kay ruled that adverse publicity meant the men could not receive a fair trial. The publicity in question was an article in the previous night's *Evening Standard* and editor Max Hastings was summoned to court to apologise. The first trial, in October 1996, had closed just two days after it opened, for exactly the same reason, and Hastings and the journalist who wrote the offending article appear to be the only media employees in London who were unaware of this situation. Unless, that is, the truth is more sinister and the one-time Falklands war correspondent turned right-wing editor, rather than making an unfortunate mistake, was doing his patriotic duty and ensuring the state's secrets remained secret. A case of investigative journalism in reverse.

By the time the trial was halted, it had become evident that the prison officers and governors giving evidence were not only contradicting one another, but were telling a substantially different story to the one they told to the government's Woodcock Enquiry conducted directly after the escape. It had also become clear that crucial pieces of evidence, mainly in the form of video film, were mysteriously 'missing'. Leaping ten steps ahead of general suspicion that 'bent screws' had assisted the prisoners in their bid for freedom, Michael Mansfield QC posed the blunt question to the media assembled outside Belmarsh Crown Court, 'Was this something where the security services set up the escape?'

If such a scenario is indeed the case, and many sources confirm entrapment as highly likely, it begs the further question as to what the purpose of such an exercise would be, particularly as the escape brought such opprobrium down on the Prison Service. There are two main reasons why such a high-profile 'disaster' would ultimately be in the state's interest: firstly, it might have been considered a way to disrupt the 'peace process' in Ireland and dismiss any demands being put forward for an amnesty for political prisoners; secondly, it might have been seen as a useful tool in the drive towards increased repression in British prisons. The counter-argument to the second suggestion is that the government doesn't *need* to manufacture excuses to attack prisoners' rights; it does so anyway, seizing on occurrences such as riots, escapes or crimes committed by prisoners on home leave, whenever it needs to. There is *no* doubt, however, that, whoever initiated the Whitemoor escape, it *was* then exploited for such a purpose.

The Woodcock Enquiry recommended a whole series of repressive measures which are now in operation, not just in high-security gaols or Special Security Units (SSUs), such as the one the men escaped from at Whitemoor, but in every prison in Britain. The Woodcock report tells of an honest but demoralised prison staff running a high-security prison where tough prisoners rule the roost, security measures are lax and prisoners have unlimited personal possessions, private cash and access to telephones. In this context the escape is described as 'a disaster waiting to happen' and has been used to justify the introduction of. among other measures: volumetric control (limitation on personal possessions to what can be fitted in two small boxes), random cell-searches at which the prisoner is not permitted to be present, Dedicated Search Teams trained to do nothing but conduct searches, restrictions on private cash and CCTV in visiting rooms.

Woodcock suggests that closed visits are the only 'completely secure' option for exceptional high-risk prisoners (i.e. those kept in SSUs — the Whitemoor escapees have been on permanent closed visits, both domestic and legal, for over two years and all judicial challenges to this have so far been rejected).

The prisoners involved in the escape refused, not surprisingly, to speak to the Enquiry team at all. Woodcock also met resistance from prison staff, as did Cambridgeshire police who were conducting their own investigation. A prisoner at Whitemoor told FRFI in November 1994 that the main preoccupation of staff who spoke to Woodcock seemed to be 'diverting the attention onto the visitors when they know they should be looking closer to home'. In January 1995 the Director of Public Prosecutions sent detectives back to re-question some officers whose statements were unclear, prior to deciding whether to prosecute the six or not; the officers refused to answer any questions.

The 'missing' video evidence concerns the first four minutes of the escape and some seconds worth of the part where the three prisoners who got over the wall, but got no further, were recaptured. This latter part allegedly shows Danny McNamee being beaten by prison officers and it is obvious why the prison authorities should want it to be lost. However, despite the standard POA denials, the beating is a matter of record. Andy Russell wrote to FRFI after his recapture: 'Outside the gaol I had them sitting on me under the same conditions (cuffed and face down) while one pulled my head back for another to kick. It was the same for Danny McNamee... More mystery surrounds the earlier film which, if the prosecution case were true, would show the prisoners cutting a hole in the fence with bolt-cutters; if the case the defence hoped to run is true, the film would show the prisoners going through a hole which had already been cut.

The question of 'who cut the fence?' is crucial to the debate as to whether the prisoners acted alone, were assisted, or were entrapped. Furthermore, given that the men were charged not with escape (maximum sentence 10 years), but with 'breaking prison' (maximum sentence life imprisonment), it was important while the trial continued that they prove that it was not they who actually substantially damaged the fabric of the prison and did the physical 'breaking'. Aware of the difficulties it was running into in this respect, the prosecution had told the judge that they would be applying to have the charge on the indictment changed to escape. But before they could actually put in their application, the trial was stopped.

There seems little doubt that this trial was halted deliberately before it got too close to the truth. Whether it would have got all the way there is impossible to guess at. Likewise, in the unlikely event that Mike Mansfield's demand for a second public enquiry is granted, it may very well be just another, better cover-up. But the 'Whitemoor story' is not going to lie down and die. Among others, the wife of prison officer Brian Curran, 'missing', like the video evidence, since March 1995 when he was suspended from his job at Whitemoor, will see to that, as will her MP, a former aide to Prisons' Minister Anne Widdecombe.

There may, of course, be no link between the escape, Curran's disappearance and the death of prison officer Marcia Whitehurst, who was on her way to court to give her second day's evidence to the escape trial when her car plunged into a river. And the Pope may not be a Catholic.

For the six prisoners concerned, the collapse of the trial is a victory and they are overjoyed. They have succeeded in sowing massive public doubt about the integrity of prison staff and have not been convicted of anything as a result of the escape. The next stage for them now will be to continue their struggle against closed visits, a 'security' restriction imposed to punish visitors as well as prisoners, and completely redundant if you accept that the Whitemoor escapees were 'assisted' by prison officers, not visitors. And there will be a further court hearing: civil action is being instigated over the beatings the men sustained on their recapture. Stand by for more revelations — this is Britain in the 1990s and beneath the facade of democracy and judicial accountability, the state is ruthless.

FURTHER COMMENT BY ME

I heard about Marcia's death because I was on duty at Whitemoor when it happened. My recollection was that she was driving to work and on a sharp right hand bend, her car had left the road and ended up in one of the rivers or water dykes, and she died because of that. I don't know anything more than that, but it didn't stop the conspiracy theorists from having a field day. But I didn't know anything about Officer Curran's dismissal or disappearance.

ARTICLE FROM THE IRISH TIMES: THU MAR 13 1997

THE British Attorney General said yesterday that he would bring contempt proceedings against a London newspaper over an article which led to the abandonment of the trial of five IRA prisoners and an armed robber.

The trial of the six, accused of breaking out of a top security prison, collapsed in January after the Evening Standard described the defendants as terrorists, accompanying the article with photos of three of the men.

The defendant's lawyers successfully argued that the article about Belmarsh Prison, where the defendants were being held, had made it impossible for them to receive a fair trial.

Legal restrictions meant that the defendant's criminal histories should not have been mentioned by the media during the trial.

The trial judge asked the Attorney General to consider contempt of court proceedings after a hearing at which Evening Standard editor, Mr Max Hastings, was asked to explain why he had run the article. A lawyer for the paper offered the court an "unqualified, unconditional apology" on behalf of Mr Hastings, the article's author, Mark Honigsbaum, the Evening Standard and its publishers, Associated Newspapers. He said the mistake was due to "human error".

Five IRA men and a sixth man were charged with breaking out of prison in 1994 and possessing a firearm with intent to endanger life. It was the second time the men's trial had been abandoned. The first last year, ended after just one day, when details of the defendants' past convictions appeared in news reports.

The judge in the January trial ruled that the case should not come before a court again. He dismissed the prosecution argument that prejudice was minimal because the jury would eventually put two and two together and assume the defendants, because of their Irish names and the nature of their imprisonment, were convicted terrorists.

Following the hearing in January, Mr Michael Mansfield, the defence counsel for one of the IRA prisoners, called for a public inquiry into the break out, saying that there were unanswered questions about events on the night of the escape.

What I don't understand is why I was never called to be one of the first to give evidence, considering that I saw everything after I had arrived first at the front and then ran down the outside of the SSU towards the back end of it. I would have thought that any governor grade would have been the last to be called. Mind you, looking at the articles I have seen, you can see why a certain governor grade was called first. Those of us trying to do our jobs properly were, in my opinion, seriously let down by senior grades in the prison, the civil service and the government of the day. I have only just come across the An Phoblacht and Nikki Jameson articles 2 March 2023, along with the Irish Times article, but just from my point of view, there appear to be a lot of unanswered questions in relation to the Whitemoor escape. Of course, I can only give my evidence based on what I saw and did that night, but what I can say is, I was never involved in any role-play before the trial commenced. When I read the articles and saw what the governor grade said, I was really quite shocked to hear their evidence, but when I raised factual things later on in my book, I can see why a clique operates in the higher governor and senior civil service grades. I am truly shocked because it seems to me as if there is some clandestine operation going on across the whole of government departments. If this is the case, then it's no wonder that people in our country are calling for radical change from what we know about politicians and others now.

I know national security is paramount, but not for the sake of truth and covering up, especially when my life and that of others were in danger. Learning some things today really makes my head spin, but why am I not surprised when I know about my own treatment by other senior governors and civil servants, which happened later on.

I personally think there are quite a few inaccuracies in The Woodcock Report. However, it still adds up to some shocking things that happened during the night, where five IRA terrorists and one armed robber were able to escape from lawful custody, but locally we called it the escape that never happened. From what I heard; prisoners were given a free rein to pretty much do what they wanted over in the SSU. Any escape planning did not happen overnight; it must have taken a fair while to manipulate staff to the extent whereby the prisoners were, in effect, in charge of the SSU and those working within it. What's interesting to note is that the Board of Visitors (BOV) monitoring board highlighted areas of concern to prison governors who did not act on the information provided to them. If the prison officer who had been shot had died, then a corporate manslaughter charge would have ensued. Something to ponder on for any future governors, managers, or politicians out there! The media had a field day about the whole thing; a lot of staff were interviewed by Woodcock's team, and the whole thing took some time to unravel to get to the truth! Conveniently enough, The Woodcock Report was designed not to apportion blame. However, heads should have rolled all the way up to government for Whitemoor's and their failures that night in September 1994. I and a lot of the staff serving there were of the opinion that there was a big cover-up going on by prison governors, senior civil servants, and maybe even up to the prime minister's office.

The escape was heading towards a trial. We had all been interviewed by the police, but somehow two large sources of information were released to the press, and in the end, the judge said the prisoners would not receive a fair trial. I always wondered who had leaked the information. One I now know to be the Evening Standard's staff, but those of us who were ex-military were of the opinion the leak before that was someone in Major's government in 1996. I do wonder whether there was any collusion between the conservative and labour governments, but most certainly there must have been people in the back offices supporting the Good Friday or Belfast Agreement. The Evening Standards article happened during Blair's government. The whole thing was conveniently put to bed from their point of view, and no one was ever hauled over the coals. A few governors were apparently promoted and moved to other posts, but they would pop up again elsewhere in the civil service in the future to cause mayhem. How can we keep rewarding failure through incompetence? Those people put my life at risk. They just love to keep rewarding failure in the prison and senior civil service, including parts of government, instead of going with the old military saying, "Mag to grid get rid," which basically means, "Sack 'em!" What do you think? Maybe that's why our country is in such a mess.

Moving on from the sorry saga of that night in September 1994 and the effect it had on various people, things took months to settle back down. Hopefully, you will remember I mentioned that I would have to go through the normal route to try and get up the promotion ladder. 1994 moved into 1995, and at the start of that year, I was eligible to sit my senior officer's paper. I had been in the prison service for just over four years, and they only held the exam at a certain time of the year. Whitemoor was around eight to twelve senior officers short, and they held promotion boards for staff, both internally and externally, to bring the number of managers up to a more respectable level. The reason for this was that it's officers who act up to the next grade, so as you can imagine, it depletes those on the coalface, which then means staff must work additional hours, accruing additional hours over and above their scheduled contractual hours - TOIL.

I think it took around two months to get the results back, and I was successful in gaining my first promotion. The governors decided to leave me on Bravo wing at the time as one of its four main senior officers. I knew everyone on the wing, so it made sense to me. I started to learn all about the role of a first line manager, dealing with shift patterns, management boards, and sick absences. When you are a prison officer, you observe a lot of what goes on, so the transition from that grade to becoming a manager wasn't difficult. The only thing I found was, some staff can make life more difficult, for whatever reason that may be. I was the T boat officer when I was originally on the ground floor. Most members of staff pay towards the fund on a wing, it's a pain in the ass role, but it worked well, so I kept doing it when I became a senior officer. Making sure staff have access to a brew is quite an important thing; you can trust me on that one!

As a senior officer, it gave me a lot more freedom to try and improve things on the wing, especially in terms of systems to make life easier for everyone, but the main role was about managing the regime through the core day. I mentioned that mainstream prisoners do not have time for certain prisoners who, in their eyes, have committed offences that they see as being below their own, even though that does not matter in the eyes of the law. If you ended up in prison, you were a criminal, regardless of the offence. Maybe it was a way of deflecting their guilt about their own crime.

One day, when prisoners were going to return to their wings from the workshops at T time, some bright spark in the control room who oversaw the process told the wings to staff the gates to receive prisoners back. Well, for some reason, all the workshops released all the mainstream and vulnerable prisoners (VPs) at the same time. They all made their way back up the main corridor, and staff were letting the VPs onto Alpha and Bravo wings, while the mainstream prisoners just carried on up to Charlie and Delta wings. I am amazed and astounded that there wasn't a riot or attacks on the VPs. It could have ended up bad, really bad, but it was a bullet the prison dodged and got away with. But I can tell you this: the staff in the control room got some flying fucks thrown at them down the phone after all prisoners were located safely back on their respective wings. It could have been terrible, like another 1990 Manchester Strangeways, when a riot took the roof off it.

Life as a senior officer was straightforward, with some handbags at twenty paces, fights, and general trouble, but there are incidents that stick in my mind from my time on Bravo wing. Officers patrol the landings, and governors visit the wings at certain times, depending on what their duties are that day. A governor turned up in the evening; prisoners love to see governors so they can try and bypass the system we had to deal with complaints. Well, this governor did not want escorting around the wing by me, but we know what's going on and how to deflect crap coming towards the governor grades.

This particular governor wanted to walk around on their own. I said, "Are you really sure you want to do that?" They just said, "Yes," and commenced their rounds off on Green Spur and managed to get around it okay without too many problems, but when they arrived on Blue 1s, they were surrounded by prisoners, who started to give them a hard time. All I could see were staff on the 2s laughing down at them and not bothering to go and help them negotiate their way through the prisoners, so I quickly went down to help sort out whatever the problem was. I managed to extricate them from the prisoners, answering any questions they were trying to put to the governor grade. As we were walking along and up the metal stairs to Blue 2s, I could tell the governor was not best happy, but we continued on our way. It's normal for staff to acknowledge governors when they walk around the wing, giving their numbers and informing them what things are going on. We eventually got around onto Red Spur 2s and walked along there to the end stairwell, and then proceeded onto the 3s. Right at the end of the landing we were walking along, there was an officer sitting on a chair with it pushed back on two legs with their legs balanced on the railings, drinking a cup of tea. Well, to say the governor grade was not amused was to put it politely. As we walked up, the officer just sat there and never said anything to the governor grade. However, I could see that the governor grade was going to burst with fury, their face was purple. They came with me down to the office, closed the door, and gave me one of the biggest rollickings I have ever had, which pretty much meant the staff were fucking lazy and had no respect for them. I said I would deal with it. Staff knew what their job was, but they, for whatever reason, decided they did not want to do it that night; maybe they just didn't like that particular governor grade. After bang up, I gathered all the staff in the rest room, closed the door, and basically gave them what I had just received in the office. I do regret shouting now, but I had to throw a few fucks out there for them to understand we and I don't need any shit from governor grades. The officer who sat on the landing, drinking tea, was not impressed with me, but they wouldn't be doing that again, not with me on duty anyway. It's the only time I have ever had to do that in my whole prison service career.

Life can be pretty challenging working in a prison environment. I had been a senior officer for around four months, and my initial appraisals were good in terms of stepping up to the management role. After the IRA escape from Whitemoor, as you can imagine, the security of the establishment was stepped up, and a dedicated search team group was set up. The uniform they wore was an all-in-one fireproof black overall. The staff would come on the wing to search prisoners' cells; this could be done because of intelligence information or as a random cell search. Prisoners had to get used to the clampdown, particularly in relation to how many possessions they were allowed in their cells. I suppose the one thing the escape had done was recheck and make sure prisoners were only allowed a more streamlined facilities list and highlight the fact prisoners will use a number of ways to circumvent systems. Prisoners used to call the staff in overalls coming onto the wing "black shirts" when they were cell searching. They came on the wing as a three-person team. Normally it was done during a lock up period, but unbeknown to me, they came on after we had unlocked. Prisoners would attend workshops in the afternoon. Spur gates were open, and the security staff were searching a prisoner on Blue 1s.

The next thing we knew, the prisoner had kicked off, and the alarm bell was activated. I, along with other staff, ran down the secure stairwell to get into the central area. I shouted at staff to lock off the gates on the wing. Some Red Spur prisoners had got through to Blue Spur. I saw a prisoner on the floor being held down by three staff, and there were other prisoners surrounding the staff, shouting and screaming at them. The officers looked dazed. This was getting way out of hand, and very quickly this could go south, and a riot develop. I was telling prisoners to back off, luckily there were staff from my own wing around us. I had to make a quick decision, and I told them to take over the prisoner from the officers who were lying on the ground. Prisoners were going to seriously harm those officers. One prisoner, who I knew very well and was sensible, was near me. I told them I would let our staff walk the apprehended prisoner to the block in no locks, and they verbally communicated that information around the prisoners. This was touch and go. My staff stood by the prisoner, and I told them they would be walking them down the block. At this point, I took a deep breath and told the staff lying on the floor with the prisoner to let them go and move away to go through the bottom secure

137

gates and make their way back up to our staff room.

I'm amazed, even now, that it happened to pass off the way it did. My staff allowed the prisoner to stand up; no locks were used, and other prisoners could see that. It helped defuse the situation. The staff walked the prisoner to the end of the wing, up to Blue 2s towards the secure corridor, and without incident walked them down the block.

Looking towards Blue 2s from the centre office.

If the spur had gone up, we would have been pummelled and got a right kicking and the chances are someone could have been killed. It's as close as I ever came to telling staff to draw their staves. If that had happened, we would have lost control; it was that close. There but for the grace of God go I.

As this was all going on, a governor grade appeared, and other staff were arriving on the wing all the time. They came down with lots of other staff and ordered the wing to lock up. Once a full contingent of staff turns up, it makes dealing with a problem a lot easier. Once prisoners had been located back to their spurs, the first thing I did was go and thank the prisoner who had helped me deal with the incident. As I said, you earn respect in this job, and I would like to believe that over the years I earned that. It's respecting the environment and understanding the consequences of who is doing what and when all the time. The person who had kicked off was now in the segregation unit and would be placed on report. The prisoner I spoke to wanted to go and see the one taken down the block, but that would never be allowed, so I said, "You need to trust me that they are fine and will be seen by a governor the following morning." They took my word at face value.

I then went up to the staff room to talk to the officers who had been in the altercation with the prisoner. One had been bitten, that's how they ended up on the floor. They were not pleased with the way I had dealt with the incident; I just said, "The prisoners down there would have killed you all if I hadn't dealt with it the way I did." I also said if they felt that way, then they should make a formal complaint. The officer who had been bitten was sent off duty to go and get checked out by their own doctor, for HIV, hepatitis etc. They made a full recovery.

We were so damn close to losing our wing. It also transpired that the three staff had not even made it known to our patrolling wing staff that they were on our unit searching a prisoner. Those staff never did make a formal complaint against me.

I really can understand why they would be upset, especially after being bitten, but that's what a manager does, make decisions. On that day, I felt I made the right one. I was told by senior managers that I had dealt with everything well, especially as we were close to losing full control of the spur. Sometimes your own staff can cause trouble without thinking too much about the job that they do or the impact on others! When I think about a lot of the incidents that have occurred, it's someone else who has caused the problem in the first place, and I have been in the wrong place or the right place, depending on your view at the time, where I have had to deal with events as they unfolded and fix them.

I used to be the allocated senior officer who held lifer boards with the wing governor so prisoners could listen to their progress reviews. It was all about risk to see whether they could move forward with their sentence. Although we had some prisoners on Bravo wing who would never be released, they were serving whole life tariffs. Whitemoor would be where they spent the rest of their natural lives, as they had received a whole life tariff. But what made me laugh in the room was that our G5 held these boards every month and wore a pair of glasses without any lenses in them. They would be going through all the documentation with the prisoner, and there would be me and another two staff in the room. As the governor was reading reports and such like, they would start rubbing their eye through the hole where the lens should have been. I used to notice it, but for some reason, prisoners didn't. I don't know why they did that, but that's also something that has stuck in my mind all these years. I used to have to bite my lip to stop myself from laughing sometimes.

Make no bones about it, top security prisoners can be dangerous, real dangerous, and one governor up on the main wings used to want to see their prisoners on their own. Personally, I would never allow that. One day the inevitable happened, and that governor was attacked by a prisoner because they had refused them something. They were very, very lucky. I saw them a few days later, and they looked like Chi-Chi the Panda. The prisoner went over the desk at them and tried to gouge their eyes out. They looked rough, but you have to be so careful when dealing with prisoners; after all, some of them in a dispersal Cat A prison have nothing to lose.

I liked the governor who had been attacked, and they were eventually promoted in situ. They worked really long hours, a bit like me; maybe that's why I liked them. But later down the line, in the sterile office areas where the main administration staff worked along with security and lots of other governor grades, those areas need to be searched as well, and I heard that an open bottle of scotch was found in that governor grades office, but I didn't hear anything more after that. Brush, carpet, sweep it underneath springs to mind if it's true.

Time flies when you are having fun. I must have been a senior officer for a couple of years when I was told that I would be moving off the wing and my next job would be in Whitemoor's security department, and as part of a forthcoming security audit, I would be required to deal with all the prison's tools, so workshops, segregation, SSU, including all wings shadow boards, which held knives, handcuffs, and such like. I think the security audit was around six months away. This really was a thankless task, and I set it up like a project management exercise so I could get it done in a logical, straightforward way and work through the prison in zones. You wouldn't believe how much of a pain in the ass this job was, but I think I was chosen because I am quite a diligent person, and I hate failure, especially my own.

I had to work closely with the locks and keys staff, who dealt with that sort of stuff, to crosscheck all their documentation against the massive amount of stuff we held in the prison. It's not as simple as it sounds. When a governing governor takes over a prison, they must personally sign for all security items under their watch. It then falls to the deputy governor, at least in my experience, to conduct an audit on a monthly basis, signing that everything is in order!

At this point, it is worth mentioning that Whitemoor had been open for a number of years, and everything had been signed for by the governing governor (remember the IRA escape) and subsequent governors after that. I was the new boy in security. I reported to a principal officer (PO) who had been a senior officer before gaining promotion to PO. I am meticulous when it comes to an audit. I worked out my plan. I held copies of all the documentation I needed, and so I started with my grand audit plan. The whole thing needed further structure added to it to comply with the forthcoming audit; this is because nothing in the prison was etched or signed for by staff in their respective areas. This was a large piece of work to ensure every tool, whatever size it was or wherever it may be in the prison, had its own individual serial number linked to equipment and audit but also etched into the item. First of all, I had to dig out and check all keys and security devices held in different parts of the establishment. You will, or maybe you are thinking that something must go wrong, and you would be spot on! The class one, two and suite keys in the prison were fine. If they weren't, heads would roll, but now I had uncovered a problem. I checked all the inventories in relation to security tools like handcuffs, keys, and other such equipment. I just closed my eyes and thought, "This can't be happening to me."

When I was checking ratchet handcuffs, I found two hundred pairs that were not logged on any inventory, along with their cuff keys. Governing governors had been signing for these items since day one, and every deputy governor on their checks were signing them all as correct. In my opinion, I don't think they had even bothered checking everything properly when the prison opened. It's rather ironic that these same types of people had the officer grades looking for security risks on our hands and knees when Whitemoor opened, and yet they couldn't even get theirs right. They must have just signed the documentation and thought, "Well, it's bound to be correct." Well, I can tell you now that was the mother of all fuckups. This was not at all good. I just thought, "Why me? Why is it me that had to find this out?" Shit rolls downwards in the prison service, never up, as prison staff know only too well.

I sat with it overnight, thinking how this problem could be sorted out without the shit hitting the fan. It couldn't. In the end, I approached my line manager the next morning and told them what the problem was. They said, "Put a memo into the deputy governor explaining the issue." I could have kissed them at that point. It would take all the crap off me that would now be raised and sit directly with the deputy governor. I duly sent the memo to them and didn't hear anything for a couple of days, and then a very, very irate security governor who shared our office sometimes came in with a face like thunder, spitting feathers, and asked me what I thought I was playing at, dropping them in the shit about the extra handcuffs we had! I explained everything to them about my discussion with the PO and what they wanted me to do, so I was just following their orders. The problem with all of this is, of course, linked to the governing governor who originally signed for all the security items, with the deputy governor checking them every month, and subsequent governors after that, including the one in front of me, trying to chew me out for their own mistakes, trying to deflect their own inadequacies and incompetence onto me.

I had to remind them of the facts in this case, and I basically said, "It wasn't my job to tell, but sometimes advise governors how to do their job, and if they and others did not account for things properly, well, then that's down to them." They said, "I had ruined his career." I said no, "The original governing governor had done that, and all the ones that have just taken everything as read, including them, instead of checking things properly."

They managed to get promoted at some point to become a governing governor somewhere up north. Leeds springs to mind for some reason. Rewarding failure is what senior civil servants do time and time again as part of their clique. All these so-called top governors in the prison service's flagship prison have been promoted and are now high up in the civil service; some may even be retired. I expect it was somehow all brushed under the carpet, but my conscience was clear. They left me alone after that. What I did was arrange for the locks and keys staff to take the cuffs back to central stores. I never heard anything else after that. There was no investigation and why am I not surprised by that! What a bunch of wankers though!

People getting paid to fail again, and a lot more than I was earning in my position I can tell you!

It took around four months for me to get around everywhere to make sure everything was perfectly correct and make sure staff were happy with the audit paperwork trail linked to the forthcoming security audit. People will know that you need clear and sustained evidence to gain markings linked to a procedure you have introduced. The audit team came in and scrutinised everything, and I mean everything, but the end result was fantastic. My area was signed off, and along with my other SO colleagues with their sign offs for different audits, Whitemoor Prison was awarded an overall 'Good' marking. As a member of the security department, I was required to have a uniform issued linked to the 'black shirts', as prisoners called them. It had to be ordered, and then you waited for it to arrive. It took around three months, but I eventually received all my stuff. I can't help but think the name prisoners made up had links to a certain party in World War II.

The next thing I had to deal with as part of my duties was linked to the Good Friday or Belfast Agreement, and that was to set up the repatriation of terrorist prisoners back to Northern Ireland. This is something that would have been happening around the country, but it felt weird. I had been part of a full circle operation: back in the military, helping to stabilise a country in what I call a bloody civil war, I then moved to the prison service to help ensure those terrorists committed to prison by the courts were kept secure, and now I was sending them back as part of a rehabilitation deal. In effect, I had been fighting against them; they against me, and now we were all buddies again! I would be lying to say it didn't play on my mind, especially when a few mates were killed in NI during the troubles, but you have to rise above everything, be professional, and

145

get on with the job in hand. Remember what I said: work is work, home is home, and you keep them separate.

Terrorists were only moved as single movement prisoners whenever I was allocated to repatriate them. It was never more than that at a time, and it was usually early in the morning, way before unlocking. When I planned and set up different movements myself, I would always be the one to see them through. What I mean by this is, I would come in to make sure on the day that the whole thing went smoothly. It may have been three o'clock in the morning, but it was a low-key affair, and very few people knew what was going to happen until it happened. I would go to the wing on my own, explain to the night duty staff on the wing what was going on, and utilise them to come with me to wake the prisoner.

Once I unlocked them, I would explain that they were being moved as part of the Good Friday or Belfast Agreement, which obviously made them very happy.

This takes out any tension from a psychological point of view between you and them, and they want to comply! The prisoner would be given an hour's notice at the most to move, so they could pack their immediate personal possessions in a bag. I would wait outside the prisoner's cell for them to get organised. Once the time had passed, they would bring their plastic prison bags out on the landing, and their cell would be sealed with a door padlock. The rest of their belongings would be searched and packed up by security staff on a cell clearance later that day, moved to reception, so it could be sent on to its final destination and returned to the prisoner at whichever prison they ended up at in Northern Ireland. I would then get permission from the control room to move them along the downstairs secure corridor to reception for processing. The transport to move them from Whitemoor was always there the day before, so it could be on its way quickly after the prisoner arrived in reception. They and their possessions were searched and processed quickly to leave the establishment.

Prisoners on the wing could hear things going on, but there was always the same reaction when I took an IRA prisoner from the wing. Once they could see them in the secure corridor, they would bang, shout, and crash about in their cells so the prisoner I was escorting to reception could hear them, and trust me, the noise was very loud. They always say there's no honour amongst thieves, but when I heard things like "Good luck, Paddy" or some other remark, they were never negative ones. They were ones of support for them, even though they were classed as a terrorist who had committed some of the most serious crimes of the day!

One more thing about the way a pegging system can be manipulated, this time an electronic one. I never knew this could be done, but I was told that some staff put the wands that were used to log their journeys around the wing, ensuring they were doing their job properly, into microwave ovens. When they were switched on, the action of cooking the wand would make it unusable. Remember the 'what if' when looking at the weakest link in any system. It's probably still happening now in prisons around the country.

Time was moving along, and then one day, I noticed on our staff bulletins that a prison called HMP Littlehey was advertising for principal officers. It wasn't that far from where we were located, so I thought, "What the hell, I may as well chuck my hat in the ring and go for it."

When you apply for further promotion with the advertisement, they stipulate the different types of skills and experience they are looking for. The prison service had around twelve core skills which they want their managers to gain experience in. It could be something like leadership, team building, networking, and decision making, that sort of thing. It all depended on what the prison wanted of their new managers. I basically responded to the advertisement, using real world experiences, and psychology cards about the roles of staff in prisons to answer the advert. I duly sent off my application and waited for a response. They only wanted one principal officer, so if fifteen people applied for the post, that number would be whittled down to around half that to call people forward for interview. A month later, I received a response. It was positive, I had been called up for interview.

They normally hold the interview over four or five days. A couple of the other SOs I knew had also been called, so it's just a bun fight to see what happens and who is best on the day. I travelled down to Littlehey for my interview, which seemed to go alright, and I felt comfortable with it all. After a few weeks, instead of receiving a letter, a governor came to see me. He told me I had not got the job. I had come a close second. One of my mates had been given it, but they said, "That it was likely another PO at that prison was going to take medical retirement." So in effect, there were two posts available, but I had to wait for a letter. A few months later, I received a notice to say I had been successful in applying for a principal officer's post at Littlehey. It has a knock-on effect in the prison you work in, and they can put a hold on you going to take up the post for up to six months at your new place of work. It meant Whitemoor could also publish a promotion board and advertise for senior officers. I think it was about four months before I was allowed to leave, but I had completed eight years in the prison service, six of those at Whitemoor, so I was glad to be moving on, and in 1998 off I was posted down to HMP Littlehey.

With the types of modern terrorism that seem to be around in society these days, where they are willing to sacrifice themselves to achieve their ideological goals as part of a bigger picture. It makes me wonder what the public now thinks about the death penalty if the country held a referendum linked to certain offence types, and whether the results of that would be yes or no!

Whitemoor seemed to be a sinking flagship prison when I uncovered the sheer incompetence of senior managers. It always made me think about the wider civil service, and if governors were rubbish at their jobs, then the whole of the civil service at the higher levels are probably the same, and radical change is needed to get rid of the people who continually fail the public, but all keep getting promoted, as they have done in the prison service. The public have a right for a decent professional service to be delivered, after all, they are paying for it through sky high taxation!

HMP LITTLEHEY 1998-2000

I was allocated to run Delta wing, which held mainstream prisoners, but I would also be taking over the enhanced thinking skills (ETS) programme for prisoner rehabilitation. I didn't endear myself to staff straight away when I arrived. I suppose I wanted to stamp my authority, and coming from a top security dispersal establishment to a Category C training prison had an impact on me. I wasn't used to this relaxed-ish atmosphere. It took me around three months to really settle down. Part of my duties were running the regime for the prison as Oscar 1, basically making sure the core day operated effectively. A smaller Category prison meant a smaller staff group, so I had more areas of responsibility in relation to my work, but I also had other things linked to me around the establishment.

The one thing I did find was, when staffing was tight or we went below certain staffing levels, my ETS groups were cancelled, which is very frustrating for prisoners, wing staff, and the psychology staff employed to deliver the course. This is a common thing that happens in the prison service. Governors didn't seem to understand, or they ignored the fact that you needed continuity in delivering the courses to prisoners, and the staff needed to see the governor and the prison supporting them in the execution of their duties. The one thing that really messed up things were bed watches, where someone was ill and needed to be escorted to hospital with a staff escort team. ETS was classed as a soft programme, and the daily detail managers used to cancel it on a regular basis. The governor grades didn't seem that interested, and my line manager, who was a G5, didn't seem to grasp the issue. I tried to be informative about what the problems would be and how we would eventually fail audits in the future, but all they said was, "Stop patronising me about the courses and their impact." But I had to fight my staff's corner so they could achieve prison service targets. I think it was around six months later an audit team arrived at the prison, which was led by a governor 4 who specialised in auditing them.

They looked at our information, talked to staff, and came to see me. They mentioned all the things that they had picked up. I explained the way the establishment operated and said that trying to talk about ETS with my line manager and the deputy governor basically fell on deaf ears. You only have so much authority and clout to be able to deliver what is required in the establishment, so the audit governor said they would chat to the governors, especially the governing governor. I think information may have been hidden from the number one by lower grade governors. In my opinion, the prison's governing governor had to ask themselves, "What is it they really want to do as a training prison?" They must have applied for funding in the first place for ETS, and if they wanted to deliver courses, they had to make sure the money was ring-fenced and make sure they were put on for prisoners.

Working in different establishments enables you to look at the regime in a number of different ways, adapting things to make the operational side work. Things still happen. One of my close mates from my military days and who worked with me at Whitemoor joined HMP Littlehey later on, following me down from there, and another close mate left the military and went to my old haunt Whitemoor. Both were specialist dog handlers, one a tracker and the other AES like me. It's a small world. Coming in for duty when things were not kicking off was really nice, but I soon found out that our healthcare department always used to say, and always at the end of a 17.00 hrs main shift, that they needed a prisoner taken to an outside hospital. So again, the regime had to be changed to accommodate these last-minute emergencies. It may still operate in the same way today: "What do you say, Littlehey staff?"

HMP Littlehey was a prison that held many elderly prisoners, not on my wing but in other parts of the establishment. As you will appreciate, the older we get, we generally all have things start to go wrong with our bodies, so we had to get on with it, but finding staff for escorts was a real challenge sometimes.

I was always early, arriving on duty in the mornings, so I could get my head around what had gone on overnight. The staff coming on duty took over from the night staff, and any prisoners that were deemed at risk of suicide and were checked throughout the night were rechecked on handover to the day staff in the morning to make sure they were fine. When all the numbers were in and unlock was called over the radio, the staff opened cells by shooting the bolts on the cell doors, which meant the doors stayed open and could not accidentally be locked again, or prisoners started playing their games by locking cell doors again, trying to give staff the runaround.

Prisoners come out to get their breakfast and sort out various personal issues that need dealing with. I was in my office when one of the wing staff came in and said to me, "We've had a death on the wing." They had radioed a code blue, which is when someone has a respiratory problem that triggers our healthcare staff to attend our location, along with a blue light call to emergency services. When the officer and I reached the cell, I said, "We need to commence CPR," but the officer said it was too late. I basically wanted to see whether there was a pulse, but when I touched the body, it was mildly cold to the touch, which meant that the person had been dead for a short while.

The deceased person was seen by our healthcare staff, who confirmed their death. They were then taken away by ambulance. I thought to myself that it must have been a lonely way to depart from the living, dying in one of Her Majesty's prison cells. We always send two staff members to see the next of kin if they have any recorded on their prison details. Normally, a governor grade and possibly the chaplain visit them to personally explain what has happened and to offer our support. After personal experience of having to take death in custody on board, it is not the greatest job in the world. The other thing we all must attend, with everyone involved with the incident, is the coroner's court. It meant they could determine what the cause of death was after listening to the evidence and questioning people to come up with an independent conclusion. The autopsy indicated the prisoner had suffered a heart attack, and with that information and other evidence, it was determined by the coroner that the death was due to natural causes linked to the heart.

The prison service is always reinventing itself, particularly when the government says it must save money or some management change must take place in the civil service. The two are normally linked, and it pretty much happens year after year. I don't think in over twenty years of service that I haven't been asked to make efficiencies or make things more effective in my area of work, usually following someone else's fuck up or some bright new initiative from up on high. I was always very good at strategy, and it certainly helped me over the years to read into things quite easily and come up with solutions to perceived problems and management of new ways of operating.

It was good to come and work in a training prison, and about halfway through my time at Littlehey, we were told efficiency savings needed to be made. In my case, this meant I had to manage two wings instead of one. They were going to get rid of two managers at PO level, so B and D wing managers would simply go through natural wastage. This meant that two staff could be managed out of the service through retirement or health grounds, and maybe that was their plan when two of us came from Whitemoor. But what it meant was doubling my workload relating to the appraisals of staff and more shifts as Oscar 1, running the operational daily routine of the establishment. I have always been a proactive, driven sort of person, so I just saw it as a challenge to overcome, but what I didn't realise was that loading extra workloads on people could also be used by senior managers in a different way, which was to weaponise it, to bully, and make someone's life a misery, so it makes them ill. Ironically, in years to come, it would be the person who was deputy governor at Littlehey who would do that to me, along with their friends at that time. Life can take many twists and turns, and its direction is normally determined by those you work with or by those who are more senior, and you have to adapt or fail.

I am a fighter, and I will always try my best to get things done. Once the new regime had settled in at our establishment, it was just carry on as normal. One prisoner who had been at Littlehey and was located on one of my wings was always protesting their innocence and had been fighting for many years to overturn their conviction for the crime they had been sent to prison for. We deal with the facts in prison; that is, we are not the judge or jury. If a person is in a convicted prison, they have been found guilty in a court of law by their peers and sentenced by a judge, so we hold them on a warrant for incarceration.

The individual was always given time by me to pursue their innocence as they saw it, and the media was starting to take interest in what was happening with the offence they had been found guilty of, which would eventually be seen as a miscarriage of justice. The media had literally started to camp outside the prison when the case was referred back to the Court of Appeal. The reason they were so interested in what had happened in this case was, first, that if the prisoner we were holding was found not guilty of a murder, who else may have committed it? And second, the person currently being held in prison had been incarcerated for twenty-seven years, a third of their life!

The governor grades, for some reason, did not want to go and talk to the press, so I said I would, which meant it was just like delivering a daily briefing, but eventually, with all the evidence surrounding the case, the individual would be set free by appeal court. I still remember the words I was told when I joined the prison service: "Treat people how you wish to be treated yourself and don't lie like a hairy egg."

I had played my own part in helping the person continue with their case, and it also made me think of things that happen in our courts so that an innocent person had ended up serving such a long sentence in prison. To be released after so long spent incarcerated must have been difficult for them to adjust to going back into the community.

I'm sure the compensation paid out by the system helped them a lot, but it could not bring back the time lost in their life. I do wonder what the person feels like today about everything that they have gone through!

Life went on after the release of that person. There is always something going on in a prison. On one particular day, I was on duty as Oscar 1. As a PO, we had duties, which meant we were in control of the unlock and lock up of the prison so that the number of prisoners could be verified during the core day. Everything was going according to plan. We had unlocked in the afternoon so that they could attend workshops, courses, and visits. It was late afternoon when a shout came over the radio, "Alarm bell visits." Oscar 1 is the designated manager to attend any incident, and it just so happened that I was in the control room with an SO from security.

We ran over to the visits complex a short distance away, which was situated above the gate of the prison, to find it empty apart from one prisoner holding onto a small child of around roughly six or seven years of age who was screaming their head off. One of the other POs was trying to calm them down, but with no success. The SO and I walked over to where the other PO was, and it transpired that the prisoner was actually off their wing. I couldn't really understand what the issue was about at the time, but the very presence of the PO was winding up the prisoner and he kept saying he was going to kill the small child. So now this had turned into a direct hostage situation. I said to the other PO that I would take over and they could back off, hoping that would help try and calm the situation down. The prisoner backed up over to the corner of the prison visits room and was shouting all sorts of obscenities to people outside as the visits windows were open. The small child was hysterical, and quite understandably so; they were crying their eyes out. When I arrived at the visits hall, thankfully, it was right at the end when people were leaving. The prisoner had been having some sort of domestic argument with their partner and decided, for whatever reason, that they were going to cut the persons throat with a blade. I had noticed some claret on the floor, but somehow the staff had managed to clear the visits hall and take the injured person out. All the doors were locked as a result, so when we arrived, we found the prisoner, child, and PO in an empty room.

My biggest concern was to try and de-escalate the situation, and that was proving very difficult, but what I tried to do was bring a connection back with the prisoner to the small child they were holding as a hostage. It was certainly a very tense moment. As the prisoner had backed over to the corner of the room, it meant we could get closer to them and they were cornered, but there was the added pressure of the child being very distressed. I had to talk above the prisoner and the small child to bring their focus of attention on to me. It took a few minutes, but eventually, I managed to get the prisoner to focus on what I was saying, getting them to reconnect with reality. I used the child's distress to tell them how upset the small child was and try and get them to listen to me. Trying to bring someone down who is in red mist territory is not easy. The SO and I sat on some visits chairs, a small distance away from where the prisoner was. Sitting down I thought would make us less of a threat to the prisoner. It meant they were bigger than us and give them the impression they were in control of events. In my mind, all I cared about was the child and how to keep them safe from harm. I kept saying to the prisoner how upset the child was and we needed to talk about what was going on. I wanted them to engage with me so they didn't cut the wee child's throat, and I was saying, "Look, we can sort this out."

I had the idea to ask the prisoner if they would allow us to bring something to them and the child from the prison canteen shop. They duly agreed, and I asked the SO to go and get some ice lollies which he did, and then placed them on a table that was about halfway between the prisoner and myself. He then came back to where I was sitting. The prisoner went over to the table with the child under one arm and grabbed the lollies, backing off into the corner again. During their ranting, they were saying how they wanted to be released from the visits hall, but that was never going to happen. A hostage on the move is not a good position to be in, so that was a line in the sand that would not be negotiated on. It just so happened that the idea of giving the prisoner the ice lollies seemed to work. It brought a connection back between them and the child. At this point, I didn't even know that the child was theirs. Hostage takers do it to use a person as a bargaining chip for something, in this case, a child, but things were finally starting to calm down. It was good to see the prisoner opening the lollies and passing one to the small child. It gave him that connection that I was looking for and also meant the child had something to concentrate on. Although the child was still sobbing, they had something that helped them stop crying so hysterically. We had managed to bring things down to a more manageable level, and the next thing I knew, an officer who worked on one of my wings came and sat down beside me. They were a trained hostage negotiator and the security SO had now left the visits hall. I was really happy that a negotiator was on duty in the prison that day and that they were available to take over from me. I had lost track of time, but I guess it must have only been around twenty minutes from the time we entered the visits hall to get to where we were now. I stayed there for around another five minutes and told the prisoner that the new person with me had come to talk to them and I would be leaving. That appeared to go okay, so I quietly backed off and left them to it.

I found leaving the visits hall a really hard thing for me to do because I had, in such a short space of time, connected and bonded with the prisoner and the small child, and I didn't want anything to happen to the little one. I made my way down to the governing governor's office, where a silver command suite had been set up, and I gave my briefing to the governing governor about where we were at that point in time. As far as things went, that's all I had to do, so I went back to my duties as Oscar 1. The person who had their throat cut had been taken to hospital by ambulance. Thankfully, they survived the ordeal.

A police tactical support unit had arrived outside the establishment, so if the prisoner had managed to exit the prison, well, that would have been something they would then deal with. "Good night, Vienna" springs to mind!

Our hostage negotiator managed to carry on with their job of dealing with the prisoner, and thankfully, were able to get the child back. The prisoner was then relocated to the segregation unit. It was good to see there was a happy ending. Not for the prisoner though, as they had been placed on report which was adjourned for the police to put a case forward through to the Crown Prosecution Service (CPS) to charge them. It did eventually go to Crown Court and the prisoner was found guilty of the offence. They would be spending a fair bit more leisure time in HMP and received a sentence of ten years for what they did. The hostage negotiator did a good job in bringing an end to the incident, and they were awarded an area managers commendation for the work they had done. I was so happy that the whole incident had ended that way. I don't know what I would have done if the perpetrator had actually killed the small child in front of me in the visits hall that day. You really don't know what's going to unfold in a prison, but as we used to say when something ends well, "jobs a good un".

The next thing you know, another notice to staff was published. This was the one I had been waiting for and for such a long time after not being selected as a fast-track governor some nine years previously. Looking back now, I'm really glad to have risen up through the normal channels because it gave me a lot of time to develop my experience and skills. So in the end, it had turned out to be a positive thing for me, even though, at the time, in HMP Lewes, it didn't feel like it. I can't really remember much about the tests, but there was a lot of psychological type stuff and interviews. It must have been about a month or so before I received my results, but luckily for me, I passed, so I was now, down on paper, an accredited governor grade.

There were more changes taking place at Littlehey, and one of the governor grades was planning to retire, and as I was the only one who had passed the selection process, I was offered a temporary promotion to governor five (G5) to cover the person leaving. It's always nice to get a pay rise, but as it was a temporary position, it meant I could still look at all the promotion boards around England and Wales and apply for jobs that became available. It wasn't long before I spotted a position being advertised, and it was as an operational governor four (G4). The prison service had been trying to reinvent itself away from governors in terms of grades, and this one was now being advertised as a grade 2C, but everyone called it a G4. Staff and prisoners would never move away from the old ranks; Guv is and was a thing steeped in history.

The new job was at HMP Winchester in Hampshire and was advertised as Governor of Westhill, which was an annex linked to the main Category B local prison. It was also a women's establishment and would be akin to a male Cat C or a restricted, closed female environment. It all seemed like an odd set up to me, but I was intrigued because you never get a prison with male and female prisoners located separately but together like that and run as one site. I think five people had been invited to attend for an interview for the position, and the questions revolved around therapy and cognitive courses. There was lots about the women's estate that I did not know about, a place where I had never worked, and in particular that there were no therapeutic prisons for females in a prison setting anywhere in the world, so the plan was to set one up. I was super excited about the prospect of being the first person in the world to do that. I had also managed cognitive programmes at Littlehey and been involved in project management, but not in relation to something like this and this big. I thought I came across really well when I was being interviewed by the area manager and the new governing governor of Winchester.

I am someone who drives things forward in life, and I won't give up on anything. The area manager at the time must have been enthused by the way I came across because, at one point, they were actually shedding a tear. To me, it was all about delivering a proper service to the prisoners, and that must have come across in my replies. It was a long journey back up and over to Cambridgeshire. It must have been a good five hours, but as I just got through the front door of my home, the phone rang. It was the Governor of Winchester, and they basically said, "Do you want to manage Westhill and become a governor who will attend the women's estate meetings?" In effect, I would become a governing governor but still report to the governor of Winchester. I had never come across anything like this before. I was over the moon and instantly replied, "Yes."

The role was bigger than I thought, and it meant setting up the world's first female therapeutic community in a prison setting. My current prison could hold me for six months whilst they found a new governor to cover my duties. However, as they were going to be advertising my position very soon, it meant I still gained experience in the short term of managing in Littlehey as a G5. It was confirmed not long after that I was to be promoted to 2C, or G4. It's odd having a boot in both camps, and I was allowed a week to travel down for a pre-visit and look for a house to buy down there. I eventually found one in a nice village not far outside Winchester and managed to get a good deal. Back then, when you were promoted to a more expensive area, the prison service paid the difference in mortgage costs and removal expenses. All in all, I was hoping this would give me more experience, and particularly in running a prison. The other part of the equation was that HMP Winchester is a Category B local remand prison, and Westhill was effectively a female Category C closed prison. The women's side held over one hundred prisoners, operating a separate regime, and had its own entrance and reception area. I had never come across anything like it, and part of my brief was to split Westhill away from the main prison's rules and regulations so it could effectively operate as a stand-alone establishment. My first governors posting, it was literally being thrown in at the deep end, but I loved the fact someone had placed their trust in me to get on with it. The timescale to move everything over was twenty-four months.

I think the one thing I could take away from Littlehey was that you don't need to be in a clique. You can progress based on your own experience and skills, but there are people throughout the prison and civil service who don't have what I have, and when they mess up, they still manage to get promoted. I have never hung on to people's coat-tails to get on, and I'm proud of that fact. A lot of people are stifled by others in positions of power and never get the opportunity to shine because it shows up those who are less able to deal with things effectively, so those people take and suck all the good ideas from others and pass them off as their own. I am sure there will be people who will read this part and think, yes, that's what happened to me. I would say to such a person, "Don't let the bastards get you down, one day they will get caught out." Karma eventually has a way of coming back to bite them, and you will have the last laugh.

Bang. The date soon arrives when your move takes place. I had managed to sort out the social side of everything with the move to Winchester. The first thing for me to do was set up the project and meet with staff currently working in Westhill, along with the union representatives, so we could make sure the transition happened in a smooth, seamless way. I needed to find out which staff wanted to become involved with the journey that we were about to undertake. For the most part, everybody did, but there were a couple who decided they would rather move over to the Winchester side, so we would need to advertise in twelve months for a 'Genuine Occupational Qualification (GOQ) to recruit prison officers.

'Genuine Occupational Qualifications' The Employment (Sex Discrimination) Act 2000 makes it unlawful for men or women to receive less favourable treatment in employment because of their sex or marital status. In very limited circumstances, Section 9 of the Act provides an exception to the requirements of the Act and allows a job to be restricted to one sex where the sex of the worker is a GOQ. A GOQ exists when the essential nature of the job or particular duties attached to the job may call for a member of one sex. It is lawful to discriminate in recruitment, training, promotion, and transfer in a job for which the sex of a worker is a GOQ.

One thing I would like to point out to the prison service is that smaller prisons have smaller staff numbers, but the policies for them are still the same number that you would have in a large prison, which means people must double or even triple up with the amount of work that they do for audit purposes. That puts extra pressure on staff to deliver and, in a lot of cases, means extra hours that must be worked to achieve the desired result. In the uniform grades, they get TOIL.

When I was promoted into the governor grades, they made us sign that we would be 'all hours worked', which basically meant, pound for pound, I would be earning less as a governor grade than when I was an officer in uniform. I think the prison service used this unfair condition to flog people to death, as we were only supposed to be working a standard thirty-nine-hour week with the odd operational duty governor twenty-four-hour shift thrown in. As the governor of Westhill, I would also still be required to perform duty governors. Victor 1 (V1) was our call sign, which meant I was having to work in the main prison on those days, running the operational side, dealing with any incidents that occurred during the core day, and be on call during the night. That was part of the conditions that attracted an operational allowance, which was in effect part of all hours worked. There was a clause that mentioned working some additional hours to deal with things. Governing governors used this contract to beat people around the head, although I would find out in years to come how some would weaponise it to become vindictive, using it to gaslight anyone if you didn't fit in with their way of thinking. They use it to try and break you. Gone was the notion of a thirty-nine-hour week, which was also in the governor grade contract. If the same contract is still running in the form I had to sign up for today, then it amounts to a modern-day slave labour programme operated by the prison service, which, in my opinion, is something that can be used to abuse people by those higher up the ladder in the civil service. The prison service doesn't like to admit it, but it is very dictatorial in the way it operates. They have some of the best policies in the world, but some follow them for their own needs and pay lip service to their responsibilities. They can hide behind policy and use it for their own nefarious ends.

There was plenty for me to do daily in Westhill, but it wasn't the Winchester Governor who abused their staff. Although I didn't know it at the time, even they could be influenced by outside forces from our own headquarters in London. I was busy and enjoying the work challenges I had, and soon I would be attending the governing governor area manager meetings, which was so weird because I was only a governor 2C/G4. I quickly learned that having two different area managers meant I had to keep them both sweet as well as bond new friendships with the governing governors from the women's prisons estate. Westhill's security category would be classed as a C, and being a fairly small place, holding one hundred and twenty-nine prisoners, it doesn't take much for people to start getting on each other's nerves. We had a small segregation unit that only had two cells, so when something did happen and a prisoner ended up in there, the staff worked quickly to organise their removal from our establishment to somewhere more secure. HMP Send had a good relationship with our staff in Westhill and always helped us to provide a quick response to our needs when we had to move someone on, so thank you to the staff there. The governing governor of Winchester had support from someone in the community who dealt with therapeutic therapies, and they were working with me so we could integrate that side of things, developing the necessary courses for women in a custodial setting.

The role of running Westhill as a governor was to be elevated to a grade D, G3, so that had to be advertised at some point. I would have to apply for it when it became available, like everyone else. As I was to find out, nothing is ever a done deal unless you know people higher up in the civil service; they stick together like glue and operate as a clique. There certainly seemed to be some sort of club operating, and probably still is, and it didn't matter how good you were at your job or how well you did it. If one of the club's faces fitted into a plan, then you stood no chance of getting promoted. I was getting my fair share of duty governors over the local Cat B Winchester side and everything that threw up. Certain individuals self-harmed and in a local prison, that can be a harder place to deal with it.

It's funny how life can throw you a googly. One day, a letter arrived for me from the treasury solicitors, which made my blood boil. It said a certain terrorist, who had been repatriated to NI as part of the Good Friday or Belfast Agreement, was suing me for misfeasance in public office. The same terrorist who had tried to shoot me in HMP Whitemoor. I was absolutely seething, and it really played with my mind for a while. It had such an impact that I needed to see the local quack at the surgery I was listed at, who referred me for some counselling. All I could think about was this fucking terrorist and wanting to kill them. It took over my mind. They wanted fifty thousand pounds for what they described as my mistreatment of them. I told the treasury solicitors that I wanted it to go to court so I could fight it all the way, and they agreed with me. After receiving six sessions of counselling, there was an awful lot of stuff going around in my head, bringing back lots of memories from my service out in NI, but it was the intense anger I felt that took some time to bring under control.

To be honest, the counselling did nothing for me, but at least I had tried to deal with the intense loathing and anger myself. I buried it in the back of my mind and just got on with my job. You make sure that you don't take any problems home with you; you leave them at the gate, and the same applies from home; don't take them to work. Staff look at governors as people who can deal with anything and have no problems themselves. I was informed by the treasury solicitors that it would take around six months for the case to be allocated to a court in London. I had bigger things going on, and a prison doesn't stop running just because some terrorist is taking the piss out of our government and the criminal justice system. Anyway, that's the way I saw it. Prisons are 24/7, and no two days are the same.

As time went by, there was a suicide on the male side. They had hung themselves in their cell. You then had to deal with an external investigator coming in to look at the circumstances surrounding their demise. The prisoner had left a suicide note, the only one I have ever seen when someone takes their own life in a prison setting. There were no issues raised by the investigatory team sent in to look at why the prisoner had taken their own life and the coroner reported that the death was indeed suicide. I guess over time, you harden up to the various things going on around you.

The advert was published for the upgraded D grade governor's post of Westhill, so I didn't waste any time sending in my application and curriculum vitae (CV). The whole thing should only take a few months to go through the process and interviews, but little did I know what was around the corner.

Westhill was shaping up okay, and the project was running along the timelines I had set out as its project manager. They always say things happen for a reason, and certainly, things on the Winchester side were not going as well as those in Westhill. The staff on our side had reacted to a challenge from the governing governor, who had given me and the head of residence on the male side a challenge to increase our regime hours. I asked my team to look at trying to increase reporting hours for prisoners time out of cell, which meant our targets could be raised from good to outstanding, and they didn't disappoint. They went through all the data we had to see where hours could be raised in line with approved policy. We ended up with hours way above those set by the prison service, so it meant keeping the wolf from our door.

The head of residence over the Winchester side of the prison wasn't doing so well with reviewing their hours, but what annoyed me was the way the governing governor would bring up Westhill's hours during the morning meeting with all the governor and uniform manager grades. Yes, it's nice to receive praise as part of your work when having your appraisal, but it felt like our hours were being used to beat the head of the head of residence on the Winchester side. It was happening once a week, but after a couple of weeks of this, I had to raise it with the governing governor because I thought it was embarrassing, but it could also drive a wedge between me and the other governors and staff. It wasn't a competition, and they were two totally different types of prison. I spent more and more of my time dealing with Winchester's problems than Westhill's. It seemed like things were going wrong in a number of different areas. The deputy governor was a fast track appointment, and in a fast-paced prison like Winchester, as much as anything, in my opinion, they did not have real life experience of dealing

with staff or prisoners. It's easy to read a book or look at targets and order people to achieve them or watch them fail, and the prison or civil service doesn't seem to understand that, and that probably fits in with the failure issues I have mentioned before in my memoir.

Prisoners and staff eat people like that for breakfast, and things can quickly escalate. Then it happened: Winchester suffered an escape, a real no-no in any prison, even in an old Victorian establishment.

The next thing I knew, the deputy governor was going to leave. I had no idea where they were being transferred to, but I then received a call from the governing governor asking me to come and see them. I headed over to their office, sat down, and, as simple as you like, I was asked if I wanted the deputy governor's job. I was rather stunned to be asked this, to be honest. I had been brought in to set up the first women's therapeutic community in Westhill, not become the deputy governor of Winchester. I said, "I don't think I have the skill set to take on that role." And in my opinion, there were governor grades who were more senior than me in terms of time in and grade. I was told that as governing governor of Winchester, I was the person they wanted for the job. It was being acknowledged to me that I was good at what I did, day in, day out, but I needed to think about it and asked if they could give me a few days. I couldn't give an answer to something like that straight away.

There was a training manager who I talked to a lot. I used them as a sounding board for a lot of things that were going on, and they used me for the same purpose. I was committed to Westhill and getting the job done, so I was thinking, could I actually take over the job I was being asked to do and still have oversight of Westhill, the reason why I had been employed in the first place. Westhill was my project, and I didn't really want to hand it over to anyone else. It had become my precious! I had to look up the statistics; the escape happened in 2001, just over twelve months of me being posted to HMP Winchester. What's odd is that I haven't found out about another escape that happened a few days after the one that was reported, so I don't know if that one was covered up to protect the governor and the prison service! Maybe they had slapped a D-Notice on the media? I went back to the governing governor to say that I had only been promoted to a governor grade in 2000 and asked them if they really thought I had what it took to step up to a deputy governor's role. They basically said yes and so I said, "I need to let the staff over at Westhill know about it all." The staff there were experienced, and my deputy could take over what I was doing. And just about then, the other escape happened, and within area office, or should I say, with the area manager. The shit hit the fan, another escape happening so close to the first one. You can only imagine what the director general of the prison service would be saying over their morning cuppa.

The escapees had managed to dig out through the cell walls, and they escaped in the same or similar place that the previous one had left the prison. Escapes can be career busters, although later down the line, the governing governor ended up leading an inspection team somewhere. Well, the next thing I knew, the governing governor phoned me to say the area manager was moving another deputy governor from another prison located down on the coast, which was in their area, to come to Winchester. It's amazing how things happen, so that was a dep's job I had been offered, and then days later, I was told it was no longer available. It was back to normal for me, and more water under the bridge in terms of my career. Incidentally, the security governor had a breakdown, went off absent on the sick and was never seen in the prison again! I heard they had been medically retired, but I don't know for sure.

The only terrorist I had come across in Winchester was a Tamil Tiger from Sri Lanka who was located in Winchester's healthcare. I used to see them when I made my rounds as a duty governor. Some prisoners stick in your mind. With this one, I wondered why they were at Winchester Prison, bearing in mind who they were and where they were from! They were a long way from home; that's a fact! They used to take out their frustration on themselves by cutting their arm with a razor blade, always on their left arm and always in the same area. As much as people tried to help them, they would do things to themselves to open the wound up, particularly with their teeth, biting the stitches out like a cannibal, and they had got to the point where they had literally cut a hole through their arm, one side to the other. They reminded me of the prisoner who had the shotgun and shot themselves through their own foot when I worked at HMP Lewes years ago. It also struck me that the human body can go through a lot of trauma and still try to recover from horrific wounds.

As time ticked by, more adverts for the various treatment roles required for Westhill were advertised, and the clinical person who had been helping me said they didn't want to apply for the job running the treatment side, which surprised me somewhat. I had booked a holiday some time ago and could do with a rest after all the things that had happened over the last twelve months, so off I went on my break. The closing date for my role was the day after I got back to the United Kingdom. I put it all behind me, resting and recuperating on a lovely island in the Maldives, and I didn't think about work at all. Remember, leave work at work! I went for three weeks, and it was such a nice relaxing place to chill out - a small island, which took me all of twenty minutes to walk around. At a height of just four feet above sea level, with the ocean as far as you could see in all directions, it was stunning. The exchange rates were great back then. I'm not so sure I could afford it now with the dollar stomping all over the pound.

Those were the days when you could get holidays in the Maldives for three weeks for the price of two, and all-inclusive. It's funny; the island resort where I was located didn't have tea or coffee, so I gave it up, and to this day, I only drink hot water with a sweetener in it. When I arrived back, I can honestly say I was really excited. I wanted to see how many others had applied for the job I wanted so much, not to mention the pay rise that went with it.

I went straight up to our human resources department when I came in for duty and was told I was the only applicant for the post. Well, in this position, bearing in mind I had been doing the job for something like eighteen months, it would normally not have even proceeded to interview, and the governing governor would get it signed off with the area manager to rubber stamp it. After the morning meeting, I stopped behind to see the governing governor, and they basically told me that the position would stay open for another four weeks. I did express my disappointment at hearing that, and at this point, the alarm bells started ringing in my head. I just got on with my work, even though I was disappointed with what had happened. You still have to be professional about these things.

Once the four weeks had passed, I was told again that no one else had applied for the role, so I think I had a real expectation that I should have been promoted to the grade D, G3 post! I went to see the governing governor and was told this time that headquarters had decided to promote someone from London. I don't mind telling you that it felt like the biggest kick in the teeth and a stab in the back at the same time. Working hard and producing the goods to get things done appeared to be all for nothing. All my reports were exceeded on my yearly appraisals, so it was beyond me why I hadn't been promoted. I was told there was a bigger plan in place. The person they were parachuting in had been moved previously from HMP Holloway to headquarters because of things that had occurred at that prison some years before. They had been located in headquarters for a few years, enough time for people to forget possible issues, and as I mentioned before, the prison service tends to promote governors who are failing, firstly by moving them to headquarters and then popping them up somewhere else at some point in time. It's a common theme. I don't know why, but it is, the clique just keeps rewarding failure and protecting each other.

In previous lower management grades that I have

operated in, if you were not up to the job, people would poor perform you, so you either stepped up to the plate or they got rid of you. That doesn't seem to be the case in the governor grades and higher civil service, and it is something that needs some serious change. That could be the reason why the clique operates – to protect their own failure. It also seems to be a common theme throughout the public sector: pay more to reward failure. I just don't get it. When you are at the top, it's almost like you have so much control it's impossible to get rid of people. That's where ministers need to get off their backsides and sack people. Mind you, a lot of them are useless as well. Our country really needs reforming, root and branch!

The person who was allocated my job was already a D grade governor, and I think the link had been female prisoners. I didn't have a choice in the matter, so I had to swallow the crap that was being fed to me and still drive things forward. A few months later, the person arrived, we sat down, and they basically said, "I hope it doesn't affect things, them being parachuted in." I said, "At the end of the day, I don't hold grudges and we are here to provide a service, to develop a therapeutic community."

I had been on a few different radio programmes like Woman's Hour and met with local media to talk about Westhill, what the whole project was about, and the way forward to make it a reality. I don't think it was too long after that, that the treasury solicitors got back to me about the lawsuit planned against me by the terrorist who had tried to fucking shoot me. They said that the prison service had decided not to fight the case against me in court. I said something like, "What do you mean, not fight it?" I had done nothing wrong. "Someone tried to shoot me, so why couldn't I sue them for trying to kill me?" They said, "The decision in headquarters had been made to pay the terrorist off by giving them fifty thousand pounds." Fifty thousand pounds of taxpayers' money, who wouldn't mind being given that sort of money tax-free. I was disgusted and felt sick after being told that someone in London, and it had to be someone very high up, probably even the director general, had authorised the payment to a convicted terrorist. It makes me wonder whether any other staff have been sued as well as me. I do wonder how much and how many other terrorists may have been paid off as well. I know it's years down the line, but if anyone knows how I can sue the prison service for mismanagement and because of their negligence in putting me in that position in the first place, I would love a chat. Rant over! I wonder how the public would feel about such a thing happening, terrorists being paid off with money that they pay in taxes.

There must be some plan going on that I didn't know about, and you do get to a point where you become a mushroom, literally fed on shit and kept in the dark. I did hear on the grapevine that the area manager in the women's estate was leaving for some reason, so their deputy was taking over that role, and I became aware that both the governing and deputy governor were also moving on from HMP Drake Hall prison up in Staffordshire. I told the governing governor of Winchester that I thought the openness and trust about the way we had been working since the escape had gone, and due to the way I had been treated over the promotion, I was looking to move on.

The person coming into my role was being set up to become governing governor of HMP Winchester, but I didn't know that at the time. I think you have to give yourself a sense of purpose and direction in life. Some people lose it and never get it back. They give up because

179

of the way they are treated in life by others. Don't give up, never give up, or, as we used to say in the military, "Don't let the bastards get you down." Easier said than done, though. I saw the advert published sometime later for the deputy governor's position at HMP Drake Hall, so I thought, "Yes, time to see if I can move on from all this going on at my current place of work." You can lose my loyalty as well as gain it, depending on how you treat me.

I travelled up to Staffordshire to look around the prison and talk to staff. It was another odd prison insofar as its category was a female semi-open, but it also had closed conditions for some prisoners and others were allowed to work in the community. It was classed as a medium sized establishment, and inside it had a fairly relaxed approach to dealing with prisoners. Although, just like everywhere else I had worked, some people who put on a uniform change the way they work with others and how they view the world in which they operate.

I went back down to Winchester and decided to apply for the role. So, a while later, after filling in my application and sending off my CV, I was eventually invited up for a formal interview. There were five or six of us invited to attend, and it was the governor and deputy governor conducting them. I came out feeling good, and I was the last person to be seen that day. I was hanging around just down the corridor chatting with one of the principal officers, who was ex-military, so we instantly got on. There's just something about people who have worked together in the forces that means they have common bonds, something I have never really seen in Civvy Street. I understand today that the prison service is sending governors on training assignments with the military in England and Wales. You can't force people into the military mindset. It's something built up over years of training and working together, sometimes in extremely difficult circumstances, and the bond grows stronger and stays even after you have left the Ministry of Defence. As I was chatting, the governing governor came down. We went into a side office, and they just said, "Do you want the deputy governor's job?" and I said, "Yes."

Once again, I disappeared down to Winchester. My new boss to be had already phoned up and informed my current governor that I had accepted the new position. When I got back, I was told that I would be held the usual six months before I could leave. I was told that the whole concept of the therapeutic community was going to be moved from HMP Winchester to HMP Send, and Westhill was going to be made an annex to the main prison as a Category C male prison. I have no idea how much money has been spent on the project to date, but the prison service holds the purse strings, and if they wanted to pull the plug and move the therapeutic community to HMP Send, then so be it. I made a deal with the governor to leave HMP Winchester in half the time, but under the provision that I sort out two things. One was to work with security from headquarters to change the whole way Westhill was. The place had to be transformed. The fishpond, which had all the koi carp, had to go. The whole ambience of the place had to change, and security beefed up to hold men.

I worked through all the plans, looking at the new buildings from a security point of view, to see that they were suitable and that things were in the right place to hold prisoners more securely than they had been previously with women. The other thing I had to do was work with the union to look at re-profiling the whole of the healthcare in Winchester because the NHS manager that was in the post had no experience of profiles in a prison setting. It didn't take that long to come up with a workable solution to deliver a new regime over there, so three months later, I moved up to HMP Drake Hall as their new deputy governor.

I think working at Winchester showed me that I was never really in control of my own destiny and life. There are forces bigger than us in the prisoner service operating in our workplace against us, mine being the clique higher up in the prison and civil service managers, but it's evident to me that a close-knit clique operates high up in the prison, civil and government services. They only care about those who are in their sphere of influence and groups. I am sure in my mind that is how the operation of government, prison and civil service now works. The whole process is corrupt and does nothing to support constitutional democracy in our country. I obviously wasn't operating in the circles of those who move in clandestine ways to reward failure, which we all see time and time again! It wouldn't surprise me to see that they have the whole secret handshake thing going on. I would ask everyone out there, "What's it like where you are? What public sector body or private company do you work in? And does it feel the same to you?" Corruption in the top echelons, from Westminster down appears to be rife in our democracy, and it needs to be dealt with properly from the top down. No wonder so many people don't vote in elections when they periodically occur. This is reinforced by the publication of the 'perception of corruption' league table, which has seen our country drop from number eleven to number eighteen in the world, suggesting things are getting worse!

MY LAST STAFF REPORT FOR HMP WINCHESTER, GIVEN TO ME WHEN I LEFT.

RESTRICTED STAFF

A System is only as good as the integrity of it's Managers.

INTERIM REVIEWS

Please record the main points made during the interim review discussions. Both the manager and the job holder may record comments and both should sign and date after each review.

14 August 2003. Discussed progress on the preparation towards the therapeutic community. Mike has a good grasp of the issues and work is on schedule.

03 October 2003. Reviewed Mike's current role as residential governor and the need for attention to physical deficiencies in Alfred. These are being attended to. Huge increase in out of cell time and purposeful activities.

When a Manager and Manager's Manager Sign off a SPDR: fraud or any

END OF REPORTING PERIOD ASSESSMENT

other Corrupt practise cannot take place like it did at HMP HEWELL

JOB HOLDER ASSESSMENT OF PERFORMANCE
Please comment on the delivery of the performance plan against the standards set

The delivereance of the new Performance Improvement programme has focused the team on the areas of audit which need improvement. I believe my team has taken on board these Concerns in balance with devolved mandatory training into prioritised and descretionary, we have a good balance to achieve a higher Status linked to a S.L.A in the future. I believe my management style has set the Solid foundations for the Success of a Complex area within the wider management of Winchester.

Signature _____ Date *15 OCT 03.*

MANAGER'S ASSESSMENT OF PERFORMANCE *Comment on the delivery of the performance plan against the standards set and provide reasons for performance level.*

Mike has done everything required of him during this reporting period and has exceeded on several key indicators. He has also put tremendous effort into planning for the change of function of West Hill prison into a women's TC. He has managed to develop the prison into a virtual stand alone and specialist site. Mike has developed several strong links with outside charities in his efforts to continue to develop West Hill. He has paid particular attention to KPI/KPT's and standards and this was reflected on a recent SAU visit and during a decency audit. An outstanding few months work. Mike should be very proud of his achievements.

During the last few weeks Mike has agreed to move to our Health Centre to help the new Head of Health Care get much needed structures in place.

This report is being closed off as Mike has recently been appointed as the deputy governor of Drake Hall. This is richly deserved and I have every confidence in his future development potential. I will be very sorry to lose him and will miss his drive and commitment, his loyalty and his personality.

Signature _____ Date *30·10·03.*

RESTRICTED STAFF

Performance Level	Definition	Tick
Exceeded	Most of the *key work to be done* has been delivered to standards significantly higher than those set whilst all other *key work* has been achieved.	✓
Achieved	All *key work to be done* has been delivered to the standard required OR. Some of the *key work to be done* has not been delivered to the required standard but this is not critical and is outweighed by other work which has been delivered to an exceeded standard. If *any* of the *key work to be done* has been delivered to an unacceptable standard an achieved performance level is not appropriate.	
Almost Achieved	Some of the *key work to be done* has not been delivered to the standard required and is not outweighed by other work delivered to an exceeded standard. Elements may be unacceptable but they should not be critical	
Unacceptable	The *key work to be done* has not reached the required standard to a critical extent.	

JOB HOLDERS COMMENTS ON MANAGER'S ASSESSMENT As part of my West Hill Governors duties I was also developing the remand centre project which was on target when I recently left to the Healthcare centre to help deliver their service. Currently there is a 80k overspend and based on current agency usage this would cost the service in excess of 180k per annum. I have produced a outline action plan to stabline the department and if managed correctly bring financial costs back under control, with a view to moving "wasted" money back into recruiting full time staff including some management to effectively deliver the Healthcare performance improvement programme for Winchester and the area manager (see enclosed working plan).

Signature [signature] Date. 31 october 2003 .

MANAGER'S MANAGER ASSESSMENT
Comment on whether the SPDR has been completed in accordance with guidelines and Equal Opportunities and Diversity Policy, and whether you agree with the performance assessment. Include any additional information/evidence regarding performance. During the reporting period you should ensure you are aware of the work of the job holder and standard to which it is produced.

A good years performace.

Signature [redacted] Date 7.11.03

FURTHER COMMENTS BY JOB HOLDER
Nil further to add.

I have seen this form following the manager's manager assessment
Signature [signature] Date 12/11/03

DEVELOPMENT PLAN

HMP DRAKE HALL 2003-2008

My Drake Hall pre-joining week took place, and I travelled up to Staffordshire to look for a property to buy and sort out my domestic stuff. Staffordshire's a lovely county and the area is really nice, lots of places to explore. Compared to HMP Winchester, HMP Darke Hall is a sleepy, laid-back prison just outside Eccleshall in Staffordshire. However, it did appear that the incumbent union representatives certainly liked to feel they were running the show; that's the impression they gave me. My job wasn't just centred around being the deputy governor; it was, unusually for a prison, to head up the resettlement side rather than security. The establishment held a lot of foreign national prisoners who, for the most part, were drug mules, and they had been caught bringing narcotics into the UK. It also held adults and young offenders, who, depending on sentence length and risk, could, at some point, have the opportunity to work out in the community, both locally and further afield. It also held life sentence prisoners who had been through the various categories in the women's estate and could be tested in the community under something called release on temporary licence (ROTL).

My governing governor had taken up their tenure something like eight months before I arrived, and they had promoted me. We both had something in common; we had both worked in the high-security estate. I will reiterate to the prison service, it doesn't matter the size of the prison; all the policies you have still have to be delivered, so it means that managers, which we all were, had to take on the responsibility to get them working properly. A governor grade could be the policy lead in a big prison, whereas in a smaller one like Drake Hall, it may have been a senior officer. Things were devolved down to the lowest level to people who could take on the work, which meant they were better skilled. It also meant devolvement worked by default and soon showed any deficiencies in the way the establishment and people operated. It brings me back to the fact that when higher management could not perform properly, the prison service moved them to headquarters rather than poor perform them and if they didn't improve, sack them. Maybe that's why I was eventually hounded out years later for actually doing my job, at least that's what it felt like. When you receive a policy from up high, you basically translate it into a local document, which is a little time consuming, so with digital technology these days, it would be super easy to have a main document that has already been translated for local use in the various categories of prison around the country. It may have moved that way now, but it's just an idea. It would make life so much easier for everyone, wouldn't it, and save money?

Drake Hall, for the most part, was a cushy prison to work in, as far as the job went, but the policy workload was heavier. The governing governor had devolved diversity down to me as part of my remit. The managers are what make a prison tick, but you need staff who are on board to deliver at the coalface. Every prison I ever worked in had a few staff who seemed to change when they put on a uniform. It must be a power thing. I would hope for the most part, that senior managers got on well together at Drake Hall. As I said, everyone is a manager, but I think a lot of staff don't see themselves as that. I would say for the most part, we tried to keep the union on board, but I wouldn't be held to ransom by them; it's all about getting the balance right. I do think the 'independent pay review body' for staff inflationary pay rises is too closely linked to the government, they are told which boundaries to use by treasury ministers before they make their decision to consult at all levels, which seems ludicrous to me. What's the point when you have already been told what the government can afford, rather than it being the other way around, and then a meaningful dialogue take place to negotiate a settlement, rather than us all seeing the result of lower inflationary pay rises affecting everyone year after year. People not being given an award that reflects price increases, etc. In real terms, standards of living drop, not only in the prison service but in all public and private sector areas.

I know that the private sector complains that the public sector pensions are high, but people who work in them tend to be paid lower wages than the private sector. Those who buy an annuity for a pension in later life should have proper inflation levels built into the process as part of the contract, so their standard of living is not eroded as well, but for the most part, annuity companies set a 5% maximum limit on it. That's something government should look at, so financial companies pay proper amounts to people who, whether in the private or public sector, receive proper remuneration for the work they do, or it stays the same where the top echelons of the richest people keep getting richer but everyone else suffers and gets poorer. I think it's time for reform. Get away from what has happened over the last forty years and vote members of parliament into Westminster who really listen to and care about the people they are supposed to work for.

In every prison, there are always a couple of staff, at whatever level in uniform and non-uniform grades, who are there to cause problems rather than solve them, and if they end up in positions that can influence others, it means they can be destructive in such an environment, which is there to support prisoners in whatever category of prison they may be held in. They cannot see that there are ways to deliver the service that are not purely seen as black and white in approach to making sure a regime operates effectively. There's just something about being put into a position of power that changes the way they are as individuals; it could be they have no real power outside of their workplace, and it makes them feel important whilst in it. The thing I found about working at Drake Hall was, for the most part, the offence was secondary to the real cause of why a woman commits a crime in the community. There is usually some sort of influence behind them, pushing them to break the law, and quite often it is a male one. Either through mental and/or physical abuse, for instance, linked to drugs, they can become dependent on the narcissist that controls their every move, and they can't escape.

They get sucked into a life of crime. It can also be compounded by the fact that they have children as well. That is probably the reason why an awful lot try committing some form of self-harm, particularly in remand prisons. It's a real cry for help, and because they don't get the help at the appropriate time in the community, they end up being incarcerated. I think because Drake Hall had, for the most part, operated a calmer approach to dealing with the prisoners (occasionally, some staff in uniform did make things worse), they did not self-harm. I would have liked to see an exchange of certain uniformed staff work at a female local prison, only for a week, so they could understand how good their lives were at Drake Hall and see what some staff must deal with, day in and day out, in a local prison's conditions.

I think from a staff's point of view, they like to see stability in terms of senior management operating in an establishment. A lot of governor grades use the system to get up the ladder as quickly as they can. They don't really care about how they do it or who they must walk over to achieve it. The other thing linked to some governing governors is that they can be narcissistic. At the time when I was serving as a governor grade, they all, bar none, received bonuses at the end of a reporting year from the area manager, which to me means even if they performed in a poor way, they still received a nice addition to their pay packet. Although I don't know for sure, I was told that in the case of Drake Hall, the governing governor received £10,000. We all could earn more through the normal process of our incremental pay scales. In my opinion, there should not be any extra bonuses outside of that unless the person reaches their maximum pay grade, but only based on the yearly appraisal score and non-pensionable, but even that is not a good argument when it is public money paying for it. I know there are incremental scales involved at all levels of staff pay, which they should use in conjunction with performance. It feels like taxpayers' money is not being used correctly. You could even say it is defrauding them, and I'm sure the money could be better utilised elsewhere. When someone isn't getting an achieved or exceeded marking, they should, in theory, not be elevated on the incremental scale, but as we will see, it can be manipulated by the clique.

Another crucial area within any prison is the governing governor's accountability for the security keys in any establishment, from class one (the highest grade) to class two (general purpose) and suite keys (offices). As you can imagine, if something goes wrong in any prison where a prisoner manages to compromise key security, it can cause big problems, and for a lock and key change to take place, it can cost upwards of £250,000 to replace them all. What normally happens is that after the governing governor signs for the prison keys and ancillary equipment, the deputy governor then conducts a key check every month to ensure they are correct. You are running the show.

The key safe was in my office and only I had access to it for issuing or taking away keys. It became apparent working with the prison locksmith that we had far too many keys, and hundreds were located in their key stores, which were surplus to our prison requirements. Outside of class one, class two, and office suite keys, along with body belt restraints, handcuffs, and their inserts, there was no real need for any other type. There was a ledger that I held that had all the different sorts of keys held within the establishment, so I decided, after consultation with our locksmith, to get rid of any surplus keys and ancillary equipment back to the prison service central locking section.

When I conducted my checks once a month, I did them in the evening when the least amount of day staff were on duty. If I was working in a dispersal prison, I would probably come in on a night shift to account for them, purely to make my job easier. If any discrepancies were found, then I could deal with the problem quickly. I could also have keys tested to see if anyone had managed to use anything to take a copy. This would normally be done as part of any security intelligence and could be done locally, but if a crime had been detected, they would be bagged, tagged, and used as police evidence for any criminal case that may develop.

Whilst I was at Drake Hall, there was a change of area manager. The prison service, in its infinite wisdom, had decided to get rid of the women's estate, and depending on where a prison was located, it would now fall under the male estate area manager. It was a cost saving exercise, but I can imagine it then meant that a women's prison ends up at the bottom of their priority list. The new area manager wasn't, in my opinion, interested at all in having a women's establishment latched onto them.

When I took over the checking of the keys after the governing governor had signed for them as being correct before I arrived at Drake Hall, I found a note in the safe in my office that had been signed off by the women's estate area manager about a discrepancy in class one keys. I never thought anything of it at the time because the keys were correct as per the ledger. It was before my time, and the letter was signed by the women's estate area manager that a class one key had been written off. The only way that could happen was with the support of locking section, so initially, I never thought any more of it. I tried to follow the paper trail to see where it led, but basically, it didn't lead anywhere, which eventually raised my suspicions as the months went by.

We had a real excess of keys and equipment in the prison. I went with the locksmith to look at the main works locking store. I was surprised by the sheer amount in there, so we had to get rid of it all, back to the prison service central locking section so I could get a handle on everything. I did wonder why all the previous governing and deputy governors had not done it previously. Maybe that's a question that they need to answer, but personally,

I think it was just laziness! The locksmith from our works department could only take a certain number of keys back at a time, so it took ages to bring down the spares and excess equipment to a level that made life easier for me and others to check all security keys and cuffs.

I sometimes sit and think, "Why me?" Maybe I'm just too diligent, but once I was able to cut through the forest, I could see the wood from the trees. I went through and inspected every single key that I held, and lo and behold, I found the missing class one key. Now, this is yet another embarrassing situation to be in and throws up all sorts of problems for what appears to be some sort of cover-up due to incompetence. There did not appear to be any investigation set up by area office or our establishment to look at why a class one key was missing in the first place or why a full relock of the prison hadn't taken place. I would also think that someone in headquarters would have been informed of this potentially serious problem. The other issue was that governing and deputy governors had been signing over the prison's full key inventory without questioning anything about the letter that was sitting in the prison key safe. Someone had taken the missing key off the inventory, so now I was sitting with an extra class one key.

I sat down and wrote a letter to my governing governor explaining the discrepancy and the current situation, and it meant the responsibility was for them to deal with it, as they had signed for the establishment keys when they took over. I would not circumvent them to report such an issue, so it was left with them to sort it out higher up the ladder. I added the key back to the inventory and made damn sure none of the identified problems were going to come back and bite me on the ass.

I know what the prison service grades higher up are now

like, and they're Teflon coated. It looks to me as if governing governors, whether that be at Whitemoor, Drake Hall, or even in the whole prison estate, just assume that their inventories are in order and sign to say they are correct. I mean, what are the odds of me finding two security problems relating to keys and cuffs in only five prisons I have worked at and being promoted to a position where I had direct control over security items after being put in post. I know what I would be doing now if I were the top person in the prison service! Again, things link to poor performance, lazy governors, and incompetence. It felt more like I was working in a circus rather than Her Majesty's prison and civil service.

A new area manager arrived, someone who had been the deputy governor at HMP Littlehey in the past, someone I knew, but I didn't expect things in my career to go the way they were soon going to go. You must make the assumption that the key issue would have been discussed with them by the governing governor. I would have expected a formal investigation to take place. The reason for that is, a new area manager would not want any surprises when coming into a whole new area. I had been at HMP Littlehey for nearly twenty-four months, and they knew me. We were doing well as an establishment in terms of audits and in general as far as a prison operates. The Release on Temporary Licence (ROTL) process was working well, I'm really proud to say that I never had a failure on releasing someone, either to work in the community or allowing them home on licence. The public expects people like me to get it right, so prisoners are not deemed a risk to the community. Unfortunately, there have been many times where prisoners on release have caused communities many problems. And to me, accountability when going through all the documents to release someone is so important because of the consequences that may occur after release into the community.

A strange request came up one day. The governing governor came to see me, and it had been requested that I be freed up to conduct an investigation at HMP Stafford Prison. I have done quite a few inquiries before, both as a uniform and governor grade. Normally they were with uniformed prison staff or other personnel, linked to fraud, expenses, bullying, and that sort of thing. But one thing you are not supposed to do is investigate any grades equivalent to or higher than your own. Well, I was asked to investigate a complaint against a grade C governor who was at HMP Stafford. The investigation itself was straightforward and took around two months to complete. I firstly apologised to the grade C governor that I was asked to investigate them, especially as I was only an E grade. When you get asked, it means you are being told to do it in prison service management language. It's worth clarifying that at this time, the highest grade in governors was A and it flowed down in terms of seniority.

The upshot of it all was that the investigation linked to health and safety. However, after a thorough inquiry, there was nothing to answer in terms of the complaint against the governor grade by a prison officer, but due to the nature of the complaint, I recommended that the radio system be fully upgraded at HMP Stafford, so there were no radio blackspots around the establishment.

As time progressed at Drake Hall, it looked like the prison services relationship with the unions across the service were deteriorating. It's normally to do with one thing: pay and conditions, but as the weeks progressed, relationships steadily got worse. One morning, coming in after the previous day's duty, I found the union representatives standing outside the main gate informing staff that they were not allowed to enter the prison due to a walkout (prison staff are not allowed to strike, as they have the powers of a police officer when on duty). I was told they were informed by their union, the Prison Officers Association (POA) to walk out. I went into the prison and phoned the area manager first to let them know what was happening, and they said, "They can't walk out," and I said, "I know, but try telling them that." They said they would inform London it had happened, who would then open the gold command suite. Locally, we would open our silver command suite to oversee our work, and if we developed any problems, we could use gold command suite to support our prison. As it happened, I was told our establishment was the first in England and Wales to walk out, but it soon became evident that others were following suit. It reinforced my view that, although we were a laid-back prison, in my opinion, the union branch at Drake Hall were quite militant and quickly showed their true colours when told to strike. They obviously had too much time on their hands.

Managers and those not in the POA union came into work. It was a tough old day for everyone. The prison went into safe mode, and we tried to keep things running, providing a basic regime for the prisoners. My legs were killing me at the end of a very long day due to some disabilities I have. Maybe I should have sued the union for breaking the law and causing me problems with my health. The POA informed their staff to return to work the following morning, but what was annoying was that the prison service took no action against the POA for the walkout, which basically meant, and in my opinion, if it ever happened again, the same thing would occur again at some point, but it showed weak leadership in the prison and civil service.

One of Drake Hall's operational managers and one non-operational manager who looked after security and education, respectively, seemed to be experiencing problems. Our head of security had to go off on long-term absence, which meant I had to take over their area and the non-operational education department under my umbrella. I was quite literally running most of the prisoner functions, but this is where my career took a turn for the worse. The governing governor informed me that the area manager wanted me to run a project for them, but I said, "You do realise I am now doing the work of three people." They said they would talk to the area manager, smooth it over, and not to worry about it, so I got on with trying to make sure things ran as smoothly as possible in the establishment. I never heard anything more about it, so I assumed things were okay.

A few months later, I had to attend a governing governors' area management meeting as my boss was on leave. After the meeting, I went to see the area manager to apologise for the fact that I did not have the time to pick up the project work for them because of the workload I had with the two senior managers being off. They basically told me, and in a tone that I knew well from Littlehey when they upset some POs with the way they dealt with them, "Don't worry, I won't ask you again." At that precise moment in time, I just thought, "Shit, my career is over." I was always told that the prison service has a little black book with the names of governors who will not get on, and I thought, "I'm never going to get anywhere now." People can ruin your career, and in my opinion, I now knew that this area manager was going to do that to me.

As time went on, they seemed to be focusing on me in my role as deputy governor, and the area team were sent into Drake Hall to try and find things going wrong. The area manager, through my governor, informed me that my area of work in resettlement management was not being delivered correctly (my annual appraisals say otherwise), even though we had great results to back that up as well. The area manager had also told me they would not support me in taking my senior operational managers exam to gain accreditation to become a governing governor.

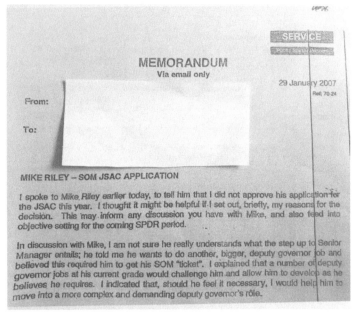

I wrote them a letter, and they did say they would support me into another deputy governor's post. Ultimately, though, the way they then dealt with me meant that wasn't going to happen!

From:	Mr M A Riley	Tel:	01785 774100
	Deputy Governor	Ext:	4201
	HMP & YOI Drake Hall	Fax:	01785 774015
To:	▮▮▮▮▮▮▮▮	Date:	8 February 2007
	Area Manager	Your ref:	
	West Midlands		
		Our ref:	DepGov/MAR/CD

I have had the opportunity to reflect on our brief telephone conversation on 29 January 2007 about you not supporting my application this year. I don't know what information you had available at that time to make the decision, but there appears to be no avenue of appeal if you decide not to support my application.

As you are aware, I have secured the Assessment Centre approval, along with a Personal Development Plan which came out of that, and I was disappointed to note your comments that it was "wishy washy" and had been agreed with the Area Development Adviser, Ruth Evans, who, I assume, would have discussed it with people, as I did with my Governor, according to NTS 42/2006. I have also passed the Silver Command and written appraisal process.

I have received feedback from the third part JSAC, which I think gives me enough information to develop myself to re-sit this year, and the Area Development Adviser indicated that I should be in a good position to re-take as well.

In taking the Operational Manager's accreditation, both my line manager and yourself approved me to go forward for the process in 2006.

In our discussion you mentioned that no grade D non-STBIC would be available in the future, which has now been highlighted under NTS 4/2007, which effectively means I have no avenue of progression to that position now.

I am currently a Deputy Governor and I identified that I needed to go to a larger prison with a typical hierarchal structure, which effectively means I can only go on a sideways move.

In applying for the SOM I indicated, even if I passed the accreditation, I would like to still be a Deputy Governor in a prison before possible employment as a Governing Governor and knew that I may even have to come out of the operational side for a period of time, to give me a further wide base experience and knowledge. However, the SOM concentrates on operational management and, as far as I am aware, I have the necessary skills to develop further in that area, and I think that is backed up by my progress so far.

I have just received your formal feedback and I am afraid I disagree with your assessment and I would like to request a meeting to discuss the comments made.

M A RILEY
Deputy Governor

A little while later, the area manager decided that the West Midlands would go through some changes based around deputy governors' skills and experience. We were all apparently going to be interviewed by human resources so that personal career decisions could be made. In the meantime, the governing governor of Drake Hall was going to be given a progressive move to another prison, and someone was going to take over the tenure. You can't make up this sort of stuff. The person coming into the post came to have a look around, and I gave them a tour of the prison. Apparently, they could not take up the post for around three to four months, so I became the temporary governing governor, and through that time, the area manager had no problems with any aspect of delivery in service. Strange that, bearing in mind what they had told me not so long ago and saying my area of work was not operating effectively. You would think they would want to bring somebody in to run the prison if I was as bad as I was being led to believe I was. It said everything to me about the way the area manager operated. In my opinion, it reinforced to me that they were just a narcissistic bully who would do anything it took to destroy anyone who was not just a "yes" person. I do wonder, even now, how many more lives they have ruined with their style of management. I certainly know of the couple at HMP Littlehey.

The other thing I had to do was re-evaluate the post of governing governor at Drake Hall. It was a grade D post, but the prison service was going through more change at the time as well. When it is top management positions that need to change, what happens is, they always mark the post upwards, never down. Governors don't like losing money, so I had to come up with a new job description for the governing governor's position at Drake Hall. A person from headquarters came to visit me in the prison and based on what I had put together, decided that the post would be reset a grade higher at level C. I think it's because the prison service director and HR had plans to make sure all deputy governors were set at grade D. Did it happen out there? I think the system should have worked the other way because the service was always looking for efficiencies at the lower grades rather than the higher grades. Funny, that isn't it!

I had previously worked in a range of prisons: male high security, local Cat B, Cat C training, female closed (Cat C), and semi-open, so my development needs indicated that I should move to a large male prison as a deputy governor, which was originally stated by the area manager in their letter.

SECTION 6: *Background Experience*
6.1 Areas of Experience

Experience of working with:

Has worked in the following types of Establishment:

Males	✓	Young Offenders	✓	Dispersal	✓	Cat C Trainer
Females	✓	Juveniles	✗	Local	✓	Specialist Units *PDS*
				Female	✓	Open Prison
				YOI/Juvenile	✓	Area/HQ/SAU/NOMS

Has the following work background:

Drugs *Winchester*	✓	Programmes *Mgr for RTS*	✓	Specialist Units *PDS*	✓
Offender Management	✓	Regimes	✓	Other	
Operations / Security	✓	Residential	✓		
Planning/Secretariat *Proj. Mgt*	✓	SAU / Area / HQ	✗		

Professional Expertise in: *Mechanical Eng. & Head Instructor Army*

6.2 Career History

Please list below all previous establishments worked in during the last 5 years. For each establishment include the grade(s) the date work commenced there and the date of leaving.

See attached Outline.

SECTION 7 – *Self-Assessment of Current Performance*

However, I was told, in no uncertain terms, that I would not be moving to another deputy governors position, even though I had been told previously in writing by the current area manager that they would help me move to a larger male prison as one.

The deputy governor at Stafford Prison was told they were being moved as well, so I said, "It's a male prison, larger than Drake Hall, just up the road a few miles, and you are telling me I can't get the job." HR reiterated that I would not be moved to a deputy governor's post. In my opinion, the area manager wanted a few of us out. We were ex-military; maybe it's because we had a voice to say when things were going wrong, and that wasn't liked by the current area manager. Mind you, that fits into the clique's way of thinking as well. You can't raise concerns with them in a positive, constructive way. They just see you as someone who is challenging their authority. They know best all of the time!

I was going through some issues with my health and needed to go into hospital for a double knee operation because they were causing me significant problems. I tried to take up the issue with the reporting line of the area manager in the hopes I would not get moved from Drake Hall in the interim or be moved to another dep's post. What was going on was clearly bullying in my eyes, but the deputy director general of the prison service, in my opinion, closed ranks with the area manager. They would not hold a formal investigation, even though prison service policies said it could happen. It appears from my perspective that, as the perceived victim in what was happening to me, I had no say in the process, which goes against natural justice. The clique was protecting themselves, and they said there was no case to answer. 'Quelle surprise'.

They stated, "That PSO 1300 required that the matter be considered and that our meeting followed by discussions with the area manager and others as necessary constituted a formal enquiry and they did not intend to commission a formal investigation under PSO 1300 as they were clear that they could address the matter appropriately and legitimately according to human resource advice."

When the person making the decision says, "That the meeting with the area manager and others constituted a formal enquiry," all I can say to that is, there was nothing ever written down from that side of things. So, to me, that means the meeting was a sham to protect the area manager. It was like the chief operating officer of the prison service was sticking two fingers up at me and manipulating things as they saw fit in the clique! I do wonder what people will think as they read this part of my memoir. I think I was unfairly treated, but people out there may have a different view.

As far as I was concerned, I had nothing to lose now but to appeal it to the director general of the prison service. That didn't stop the process of the area manager moving me. The new governing governor of Drake Hall had a few chats with me, reiterating that I would not be going to a deputy governor's post, but the area manager said I could go and work in area office. I said, "I have always worked on the operational coalface, and there was no way I was going to become a further target for the area manager working in their office. I wasn't going to get anywhere." A funny comment was then made to me, they said that I wasn't "politically astute". I took that comment to mean that I don't lie well enough, as politicians and some other senior managers do. I was then told that the governing governor of HMP Hewell, who was a very close friend of the area manager, had said they would take me at their prison, in effect a demotion in my eyes from deputy governor to take up a post at HMP Hewell down in Redditch as the head of interventions.

There were three different prisons on the site where the area manager posted me. The idea was that I would be used to integrate all the systems which linked into my area of responsibility so they could operate as one establishment. I would report to a head of function, who, in turn, would report to the governing governor. This just reinforced to me that I was being penalised and demoted.

In the meantime, about a month before I was due to move, I went into hospital to have surgery on both legs. I was signed off for the rest of the time I was supposed to be at Drake Hall, but ten days after I left hospital, I phoned up the governor of Drake Hall and said, "I would come into the prison on light duties and sort out my stuff." A new deputy governor was already floating around. They couldn't wait to get rid of me, so it was easy to pass things on, and I signed over the key safe and thought, "Good luck to you."

They sent me down to HMP Hewell on a public expense move as the head of interventions. They had to, due to the distance, and I wouldn't have been able to afford to live in two places at the same time. What it does show is that they are willing to use taxpayers' money to shore up their bullying ways. This, in effect, meant the area manager was willing to use public money as part of their nefarious plans to get rid of those who were willing to constructively challenge them on their thought processes. I was still pursuing my grievance for the treatment that the area manager had dished out against me. You need to understand how the hierarchy operates in the prison service. They just close ranks and put up a brick wall. They were all friends at senior civil service, area manager and governing governor grade levels.

After arriving at HMP Hewell, I was soon called to see the governing governor. They and their team had been in the prison for over twelve months, and it seemed to me as if, although part of their team now, I wasn't part of the team. When you are the governing governor, you are directly responsible for running the NHS operational contract. The deputy governor would normally be the one overseeing it due to the important nature of the work in a prison setting. However, I was told by the governing governor it would fall to me to manage and that I would report directly to them in terms of that element of the work. It didn't make sense to me at the time because I had a line manager to whom I reported, so if the governing governor wanted the NHS looking after and for whatever reason, the deputy governor wasn't doing it, then it should have been allocated to my line manager.

As I tried to negotiate my way around three different sites, I deduced as time went on that one of the biggest issues affecting the three prisons was the contractual work. Systems and accountability for them were very limited. I was going to be used to pick up their lack of progression in the three establishments, as an individual and as part of my team. How the previous prisons operated on such poor contracts I will never know, and with all the problems I had been experiencing with the area manager, I knew inside they were going to continue to try and demolish me. They had a governing governor in their pocket whose higher managers appeared to be in their pocket, and as a group, they just wanted to bury me. It felt as if I were some sort of threat to them all, something I couldn't quite put my finger on at the time. But what I did know was that my sixth sense was telling me something was very wrong; I was now a target. Imagine commencing a new job, and before you arrive, you are given your areas of responsibility to deal with and have work outside of that dumped on you. No discussion, just dumped on you.

For me, the whole issue of bullying needs to be tackled throughout the prison and civil service. The way people abuse their authority to destroy other people is unforgivable, as is the way the rules are blatantly ignored to justify doing something because they get away with things by abusing their power through corruption. Do bullies enjoy doing what they do? Yes, until they get caught out. The problem with this is that these bullies are protected by others who are just like them and think the same way, and they are all working in the top grades in society. They look down on us all, and they think they can get away with treating people like shit. They require people around them who think the same way they do, so it ends up with nobody challenging them, and they can just get away with it with impunity. It must stop. We can stop it, but it needs us all to stand up to them and be counted, and I know from experience that is very difficult when they are senior managers, civil servants and politicians. Our nation, as a family, deserves better. We should be a family nation, but we are not. They have divided us, and in doing so, we are failing. It's surely up to us, the majority, to take back control of a fractured country, so the dog is wagging the tail and not the other way around.

HMP HEWELL 2008-2009

I arrived at HMP Hewell, and it quickly became evident that I was going to have lots of extra work over and above the job description pushed my way. When you want to allocate extra workload to someone, you are supposed to risk assess it to see whether individuals have the capacity to be able to deal with the workload and make sure their work-life balance is okay. Bearing in mind my disabilities, it never happened to me. What I found was that my experience and skills were better than those of my line managers and most but not all the other senior managers.

The one person I respected was the head of resettlement. We worked well together in making sure risks were managed appropriately in terms of the prisoners. What the area manager and governing governor had not done and made a fatal mistake in their planning to bring me down was they left my deputy governor status on the computer systems. Depending on what management grade you were, meant how much you could interrogate it and the depth of information you could see and pull out of the prison data system. I kept this to myself. I was now like a spy in their camp, it meant I could keep an eye on all the governor grades. Happy days.

I travelled to London to have my grievance heard by the director general of the prison service, who had a governor grade from the Prison Governors Association (PGA) and a Human Resource (HR) manager available to hear it. The director was asking where all my documentation was, and I said, "It's all with your deputy just down the hall, and it should have been given to you." For some reason, the board didn't have it. You would think someone working a few doors away would have provided them with the information. It felt like I was now going through a process to just get things over with. My complaint was not upheld, but the group had not followed due process. The only option left to me after that was to take it to the permanent secretary's office to complain about the director general. That office basically ignored the complaint. They would not entertain it at all. That was the only avenue available for me to go down, but I was being stonewalled.

I would think at the top of the chain some expletives were being thrown in my direction and probably at the director general. The system was silent, so I had to leave the complaint. Silence is golden, but it taught me a lot. Our policies are some of the very best, but only when used correctly with integrity and honesty. As I was working towards getting my areas of responsibility sorted out, the prison was gearing itself up for a security audit, so a lot of those managers and staff who worked in that area were pulled from their normal duties, which left the rest of us to pick up the slack, including duty governors.

My legs were not doing very well at all after the double leg surgery. I was struggling to get around the three separate sites, especially the old open part. I was talking to my line manager about it, but I was being ignored, and the work kept coming. It was extremely stressful, trying to make sure everything was working and trying to support my staff group whilst I was being overloaded and suffering with my disabilities. The higher-ranking governors just didn't seem to care about the impact things were having on me.

There were some staff, but one in particular on one of the residential wings causing problems with our enhanced thinking skills staff and the prisoner group. It was suspected they had wiped some of the recorded tapes of the groups, which meant the whole audit section for that would score no points. It was raised with the relevant functional head of residence, my line manager and the governing governor, who, in my opinion, did not deal with it effectively. It was alleged that some bullying by an officer on my staff group members was taking place in the wing where the courses were delivered, as well as abusing their authority to bully prisoners. The head of residence at the time would not initiate an investigation into the bullying and bringing it to the attention of my line manager and more senior grades did nothing to sort out the problem either.

Some years later, after I had left HMP Hewell and the prison service, I was told by a contact at the prison that a new governing governor later on down the line eventually sacked them for the same sort of thing. That's only what I have been told, though. It's a pity the functional head and governing governor did not investigate it at the time in a proper manner, but hopefully the person has gone, albeit years later. I do wonder how many more people have been subjected to their bullying ways over that time. At whatever level bullying is an issue, it needs confronting so people can get on with what they need to do to without the fear of what will happen next!

I was really struggling with my legs, and I was in lots of pain. I kept asking for an adjustment to support my daily working because of my disabilities, but it fell on deaf ears. In the end, I wrote to my line manager to say that they were not supporting me. The senior managers were having their shifts changed to cover security audit work, but here I was with damaged legs having to cover more duty governors, and they were not helping me at all.

After all the previous treatment against me, I thought, "Things need to change now." I really needed to raise my fight to a much higher level instead of being used and abused. After being fobbed off with silence from very senior managers in the civil service, the permanent secretaries office, and the localised treatment I was receiving at HMP Hewell, I had to get tougher in my approach to people bullying and gaslighting me. What I was going through did make me want to stick my head in the oven, that's for sure. It is also an odd situation to be in, as all the people doing it to me in the prison were of the opposite sex.

My manager must have gone to see the governing governor, who, instead of going through the proper process of dealing with a disabled person, referred me straight away to prison medical services to try and get me medically discharged from the prison service (this is the end process after all other avenues have been exhausted). I informed them that they cannot just get rid of staff like that, never mind me, and there is a whole procedural process that has to be followed, but in the meantime, they were still ignoring my pleas for help. It's horrible having to beg for that, but that's what it felt like. However, they could still allow security managers to be taken off duties to complete audit work. I thought, "To hell with this, I'm going to take them to a disability tribunal."

Something at some point must have clicked after I told them about going down that route because they had left me no other option. A while later, they backtracked on the medical discharge and referred me to our prison occupational health advisor (OHA), who swiftly told them of my condition by letter. I wasn't trying to dodge out of duties; that's not my style. What I requested was to be given main prison duty governors rather than go around the three prison sites. I also had to introduce a new initiative into the main prison called the Intensive Drug Treatment Service (IDTS), which meant some really big changes needed to take place.

A MEDICATION COUNTER FOR IDTS

The integration of three prisons into one site blended itself perfectly for a cost reduction exercise, so I had to work out a strategy for my group to see where savings could be made as the project proceeded. After all, it's taxpayers' money funding everything. All during my short time at HMP Hewell, I was not supported by the governing governor or my line manager to progress towards the senior operational managers JSAC to become accredited to apply for governing governor posts.

Then it happened.

I was looking at the end of year appraisals for my staffing group, and I can hand on heart say that whatever appraisal marking individual staff ended up with through me or their line managers was a true and accurate reflection of the targets set, but with my access to the whole data system in the prison, I was extremely shocked to see what other managers were doing to manipulate the system along with the counter signatories!

TARGETS FOR HMP HEWELL 2008/2009

HMP Hewell KPT Outturn 2008/09

Security	Target 2008/09	Outturn 2008/09	
Absconds rate /100,000 prisoner days	26.2	25.38	
Escapes	0	0	
Mandatory Drug Testing	10.20%	9.00%	
Security Audit	80%	85%	
Maintain Order & Control	**Target 2008/09**	**Outturn 2008/09**	
Accidents	8.10%	7.57%	
C & R Training	80%	87.00%	
Contingency Exercises (all)	6	14	
Cont Exercise (hostage)	1	1	
Operational Capacity (monthly)	97.60%	97.90%	
ROTL	95%	99.95%	
Searches	100%	102.80%	
Serious Assaults Rate	2.45%	2.78%	
Tornado Commitment	21	29	
Reducing Re-offending	**Target 2008/09**	**Outturn 2008/09**	
Accomm Settled	81.80%	97.80%	
Accomm - Housing Assessment	90%	99.70%	
CARAT'S	1675	1,715	
Drug Treatment Starts	240	240	
Drug Treatment Completions	125	143	
OBPs	81	83	
Resettlement % Employment	28.90%	34.70%	
Resettlement % Educ & Training	3%	2.70%	
Work Related Skills	250	769	
Voluntary Drug Testing	320	371	
Decency	**Target 2008/09**	**Outturn 2008/09**	
Overcrowding	35.30%	29.60%	
Purposeful Activity	26.7	26.9	
Request & Complaints	95%	95.9%	
Self Harm Audit	80%	80%	
Time Unlocked	12.3	11.3	

Race & Diversity	Target 2008/09	Outturn 2008/09
Race Equality (Monthly)	5.30%	4.70%
Race Equality (Prisoners) Qtrly	70%	73.40%
Race Equality (Staff) Qrtly	70%	82.80%
Organisational Effectiveness	Target 2008/09	Outturn 2008/09
Classroom Attendance	80%	77.90%
Correspondence	95%	96.50%
Discharges for Court	90%	98.80%
Energy Efficiency	456	449.2
Water Consumption	27019	33,073.80
PPM	100%	100%
SPDR Opened	95%	99.10%
SPDR Reviewed	95%	99.10%
SPDR Completed	95%	99.90%
Standard Audits	80%	85%
Staff Sickness	11.2 days	12.4
Staff Training	6 days	7.3

The highlighted numbers are the failures, of which there are seven. Do you think exceeded markings should have been awarded, or by doing so, do you think corruption and fraud were rife at HMP Hewell at the time of reporting, bearing in mind that for the governing governor, the SPDR must be signed off by the area manager and the deputy director general of the prison service. The deputy governor will have been signed off by the governing governor and the area manager etc. The point I'm trying to make is that signing off by two managers should cut out corruption and fraud, but I guess that depends on who is in the clique!

The governing governor is in overall charge of all the prison's targets. The deputy governor maintains order and control in the establishment, as well as decency.

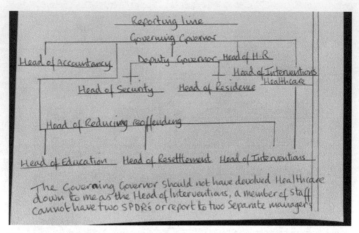

Reporting line
Governing Governor
Head of Accountancy   Deputy Governor   Head of H.R
                                         Head of Interventions
                                         Healthcare
      Head of Security   Head of Residence

Head of Reducing reoffending

Head of Education   Head of Resettlement   Head of Interventions

The Governing Governor should not have devolved Healthcare down to me as the Head of Interventions, a member of staff cannot have two SPDRs or report to two separate managers

People out there will not know this, but with SPDRs, there is a paper trail, so you can look back years if necessary to spot any issues such as corruption and fraud. I am told that through the shared services in Newport, that they are now only going to have two years' worth of SPDRs on the prison system, so investigators looking into criminal activity cannot and will not be able to uncover anything over two years old. To my mind, that means people can literally get away with things unless a proper audit system is in place, and as we have seen, the two manager system does not work when corruption by people in a clique is leading the way.

STAFF PERFORMANCE

Michael Riley staff performance and development record (SPDR) HMP Hewell

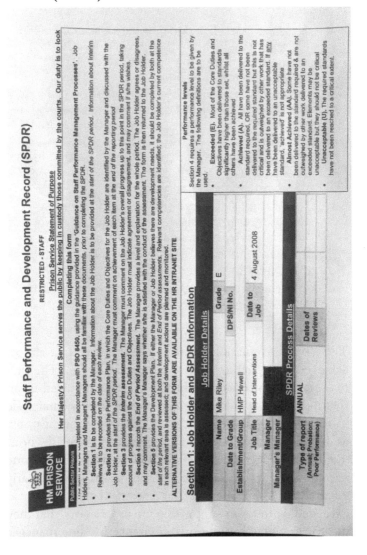

Appraisal sheet performance levels

Performance levels

Section 4 requires a performance level to be given by the Manager. The following definitions are to be used.

- **Exceeded (E).** Most of the Core Duties and Objectives have been delivered to standards significantly higher than those set, whilst all others have been achieved
- **Achieved (A).** All have been delivered to the standard required, OR some have not been delivered to the required standard but this is not critical and is outweighed by other work that has been delivered to an exceeded standard. If <u>any</u> have been delivered to an unacceptable standard, 'achieved' is not appropriate
- **Almost Achieved (AA).** Some have not been delivered to the standard required & are not outweighed by other work delivered to an exceeded standard. Elements may be unacceptable but they should not be critical
- **Unacceptable (U).** The required standards have not been reached to a critical extent.

The appraisal markings are unacceptable (U), almost achieved (AA), achieved (A), and exceeded (E). The first two gradings of unacceptable and almost achieved mean that individuals could not step up their incremental scale to receive a pay increase. It's a good system, but it's only as good as the person making an informed, non-judgmental decision. My staffing group had done exceptionally well, exceeding all the prison service yearly targets. As their manager, it meant that I had also exceeded, with them supporting me in the work that they did for me linked to my prison targets. My line manager had other ideas about me and basically said that even though I had exceeded all targets, I had only achieved and not exceeded on my appraisal, even though the prison service targets in my area were all surpassed.

The other thing of note is that the U, AA, A, and E have values linked to them of 0%, 1%, 2%, and 3%, respectively. For those managers at the top of their incremental scale, they could receive a non-pensionable bonus on those percentage rates. Those are part of the rules, but you could also argue that if they are at the top of their incremental scale, they should not be getting any extra bonus money for doing what they are paid to do (even though it is not added to their pension rights). When people talk about the use of public money, being at the top of your scale is a good example of saving money in the civil service; after all, we are paid to do a job, and staff receive inflationary uplifts through government most years, albeit they are usually lower than the inflation rate set every September. I'm sure there are lots of people out there who don't receive bonuses in their work.

Things like that reinforced in my mind that they were discriminating against me. Appraisals are linked to the national pay structure in terms of incremental advancement, so a pay rise can be allocated based on an almost achieved, achieved, or exceeded score. Where someone has reached the top of their scale, an almost achieved marking attracts a 1% payment, an achieved 2% and an exceeded 3% award. The money does not go towards any individual pension built up in the civil service. It was good to see that all the hard work put in by staff in our group meant they were rewarded appropriately. After all, it meant they could progress through their incremental scale and know that they had earned it.

I made sure my line manager knew I was not happy with the way they and the governing governor were marginalising me. It didn't matter what I said, but you must take into account the work the governing governor should have done, who had conveniently dumped their work on me because they were the lead on it; that part of the appraisal has to be written up by them. I had exceeded, and it meant that part of my appraisal should have gone to the area manager for signing off. That never happened. The governing governor knew they should not have dumped their workload on me. I wasn't at all pleased with the way they were treating me now, so I added all the documentation to my submission for disability discrimination. As far as I was concerned, they had all dug their own graves, from the area manager downwards, and it would be up to a tribunal to decide whether what I was saying was, as I thought, discriminatory.

You will remember that I said I still had my deputy governor status left on me as part of data access, so taking everything that was happening to me into account, I interrogated the system to have a look at all the targets for the prison as a whole and the different groups within it to see what everyone else above me and my peers had scored in relation to their targets. It's worth noting that, from the governing governor down to include all my peers, they had all been given exceeded markings. I was flabbergasted and angry. The reason for this is that only one other person besides me in my peer group had exceeded their targets. The governing governor, deputy governor, my line manager, and all the rest of my senior management peer group had not even achieved their targets. Some of those managers fell into the unacceptable box. Even if they were awarded an almost achieved, they could still pick up a 1% bonus and the only way they could receive an incremental increase is by achieving their own targets as a minimum. Looking at my peers and those governor grades above me, when they had not hit targets, meant they should not have received any incremental increase or bonus. In my opinion, there is a simple name for that. It's called fraud, which also involves the act of corruption when defrauding the public purse using favouritism to make personal gains!

PAY ON PROMOTION AND PROGRESSION
THROUGH THE INCREMENTAL SPINE POINTS SCALES OF PAY

Pay on Promotion & Progression - Managerial Pay Ranges 2009   Appendix 1

		Spine Point Steps:	£1,320	£1,295	£1,250	£1,425	£2,297			
		From Basic Pay G	£24,235	£25,555	£26,850	£28,100	£29,525	£31,822		
		To Basic Pay F	£27,690	£27,690	£27,890	£28,970	£30,420	£31,825		
		Uplift £	£3,455	£2,135	£840	£870	£895	£3	Min	Max
		Cash Balance £			£503	£535	£581	£1,588	£503	£1,588
		Total Uplift £	£3,455	£2,135	£1,343	£1,405	£1,476	£1,591	£1,343	£3,455
Underpin %	5.00%	New Rule New Structure	14.26%	8.35%	5.00%	5.00%	5.00%	5.00%	5.00%	14.26%
		Old Rule Old Structure	12.14%	5.83%	5.13%	5.84%	5.11%	4.40%		
		Old Rule New Structure	14.26%	8.35%	7.90%	6.26%	7.79%	0.01%		

		Spine Point Steps:	£1,280	£1,450	£1,405	£1,865	£4,964			
		From Basic Pay F	£27,690	£28,970	£30,420	£31,825	£33,690	£38,654		
		To Basic Pay E	£31,210	£31,210	£31,210	£32,635	£34,525	£40,495		
		Uplift £	£3,520	£2,240	£790	£810	£835	£1,841	Min	Max
		Cash Balance £			£731	£781	£850	£92	£92	£850
		Total Uplift £	£3,520	£2,240	£1,521	£1,591	£1,685	£1,933	£1,521	£3,520
Underpin %	5.00%	New Rule New Structure	12.71%	7.73%	5.00%	5.00%	5.00%	5.00%	5.00%	12.71%
		Old Rule Old Structure	11.05%	5.64%	5.11%	6.70%	13.85%	3.88%		
		Old Rule New Structure	12.71%	7.73%	7.28%	8.48%	20.20%	4.76%		

		Spine Point Steps:	£1,425	£1,890	£3,875	£2,095	£5,073			
		From Basic Pay E	£31,210	£32,635	£34,525	£38,400	£40,495	£45,568		
		To Basic Pay D	£41,715	£41,715	£41,715	£41,715	£41,715	£49,365		
		Uplift £	£10,505	£9,080	£7,190	£3,315	£1,220	£3,797	Min	Max
		Cash Balance £					£805		£805	£805
		Total Uplift £	£10,505	£9,080	£7,190	£3,315	£2,025	£3,797	£2,025	£10,505
Underpin %	5.00%	New Rule New Structure	33.66%	27.82%	20.83%	8.63%	5.00%	8.33%	5.00%	33.66%
		Old Rule Old Structure	28.65%	23.34%	16.71%	14.13%	18.48%	10.24%		
		Old Rule New Structure	33.66%	27.82%	20.83%	28.55%	21.90%	12.88%		

		Spine Point Steps:	£3,665	£3,985	£2,070	£4,275	£4,723			
		From Basic Pay D	£41,715	£45,380	£49,365	£51,435	£55,710	£60,433		
		RHA £	£5,474	£5,474	£5,474	£5,474	£5,474	£5,474		
		Total £	£47,189	£50,854	£54,839	£56,909	£61,184	£65,907		
		To Basic Pay C	£55,060	£55,060	£55,060	£57,170	£61,485	£66,830		
		Uplift £	£7,871	£4,206	£221	£261	£301	£923	Min	Max
		Cash Balance £			£2,521	£2,584	£2,758	£2,372	£2,372	£2,758
		Total Uplift £	£7,871	£4,206	£2,742	£2,845	£3,059	£3,295	£2,742	£7,871
Underpin %	5.00%	New Rule New Structure	16.68%	8.27%	5.00%	5.00%	5.00%	5.00%	5.00%	16.68%
		Old Rule Old Structure	19.56%	9.39%	4.07%	8.85%	5.12%	1.83%		
		Old Rule New Structure	16.68%	8.27%	4.25%	8.04%	9.23%	1.40%		

		Spine Point Steps:	£2,110	£4,315	£2,865	£2,480	£4,910			
		From Basic Pay C	£55,060	£57,170	£61,485	£64,350	£66,830	£71,740		
		To Basic Pay B	£58,165	£58,165	£62,515	£64,990	£67,480	£74,210		
		Uplift £	£3,105	£995	£1,030	£640	£650	£2,470	Min	Max
		Cash Balance £		£1,864	£2,044	£2,578	£2,692	£1,117	£1,117	£2,692
		Total Uplift £	£3,105	£2,859	£3,074	£3,218	£3,342	£3,587	£2,859	£3,587
Underpin %	5.00%	New Rule New Structure	5.64%	5.00%	5.00%	5.00%	5.00%	5.00%	5.00%	5.64%
		Old Rule Old Structure	4.07%	8.85%	5.12%	4.07%	4.59%	3.88%		
		Old Rule New Structure	5.64%	9.35%	5.70%	4.86%	11.04%	3.44%		

		Spine Point Steps:	£4,350	£2,475	£2,490	£2,870	£3,860			
		From Basic Pay B	£58,165	£62,515	£64,990	£67,480	£70,350	£74,210	£79,661
		To Basic Pay A	£62,515	£64,990	£67,480	£70,350	£74,210	£79,665	£79,665
		Uplift £	£4,350	£2,475	£2,490	£2,870	£3,860	£5,455	£4	Min	Max
		Cash Balance £		£651	£760	£504			£3,979	£504	£3,979
		Total Uplift £	£4,350	£3,126	£3,250	£3,374	£3,860	£5,455	£3,983	£3,126	£5,455
Inderpin %	5.00%	New Rule New Structure	7.48%	5.00%	5.00%	5.00%	5.49%	7.35%	5.00%	5.00%	7.48%
		Old Rule Old Structure	6.85%	5.12%	4.07%	4.59%	6.17%	4.59%	3.03%		
		Old Rule New Structure	7.48%	3.96%	3.83%	4.25%	5.49%	7.35%	0.01%		

Basic Pay A	£62,515	£64,990	£67,480	£70,350	£74,210	£79,665	£82,071

221

The area manager had signed off the governing governor. I did wonder what the area manager had received as a marking from the deputy director general and signed off by the director of the prison service when their appraisal was marked, but because they had effectively given out exceeded grades to or supported governors locally as the counter signatory, in my opinion, it meant they were complicit and helped them commit fraud. I also wonder if the deputy director general of the prison service had actually countersigned the governing governor's appraisal after the area manager had given the governor an exceeded marking, as they should do that to ensure corruption does not take place! I'm assuming they did because nothing changed on the system, meaning they would be complicit to the fraud taking place.

I received my tribunal date, so I informed my line manager about it and requested from them that I needed time to attend it. I was flatly told that I couldn't have the time off to attend the hearing. I said, "I would have to contact the tribunal and inform them of their decision." A few hours later, they came back to see me, saying that they had contacted prison service headquarters, who had informed them that I must be released to attend the hearing. Again, it was like I had to battle for everything, but at least I was now set to attend and take these governors on. I was still being turned down by my current governors to attend the senior operational manager (SOM) to gain accreditation as an operational governing governor. It wasn't long after this was all happening that we were informed the current area manager was leaving and a new one would be taking over.

The new area manager turned up. I didn't know who they were, and the first time I was going to meet them was at the tribunal when I found out that they, along with a few treasury solicitors, were going to be their supporting team. Before the case was due to start, there was a prehearing in early September 2009, and my support team would meet with their side. They appeared to want to try and sort things out before going to the tribunal. Even though I knew I had a good case, I loved my job, and I thought with the old area manager leaving, things could be different. In my opinion, the biggest issue was my perception of effectively being demoted, moved, and further bullying against me, now linked to my disabilities, by the old area manager and people linked to them. I did not mention anything at that time about the data I had uncovered on the prison system. I was asked what I wanted, and I pretty much said I was looking to be appointed back to a deputy governor's position.

Through our newsletters, I knew that the deputy governor's post was available at HMP Shrewsbury. I was informed by the area manager that I could not have that position, but they could offer me the deputy controller's job that had been advertised covering HMP Dovegate. I really should have pushed for HMP Shrewsbury, as it was my home town, but I really needed to get away from all those people who were harming my mental health, so I said I would take the deputy controller's post as a compromise. I said I just needed to sort things out because I was suffering, so a date was agreed to move to HMP Dovegate: 18th December 2009, ironically twenty years to the day I joined the prison service in 1989.

What I didn't realise was that bringing closure to one thing didn't necessarily mean it was over in the eyes of prison service managers. The governing governor called me up once they knew the result of the tribunal in terms of me being moved to a new position. Unbelievably, they said, "I will speak to the area manager and get the move stopped," because I was covering some Christmas duties at Hewell, but I said, "I'm sorry, but I have an agreement with the tribunal and the new area manager was the prison service lead on it." They didn't like it one bit. It was like I had got one up on them, and they basically told me, "To wait and see." They had no power, of course, to stop my move. It was like trying to drive a nail into me one last time. I would really have loved to tell them to fuck off at that point, but I just bit my tongue, and I don't think anyone could have blamed me if I did. I had a leaving meeting with my staffing group just to say I was being allocated a position to help oversee a contract on behalf of the secretary of state with a private prison. The reason there is a contractual oversight is because the private prison was operating in a public, civil service role because of its HMP status. A few of us went out for a meal. I really did appreciate them as a group. They worked hard, and I hoped they would go on to better things. I do hope you all made it out there.

I honestly thought things were going to get better, and at this point, I decided now was the right time to whistle blow because of the fraud and corruption I believe I had uncovered. I sent an email to the new area manager (who had negotiated my move at the tribunal) informing them there was a problem that I had uncovered, which could be considered fraud, linked to corruption by senior managers. I left it for a few days and there was no response, so rather than keep pestering them, I sent emails to someone (staff officer to the area manager) in their office, asking if the area manager could contact me about an email I had sent them. Before I sent the area manager an email, I made sure I had downloaded all the evidence about the fraud I had uncovered because I knew as soon as I raised it, my deputy governor status on HMP Hewell's data system would be withdrawn.

From: Riley, Michael [HMPS[
Sent: 23 September 2009 08:18
To: ███████████[NOMS]
Subject: Ref: Grievance over SPDR.
Dear ███████████

After our meeting last week to discuss 2 grievances one relating to the further victimisation based around my SPDR, I spoke to the union representative and it dawned on me that after informing you that people had been given exceeded markings and bonuses, that professional standards have probably been breached in terms of misuse of public funds and about what I was saying in terms of a clique operating under the saying "of its not what you know but who you know" which decides whether you progress within the service and even worse it would appear if you are disabled. This would also appear to link in further to my original grievance because the person I complained about would of given in the first instance the exceeded to the Governor which I believe confirms what I am talking about.

Regards

Michael Riley
Head of Interventions
HMP Hewell
Redditch
Worcestershire
B976QS

███████████

michael.andrew.riley@hmps.gsi.gov.uk

"The simple step of a courageous individual is not to take part in the lie."

Alexsandr Solzhenitsyn

PRISON SERVICE ORDERS: CONFLICT OF INTEREST, FRAUD AND INVESTIGATIONS.

DECLARATION OF CONFLICTS OF INTEREST

It is an offence for a civil servant to corruptly accept any money, gift or consideration as an inducement or reward for:

> ➢ *Doing (or not doing) anything in their official capacity or;*
> ➢ *Showing favour (or disfavour) to anyone in their official capacity.*

Staff must report any conflicts of interest, including any offer of gifts or hospitality (whether accepted or not), to the Governor. A local register at establishment level must be maintained to record all potential conflicts of interest.

EXAMPLES OF INSTANCES OF FRAUD – dictionary definition of each term is in italics

Theft – an act/instance of stealing

A global term for stealing, for example a colleague's personal belongings or cash being sent to a jail for a prisoner.

Corruption – abuse of official position for personal advantage or gain

Eg. staff who can self certify authorising false expense claims.   Public funds. SPDR's

Extortion – to obtain money or favours by intimidation, violence or misuse of authority

Using authority or information against a colleague to gain an advantage, eg a manager instructing a junior officer to place an order for goods/services with a specific supplier with whom the manager has a relationship.

Deception – the act of deceiving someone

Providing information that is untrue to gain benefit, e.g. giving false information about domestic circumstances in order to gain additional expense payments (for example, under public interest transfer conditions)   SPDR's 11

Concealment of facts – to cover and hide, to keep secret

E.g. not informing pay section when a retired officer receiving a pension dies, with the result that payment is still made, or not informing pay section when an overpayment has been made

Misappropriation – to take and use money dishonestly

Stealing money for personal benefit and then replacing the original amount, e.g. borrowing from the cash box and replacing funds on pay day

Forgery – illegal copying, crime of making fraudulent imitation

Falsifying authorising officers' signatures on documents for gain or to conceal other misdemeanours, e.g. authorising signature on invoices.

PRISON SERVICE ANTI FRAUD STRATEGY

The majority of our staff are scrupulously honest. They are tireless in their efforts to ensure that we run the Prison Service in accordance with our values and the highest standards of public service. But in an organisation of this size there will always be, from time to time, a few people who betray those values and, for whatever reason, abuse their position. Internal fraud can take a number of forms, from theft to misuse of confidential information.

That is why we need robust systems and detection mechanisms if we are to maintain a secure, honest and open working environment. It is also why the Board agreed some time ago that we should thoroughly investigate all suspected frauds. Wherever we find fraud proved and a member of staff is involved – whether the fraud is internal or external – we will take disciplinary action against the person or people involved. Penalties can include dismissal; people involved in serious fraud can also expect to face prosecution.

The Prison Service expects its staff to work with absolute honesty and integrity. It details its requirements in Prison Service Orders and Instructions, the Staff Handbook and the Code of Conduct and Discipline. The Prison Service will discipline, and consider dismissing any employee who fails to carry out their work in accordance with the expected standards of behaviour and the professional standards and codes of ethics of professional bodies to which many specialist staff are affiliated. These standards will equally apply to independent consultants and other temporary or agency staff employed by the Prison Service.

The Prison Service has a statutory duty to protect public funds. In doing so, it encourages a culture of openness and transparency. All allegations of fraud must be investigated. Where appropriate the police must be informed. Action must be taken where fraud is proved.

DEFINITIONS

Fraud is described in the dictionary as:

"the use of false representation to gain an unjust advantage; a dishonest trick; a person not fulfilling what is claimed or expected of them".

Fraud includes, but is not limited to, theft, corruption, extortion, deception, concealment of facts, misappropriation, forgery, embezzlement, conspiracy, bribery or collusion.

The effective eradication of fraud starts with all managers and they should try to create the conditions in which staff have neither the motivation nor the opportunity to commit fraud. It is the responsibility of all managers – at every level – in the Prison Service to ensure that they manage the risk of fraud within their respective work areas. The risk of fraud must be regularly reviewed as part of managers' overall assessment of business risk. Steps that managers must take are described at Appendix B.

All staff who suspect fraud or theft must report it either to their line manager or to the wrongdoing line (01527 544777). Professional Standards Unit refers all cases of suspected fraud reported via the wrongdoing line to the Fraud Investigation Unit for investigation. I did report this; no one was interested

139

PRISON SERVICE ANTI FRAUD STRATEGY

INTRODUCTION – SUMMARY

All allegations of fraud must be investigated. Where appropriate the police must be informed. Action must be taken where fraud is proved.

The risk of fraud must be regularly reviewed as part of managers' overall assessment of business risk.

Staff must report any conflicts of interest, including any offer of gifts or hospitality (whether accepted or not) to the Governor or Head of Group. A local register at establishment level must be maintained to record all potential conflicts of interest.

The fraud response plan sets out how suspicions must be reported and how investigations must be conducted and concluded.

Managers must report all cases of suspected fraud to the Head of Internal Audit (020 7217 8766; e-mail: ~~~~~~~~~~~~~~~~ immediately they become aware of them. ↑ I phoned up and informed them.

Where assets have been stolen, the Prison Service must make every effort to recover them.

All investigations must consider what action needs to be taken to prevent a recurrence. This must be included on the fraud/theft investigation report.

The Level of Investigation

1.3 Overview

1.3.1 *The level of investigation into an incident, allegation or complaint must be decided by line management and be based on a judgment of its nature, seriousness and how much is known about its circumstances.*

1.3.2 Managers regularly deal with minor incidents, allegations and complaints as part of their everyday activities without recourse to an investigation and this should continue. Also there may be no need for an investigation in more serious cases where the facts are clear and unambiguous, e.g. where a member of staff receives a criminal conviction. However, in most cases there will be lessons to be learned from incidents and an investigation would prove useful. In certain circumstances, disciplinary action may be taken prior to a court hearing. Consultations should take place with those leading a criminal investigation prior to any disciplinary action or investigation taking place which might compromise the prosecution of a serious crime.

Types of Investigation

1.5 Simple investigation

1.5.1 Managers are encouraged to make greater use of simple investigations where there is no need for a formal investigation or the need is uncertain. This will reduce the number of lengthy and expensive formal investigations that are currently commissioned unnecessarily.

1.6 Formal investigation

1.6.1 A formal investigation will be necessary if, from the findings of a simple investigation or from the outset, it appears that any of the following apply: -

General

- The incident has major consequences (disorder, damage, injury etc.).
- There was serious harm to any person.

Specialist

In addition to the above:
- It is likely that misconduct has occurred which may require formal action under PSO 8460 Conduct and Discipline.
- Where a formal investigation is made mandatory by another instruction e.g. PSO 1301 Investigating Deaths in Custody.
- Where there is a specialist element to the investigation apart from the two mentioned above for example, financial impropriety/fraud and sexual or racial harassment or discrimination. (see the orders and instructions listed at 1.1.4)

1.6.2 It is for the Commissioning Authority to make a judgment of the seriousness and nature of the incident or allegation in all cases, having examined the information available at the time. *nobody investigated as simple or formal process of investigation*

1.6.3 Normally the investigation will be carried out by a local team, except where the Commissioning Authority judges that a greater level of independence is needed. When an incident prompts high levels of public concern or there is potential to cause embarrassment to Ministers or the Service, an investigation might well need to be independent of the establishment or group in which it is conducted. The Commissioning Authority may also need to bring in outside investigators where specialist skills or team members are not available locally. *Police .*

1.6.4 In exceptional circumstances, such as major and/or simultaneous incidents, an independent external investigation, from outside the Prison Service may be commissioned by Ministers or the Director General. Such investigations are beyond the scope of this Order.

P5 29

1.2.1 The purpose of any investigation into an incident or allegation is to inquire into what has taken place, to establish the facts, to learn from them and to establish any accountability.

1.2.2 The main issues to be identified in investigations, which should normally be included in terms of reference, are:

    i.   what happened and why;

    ii.   identifying weaknesses in procedures or performance, either locally or nationally, so that they can be remedied and action taken to prevent them recurring;

    iii.   determining whether the response to any incident or event was proportionate and managed effectively and what can be learned from it;

    iv.   identifying any failures in physical security or equipment in order to enable improvements to be made;

    v.   identifying any individual or corporate failings or accountability; and

    vi.   commending points of good practice, good individual performance and positive actions.

P5 87

Not the Life of Riley

EXTRACT FROM CONDUCT AND DISCIPLINE POLICY

3. **Behaviour which may attract management action**

3.1 All NOMS staff are expected to meet high standards of professional and personal conduct. All staff are personally responsible for their conduct. Failure to maintain the required standards can lead to action, which may result in dismissal from the Service.

3.2 For detailed guidance on areas of misconduct, please refer to:

- Professional Standards Statement;
- Misconduct;
- Gross Misconduct

3.3 Not every breach of the required standards will lead to formal disciplinary action. *A manager's primary objective must be to encourage improvement in an individual rather than impose a disciplinary sanction.*

3.4 Day-to-day activities can sometimes bring up issues that a manager may need to act on. Line managers may need to meet with a member of staff solely to establish the nature of an incident or to establish the basis of an allegation or complaint. This is good management practice and line managers are expected to do so in the course of normal line management duties.

3.5 Where a line manager needs to meet with a member of staff to find out what happened, the line manager should make it clear to the employee involved that this is not a disciplinary meeting. *Line managers must tell the employee of the range of options for further action available to them and should be clear about the purpose of the meeting (i.e. to establish the facts or the basis of a complaint). Line managers must not continue with such a meeting if it becomes clear that a disciplinary investigation is necessary.*

3.6 *If there is an issue to be addressed the line manager must decide whether to:*

- *deal with the matter informally (e.g. the line manager may consider mediation, training, coaching, etc.);*
- *deal with it as a performance or capability issue (action must be taken in accordance with the Performance Management policy and/or the Management of Attendance policy);*
- *arrange for it to be investigated formally under the procedure set out in this Instruction; or*
- *if fraud is suspected, you must refer it to the Head of Audit and Corporate Assurance Unit and follow the other mandatory actions in the Anti-Fraud Strategy.*

3.7 *Whichever course of action is taken, the line manager must make brief notes of what is said and record their decision. The line manager must keep a copy of this locally. Records must not be kept on a member of staff's personnel file.*

3.8 See also: Advice & Guidance

PSI 06/2010 – AI 05/2010   Issue Date 04/03/2010

P710

Staff who report misconduct

2.13 *Staff who report misconduct, including those who make corruption prevention reports, must be aware that the information they provide may be required to support disciplinary proceedings and/or a criminal investigation. This means that their reports, and/or the information they provide, may be disclosed and they may be required to give evidence both internally and to external bodies such as criminal courts or inquiries. If this is likely to arise, the situation must be discussed with that member of staff and arrangements put in place to manage the process prior to disclosure.*

2.14 *It is important to ensure that the appropriate support is available to staff. Any member of staff who comes forward to report their concerns or who makes an allegation of misconduct must not be victimised, harassed or bullied as a result of doing so. Such behaviours are totally unacceptable and may lead to disciplinary action.*

2.15 Staff who raise concerns about wrongdoing are protected by the Employment Rights Act (ERA) 1996 as amended by the Public Interest Disclosure Act (PIDA) 1998.

2.16 Additional guidance about protected disclosures can be found in the Reporting Wrongdoing guidance on My Services

232

Not one person got back to me at all, and I couldn't understand why, bearing in mind the seriousness of what I was saying about senior managers taking money to which they were not entitled from the taxpayers of our country. We had people incarcerated in our prison for committing fraud, and all those managers who were cheating the public purse, probably, and in most cases, were then building up their future pension pots, in effect committing further fraud. When they retired, they would still be drawing a higher pension after they left service, and probably still are, based on fraudulent reporting and a group that worked together to take money to which they were not entitled. They would also be receiving yearly uplifts based on the consumer price index (CPI), so the fraud keeps adding to pension pots and more and more taxpayers' money is lost.

The system for any appraisal can be manipulated for either yourself or someone else's gain, but when the system is corrupted by those who are at the top of it, bearing in mind that a second higher manager has to sign off the appraisal as being correct and doesn't challenge it, then it needs total reform to stamp out abuse of process, power and manipulation, committing offences by senior managers at the highest level of office in prisons and the civil service. I wonder how staff in prisons or elsewhere will feel if they decide to read my book. Surely there must be a whole review of civil servants and how they operate. There are many good people who work in the organisation, but as I have shown in this memoir, there are also people who put their own and their friends needs over and above everybody else's, not only the staff taking money illegally from the public purse but also their line managers who are supporting them by countersigning the appraisals!

Looking back at my public sector prison service career, and particularly around the incompetence that I have personally uncovered and witnessed, I would say that prisons in England and Wales must first and foremost protect all that operate within them at whatever level the prison is in terms of their security category, for not only the safety of the staff but also the prisoners and visitors. There may be disagreements between governors and unions, which can happen in any business, but security and safety must always come first. Certainly, in my time, that has always been the number one consideration, because if you get that right, then everything else flows from it. Ever since I joined the civil service, every year ministers expected governors to make savings, but there comes a time when there is no meat left on the bone, so when that is the only thing left to hack at, the integrity of the structure will weaken and break. You have to listen to people to get a full understanding of the environment you operate in, and for me, I learnt all about that by starting off as an officer and working my way up in various establishments. This allowed me to risk assess everything appropriately and ensure that the correct resources were available.

Safety is paramount, but when that is underpinned by incompetence, then it's a recipe for disaster in any environment. If I were a prison minister, I would order a complete review of the prison system to change the way it operates, root and branch, but I have come up with my conclusions and recommendations at the end of my memoir. An organisation that investigates itself invites corruption as part of its foundations by people that work within it, but it also needs to change the way employers look at the way they recruit ex-prisoners into their workforce. As I mentioned previously, 80% of offenders cause 20% of crime in England and Wales, and they then go on to commit no further offences, so employers should reflect on that when recruiting for their workforce. I have seen recruitment documentation by some large national employers that just asks, "Do you have a criminal record?" with a yes or no answer. They use that to disbar people straight away, instead of looking at them in more depth and the circumstances surrounding why someone offended in the first place. They could be turning away the best employee without actually giving someone a chance to change and turn away from a lifetime of crime. That links in with early intervention in some people's lives because prisons are expensive places to operate. Again, safety is paramount for the employer, but don't just turn away 100% of the people applying for a job because of a criminal record. Giving some a chance really can make a difference in society, and they will go on to be useful citizens, providing a positive contribution in our communities.

Incidentally, I also raised the fraud with the HR shared services section at Newport in Wales, who also conveniently helped hide it by trying to deviate from the performance appraisal rules to cover up the senior management fraud.

PUBLIC SECTOR CONTROLLER'S OFFICE
HMP DOVEGATE 2009-2011

I transferred to the controller's office at HMP Dovegate and met my new line manager. We got on well, and I explained the JSAC SOM situation to them. The next one was not due for some twelve months. I had been turned down twice by the old area manager and their cronies who were trying to ruin my career, so I thought, "I must get on with the job in hand and prove I am the person I was before my problems started with the old area manager."

HMP Dovegate is operated by SERCO, and I felt like a fly on the wall with a contract to help support their delivery of services under the home secretary. They do have different ways of conducting business, and I was a public sector operational governor there to help advise them to make sure they did it properly. As deputy controller, I had my own areas of responsibility reporting to the controller, and they had theirs. They got to know me and watched the way that I operated, to the point that they said that they would support me for the JSAC SOM to become an accredited governing governor.

When the time came, I submitted my application, which the area manager endorsed. I think they would have found it difficult to knock me back. It had been a few years since I was hounded out of HMP Drake Hall and knocked back by the old area manager and their friends. I had to attend some testing days, and it now included a psychometric evaluation. At the end of it all, I had to sit down with a governing governor from headquarters and run through everything. Although I had a couple of skill gaps, they supported me to go forward and take the JSAC SOM evaluation. They said all my data from the last couple of days would be sent to the area manager first, so they could rubber stamp it.

Around about the same time, I saw an advert explaining that there was a shortage of senior managers from black and minority ethnic (BAME) and disabled backgrounds in the senior grades of the civil service. It was asking for staff to become involved in a programme for managers and to apply to attend a two-year programme, which would help teach us the skills and provide experiences to enable us to apply for positions higher up. I sent in my application form, and within six weeks, I received a reply informing me that I had been accepted.

What happened to me next was rather bizarre, but if you add it to previous experiences of people targeting me, you can draw your own conclusion about whether it was carrying on and whether I am right or wrong based on what I'm telling you now. The information about me from the prison service away day, which included personal data, was sent to the director of SERCO at HMP Dovegate, a private prison. I have no idea why it was addressed to them rather than me, but I found out as their secretary came around and handed me the envelope, which had already been opened. I was not best pleased, not with the director of the private prison but with the prison service for sending it to them. I was a public sector employee with a public sector line manager.

The next thing that happened was linked to all my psychometric documentation. It had been sent to my new area manager, the one that had negotiated the prison services side tribunal outcome and the one I raised the fraud with, which meant I could move to the controller's office at HMP Dovegate. They came to the prison as part of one of their routine visits. When they came in, they said they had left my documents at the front desk, which I didn't think about very much. On the way out of the prison, I forgot to ask for them, and I wasn't in work the next day, but the following morning, as I was entering the establishment, I asked for them. The gate staff handed them over after I had gone through the security process for entry into the prison. I realised immediately that the package they had been given was in an open folder. It had not been sealed in a proper envelope, so people could access the data inside. I couldn't believe this. I just thought to myself, "I had been suckered into withdrawing the tribunal case and now things were happening to me again."

I was so angry with the way things were heading. I phoned up the area manager to ask if they had left my documents sealed at the front gate when they handed them in. They said they had left them in an open folder. I just replied that I had picked them up that morning and people could access them, but the area manager didn't say anything. It's as if they either didn't know what data protection was all about and the security of my personal information, or they didn't care. I cannot for one minute think they didn't know or understand the rules as they were the area manager, where all the information for prisons filters down to establishments through their office, including data protection. I think it's telling when the area manager and prison service signed off the tribunal deal and then went on to do what they did to me at HMP Dovegate!

The prison service was running a voluntary exit scheme, so I enquired how much I could receive if I left the prison service. That was in January 2011. It was now the end of February, so I submitted a complaint form about what had happened recently against the organisation, asking why the prison service had sent my personal data to the director of SERCO and the area manager had left my personal information open with the front desk staff at HMP Dovegate. It felt like senior prison civil servants were playing a game with me again and just wanted me out.

> **"Look well into thyself;
> there is a source of strength which will always
> spring up if thou wilt always look."**
>
> Marcus Aurelius

They were playing with my mind, and I was trying hard to keep it together. The prison service had twenty-eight days to respond to the complaint, so I had to take them on again. The prison service area manager had not responded or held a formal investigation into my whistleblowing complaint about corruption that I had uncovered. I had all the documentation available, so I kept it safe. They were protecting each other, and it would seem whatever I did in my career, it was over. The pressure felt immense. I was just trying to do my job. Why had everything changed so much that they hated me like this? They also did not deal with the fraud I had informed the area manager about. They were all just trying to brush it under the carpet. Everything they had done to support their clique and protect senior managers flew in the face of investigatory common sense and policy. When I think of all the investigations against prison officers and other various personnel who were sacked on the spot for things like expenses fraud, what I had found was far worse than that. It seems to me that the higher up the ladder you go in the civil service, the more you can do what you want. Senior civil servants, in my opinion, were institutionally corrupt, and that needed dealing with, especially when they were investigating themselves.

The time seemed to pass slowly as the twenty-eight cut off day for my complaint drew near and then ticked on past it, so on 29th March, I phoned up the group that were dealing with the voluntary exit scheme and asked straight out if I could be let go. I told them I'd had enough of working for the prison service and the way it had treated me. I received an email later that day saying I could leave. I left everything in terms of my workload, cleared my personal effects, told my line manager what was happening and that the following day, the 31st of March 2011 was to be my last day working in Her Majesty's prison service.

PROTECT – PERSONAL

Early Departure Team
MoJ Shared Services
PO BOX 3005
NEWPORT
Gwent
NP20 9BB

Michael Riley

9th April 2011

Dear Michael,

Voluntary Early Departure

Thank you for returning your signed acceptance of the offer of voluntary early departure made to you. Your departure is now confirmed

Arrangements are currently being made with regards to the administration of your departure with My Civil Service Pensions (MyCSP) and Shared Services will be in touch with you to confirm these arrangements.

Your last day in service was therefore 31st March 2011. You will be paid your salary up to and including this date.

Compensation in lieu of notice arrangements

Under the terms of the Civil Service Compensation Scheme you are entitled to 3 months' notice.

Your period of notice began on the 29-03-2011, the date you signed your agreement to leave.

As your leaving date is before the end of this 3 month period, we will pay you Pay in lieu of notice (PILON) on the balance. Accordingly you will be entitled to 12 weeks and 4 days pay as pay in lieu of notice.

In addition you will be paid Compensation in lieu of notice (CILON) an amount due for the loss of pension benefits within the unworked period of the notice period.

I had tried to sort out my complaints against HMPs but nothing happened, so I phoned the early departure team and said I wanted to leave as the prison service failed to deal with my complaint   Submitted 1st March 2011

This links in with the judge's comments, who said I had accepted a VEDs offer before I actually had and phoned up the early departure or VEDs team to say I wanted to leave. The letter above relates to when I actually received my VED and shows my period of notice commenced on 29th March 2011, the date I signed my agreement to leave. This letter shows that the judge who said I applied for

VEDs in January and accepted it was incorrect. In my opinion, they made that part up. I informed them that everybody asks for a statement to see how much they may receive if they leave the prison service. It's just what people do; everyone does it and people are curious to see how much they are worth! The information, in my opinion, had been manipulated to suit the narrative in the Ministry of Justices' favour. I signed to leave 29th March 2011 after my complaint was ignored by the prison service, and a reply to it was not received by me from higher management until way after 28th March 2011.

In the prison service and senior manager's eyes, they will have won and driven me out, but it wasn't the end of things. My line manager and the admin person in our team met up with me a few weeks later for lunch. They had brought my operational prison service medal which the late HM Queen Elizabeth II, God bless her, had authorised for all staff who had served over twenty years in continuous operational service. Two weeks later, I had a complete breakdown. It was like someone switching a light off inside my head, and it was awful. I went to the doctors, sat down, and burst into tears. Everything had caught up with me from an emotional point of view, and my hatred of those who had hurt me became a mission. I found it difficult to function and it had a profound effect on me. Relationships broke down. I was so angry, and that rage was solely directed at those who had destroyed my life.

I started the process of seeking legal help to go to a tribunal once again, this time an employment one. I engaged the services of a very well-known solicitors, who, after looking over my documents, said I had a case against the prison service. In the meantime, nothing had happened with the complaint I had submitted against the prison service. I was receiving information during April about the whole leaving process and how things would work out. Apart from a few errors, things seemed to be correct. When you leave somewhere, and because I had a contractual leaving date of age sixty, I could not apply for my pension until that time.

With cancer hitting me in 2017, I didn't even know if I would reach that age, and with me having more and more things going on in relation to that, my life expectancy was cut down to the extent that I could die within twelve months. The paperwork was submitted to the relevant authority with all the supporting documentation, and I started to receive a pension. I had a choice of a lump sum or I could receive a monthly pension. It was like a toss of the coin lottery, but in the end, I am a fighter. I didn't want to die, so I took the monthly option. It looks like it paid off, as the lump sum wasn't that much, but if something does happen, at least my son will be the beneficiary until he is twenty-three because it is built into the process that if I do pass on, he will receive half of my monthly pension. I wanted my son to see that if I wasn't around anymore, the hyphen that they put between the year of birth and death on my gravestone meant I'd had a life, and he could read about a part of it and understand a bit more about me as a father and person.

There was a bit of a kerfuffle over the complaint I had submitted. I had pushed it to the next level because nothing had been done. The prison service was saying that because I had left, I should not have the complaint heard. You have to bear in mind, I only left after they failed to deal with it at the correct time. From a human resources point of view, they told them it still had to be dealt with, so it was passed up to the head of HR in the prison service to deal with. They set up a meeting sometime after I had left under the voluntary scheme. When I met them, I explained everything, and I was surprised at the end of it to be asked whether I wanted my job back. I said to them that, as far as I was concerned, after all the treatment I had received in their employment, I could never return to the same environment that I had experienced for so long under the hands of those senior governors and civil servants. They asked me what I wanted, and the only thing I could think of was to tell them I wanted compensation for everything that had happened to me. They asked me how much and I said, a couple of million would do it. I based it on the fact that I left the service just after my forty-ninth birthday and could expect at that time to continue working until I was way past sixty!

Things progressed towards a tribunal of which I had very little knowledge, and then the solicitor who said I had a case against the prison service sent me a letter saying that they could no longer represent me and take my case forward. I must ask the question, "Why would a solicitors take me on and inform me I had a good case, and then months later inform me they could no longer act for me?" Draw your own conclusions from that one.

The prison service knew which solicitors were covering my case, and with the way things had gone, it would not surprise me that the solicitors had been warned off against acting for me, although I could never prove that without evidence. It felt like the system was heavily weighted against me, but I ploughed on as they had told me I had a case. There is an old saying, "You can't beat the system." Those in charge know the rules inside out, and with the weight of the treasury solicitors against me, it was such a long arduous process to carry on regardless. It certainly felt like the world was on my shoulders. They didn't care about me, my life, and the damage it had caused me.

The judge in my case held sporadic case management meetings as things progressed. I had a very steep learning curve, managing through the whole thing. At every step along the way, the other side wanted my case thrown out, but two years later, the time came to hold the tribunal. The barrister for the prison service came to see me before the case, introducing themselves to me and saying, "They hoped I wasn't nervous about the whole thing." I thought that was rather an odd way of introducing oneself. It felt like I was being put down from the start. After everything I had raised about previous treatment, the judge said that because I had signed an agreement with the prison service that evidence could not be used in their hearing. I just wondered why they had not made that order during case conferences. I asked the judge why they would do that when the person signing off the issue for the prison service at the disability tribunal was the same person who had carried on the whole process of damaging me after I had moved to HMP Dovegate, but it fell on deaf ears; they were not interested and told me to carry on. I suffer from post-traumatic stress disorder (PTSD), something that developed when I had a breakdown due to suffering at the hands of others sometime down the line. This has been verified by medical professionals.

During the tribunal process, I was having a rough time of things, and when I told the judge about my health issues, all they could say was, "Well, you are not ill now." I just said to them, "How do you know I'm not ill? Are you a qualified doctor now?" That probably didn't help me, but it appeared to me that the judge was biased as the tribunal was progressing. They also set timelines on the first day for evidence from the time I submitted my complaint until I left the prison service on 31st March 2011, and nothing outside of those dates could be heard in the tribunal. It felt like my hands were being tied behind my back, and it also felt like I was unable to say anything or contribute fully to the whole tribunal process.

After it had ended, the judge and two panellists (I don't know of any process where the two others who were sitting did not question me at all) did not give a decision straight away. The judge said I would receive a reserved judgement sometime after the tribunal ended. A few weeks later, the judgement turned up in the post. The judge said there was no case against the prison service and said they would hold another court day to award costs against me to the prison service. The judgement against me was skewed, in my opinion. The other side said I had vexatiously brought the case, but my argument to that would be, why would a legal firm take me on based on the information I had provided to them. If the advice was that I had a case at the outset, then it, in my opinion, also follows that I did not bring the case vexatiously. The judge also used information outside of their own judgement parameters they had set in the court when coming to their final decision against me. I wanted to introduce to the tribunal, documents outside of those times, but they wouldn't let me, but they then did themselves in the reserved judgement to strengthen their judgement against me! Why would they do that unless it was to protect the interests of those very high up in power in the prison and civil service? I am not intelligent enough to ask all the necessary questions, but what I am sure about in my own mind is that when things get used against you that are not set appropriately in case conference before a tribunal starts, but then, in my opinion, the judge made up things as they went along and used information outside of the set process with the rules they had set in court to come up with a biased decision to turn down my case, is and was in my opinion fundamentally wrong to do that. In my opinion, it certainly feels like an injustice. I do know that.

Extracts from Employment tribunal.

████████

that the Employment Tribunal did not have jurisdiction to hear them. I restricted the scope of the constructive dismissal claim to events arising after 30 October 2009 and prior to 31 March 2011. I restricted the victimisation claim to events occurring after 12 November 2008 and prior to 31 March 2011.

26   On 5 January 2011, whilst awaiting the outcome of his Stage 3 appeal, the claimant applied for VED. On 18 February 2011 (after the determination of his appeal), the claimant received a statement of what payments he was entitled to upon the termination of his employment under the VED scheme. On 31 March 2011, the claimant's employment terminated under the VED scheme.

27   On 1 March 2011, the claimant raised a detailed grievance about what he saw as unacceptable treatment of him by the prison service over many years. The grievance sought to re-open many of the issues which have been the subject of the earlier tribunal claim. The grievance was initially passed to ██████████ to investigate.

The Judge states I applied for VED's, I applied for a statement of how much I would receive if I were to leave HMPs employment. I had not applied for VEDs at that point in time

43   So far as the grievance is concerned, in our judgement, the respondent dealt with the grievance in that manner beyond that which were strictly required of them bearing in mind that it was raised after the claimants VED had already been agreed. Many employers in the circumstances would have refused to investigate the grievance on the basis that such an investigation was clearly unnecessary in view of the impending termination of the employment contract. We did not hear evidence from ██████████ ██████████ but we did have the opportunity to review the grievance documentation and their correspondence with the claimant. It is clear that the claimant received a detailed response to his grievance and, whilst he may not agree with the outcome, he has adduced before us no evidence from which we can properly infer that the response was anything other than genuine finding of Mr Harnett and Mr Wilkinson or that it was in any way related to the earlier claim. *

The VED had not been agreed, (Judge appears to be showing bias (See early departure team letter dated 9 April 2011) I asked to leave HMPs because of my treatment 29 March 2011. They effectively said I signed my agreement to leave because of that.

In relation to Para 43, the tribunal judge restricted everything in the case to before 31 March 2011, having put that information in a reserved judgement, which was after 31 March 2011, surely that cannot be right and may have some influence in other areas within the scope of the judgement.

Case Number 1306471/2011

37   We reject the claimant's account of the conversation with ▓▓▓ ▓▓▓▓, we prefer her account. Nothing in what was said can possibly amount to a detriment.

38   The matter complained of at (f) above was the product of the claimants appeal being fast tracked. Had it not been fast tracked, he would have missed the Assessment Centre in September 2010 altogether. Following his successful appeal, he was offered a later Assessment Centre but the claimant declined the offer. There was no detrimental treatment. *I didn't decline the offer I was on holiday! They wouldn't give another date.*

39   ▓▓ ▓▓▓▓▓ dealt with all of the appeals from the 2010 Assessment Centre – he not only deal with the claimant's appeal. All appellants were, to a greater or lesser extent, appealing against decisions taken within ▓▓ ▓▓▓▓▓ department. Whether one views that is appropriate or inappropriate there is no basis for the suggestion that the claimant's treatment was detrimental; he was treated in exactly the same way as all other appellants.

40   So far as (e) and (i) are concerned – we accept that the claimant was extremely disappointed by the results of both the Development Centre and the Assessment Centre. But he has not even suggested, still less has he adduced any evidence to indicate, that the results were anything other than a genuine assessment of his performance.

41   To the extent that any of the matters complained of can truly be described as detrimental treatment, the claimant has established no facts before us from which we could properly infer any connection between the claimant's treatment and his earlier tribunal claim. The matter complained of at (d) above was a simple administrative error and there is no basis to suggest that it arose from deliberate action on the part of any individual. The matter complained of at (k) above arose out of a genuine effort on the part of ▓▓ ▓▓▓▓▓ and ▓▓ ▓▓▓▓▓ to try and assist the claimant to understand his lack of success at the Assessment Centre; furthermore, the claimant had the opportunity to retrieve the package from the gate staff almost immediately such that there would have been no possibility of detriment in any event. ↑ *This is not true, the fudge has made this up.*

42   When ▓▓ ▓▓▓▓▓ gave evidence the claimant did not suggest to him that, but for the earlier claim, he would have allowed the Stage 3 appeal. We find that ▓▓ ▓▓▓▓▓ refused the appeal for reasons which he genuinely believed were justified and which were unrelated to the earlier claim.

43   So far as the grievance is concerned, in our judgement, the respondent dealt with the grievance in that manner beyond that which were strictly required of them bearing in mind that it was raised after the claimants VED had already been agreed. Many employers in the circumstances would have refused to investigate the grievance on the basis that such an investigation was clearly unnecessary in view of the impending termination of the employment contract. We did not hear evidence from ▓▓ ▓▓▓▓▓, ▓▓ ▓▓▓▓▓ or ▓▓ ▓▓▓▓▓ but we did have the opportunity to review the grievance documentation and their correspondence with the claimant. It is clear that the claimant received a detailed response to his grievance and, whilst he may not agree with the

They did not hear any evidence from the people because they were outside the fudges scope dates, but now they enter that they reviewed the grievance outside the timescales. The fudge could bring it all up here, but they refused me the right to call those people to give evidence. !☺ This is not natural justice. The VED had not been agreed, fudge appears to be showing bias (See early departure team letter dated 9 April 2011) I asked to leave HMB because of my treatment 29 March 2011. They effectively said I signed my agreement to leave because of that!

outcome, he has adduced before us no evidence from which we can properly infer that the response was anything other than genuine finding of ▓▓▓▓ and ▓▓▓▓▓ or that it was in any way related to the earlier claim. ⁂

44   With regard to the allegation at (a) above. As stated we reject the claimant's account of the conversation and on ▓▓ ▓▓▓ account, which we accept, there was nothing said which was detrimental. We also find that nothing which ▓▓ ▓▓▓ said was in any way related to the claimant having brought his earlier claim. For the sake of completeness however, we have also considered the time issue urged upon us by the respondent. The incident with ▓▓ ▓▓▓ took place on a specific date on 10 December 2009. The next incident about which the claimant complains did not take place until the period May – September 2010. ▓▓ ▓▓▓ has not been involved in any subsequent incident. Accordingly, we find that even if ▓▓ ▓▓▓ conversation amounted to detrimental treatment, and even if it linked back to the earlier claim, it was clearly a *stand-alone* incident, and not part of an ongoing series. The claim was presented on 19 April 2011, some 16 months after the incident complained of; it is clearly out of time by reference to Section 123 EqA and the claimant has adduced before us no basis upon which could conclude that it would be just and equitable to extend time. Accordingly, if for no other reason, the claimant's complaint at (a) would be dismissed for want of jurisdiction.

45   For the reasons given the claimant's claim for victimisation against the 1st respondent, ▓▓ ▓▓▓ ▓▓▓▓ and ▓▓▓▓▓ fails and is dismissed.

Constructive Dismissal

46   It is the claimants case that those matters which he claims amounted to a campaign of victimisation also amounted to a series of events which either individually or collectively amount to a fundamental breach going to the root of his employment contract. We find that there is nothing in what he complains of which could properly be said to amount to a breach of the employment contract let alone a fundamental breach. Of course an employer has an obligation to deal appropriately with an employee's confidential information. But mistakes will happen and incidents of misdirecting items in the post accidentally do not, in our judgement, amount to fundamental breaches of that obligation. It is trite law that where there has been no breach of contract there simply cannot be a successful claim for constructive dismissal.

47   In any event, we find that the claimant did not resign in response to the alleged breaches. He took advantage of the VED at a time when he knew that he had been unsuccessful in this Stage 3 assessment for senior management.

48   Finally, there is a point which was not argued before us - and for that reason we make no specific finding with regard to it, but, in our judgement, it is properly arguable by the respondent that even if its conduct in the period between November 2009 and January 2011 amounted to a fundamental breach of the employment contract, the claimants very action in choosing to depart with the benefits of the VED scheme (which

In relation to Para 43; the tribunal Judge restricted everything in the case to be before 31 March / 7 ⊘ 2011, having put that information in a reserved Judgement which was after 31 March 2011, Surely that cannot be right and may have some influence in other areas within the scope of the Judgement.

Links into page 221, *Pay and Promotion on Progression*.

Case Number 1306471/2011

were essentially part of the employment contract) could be said to amount to an express affirmation of the contract. We make clear that we do not determine the case on that basis; but, for the reasons given above, we find firstly that the respondent was not in breach, and secondly that the claimant did not resign in response to what he now alleges to have amounted to a breach. Accordingly, his claim for constructive dismissal must fail.

49   Therefore we find that the claimant was not dismissed. The claim for unfair dismissal is not well-founded and is dismissed.

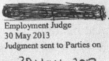

Employment Judge
30 May 2013
Judgment sent to Parties on

30 May 2013

When I turned up at the costs hearing, the barrister from the treasury solicitors was there, and they informed me that the total costs from the prison service side were £53,000. I had furnished the tribunal judge with all my information. The barrister said the prison service would limit their costs, capping them at £20,000. I didn't have the money to pay that sort of amount, so it looked like the judge wanted to take it from future monies I may earn.

After it had ended, I was left thinking, "How come a full tribunal of three could be making a reserved judgement decision and then a single judge decides about costs without them being present?" It certainly felt like bias again to me, just as it had throughout the tribunal. The judge seemed to think I was not telling them everything. They seemed to think I owned property abroad, which I didn't and never had, but they kept pushing it, in my opinion, trying to make me out to be a liar!

I decided to appeal the whole process of the tribunal

judge, but the only part they would look at was the costs. I managed to secure the services of a pro bono barrister who would help me, and we attended the high court in London so they could look at the case. Before the case started, a message was sent to me asking what I could afford to pay. I said, "£5,000," which was sent back to the treasury barrister. However, they thought I could pay that there and then, which I couldn't, so I said I could only pay it out of any pension in the future. We ended up going into the appeal tribunal because I could not pay anything at the time. My pro bono barrister told me not to worry, as they would put my case forward to the three judges at the appeal hearing. There was a fair bit of stuff being put forward by the treasury solicitor's barrister.

The judgement is here for you to see. However, what I can say is, the other side did not go back as per the appeal tribunal's recommendation and just dropped it all. In my opinion, I think there were exceptional circumstances for the appeal court to look at bias within the case itself, but I think they said I was over a three-month ruling to do that, but in the interests of justice, I think exceptional reasons were there for them to do it, but once they made the decision, well, I couldn't do anything more. I believe that all the prolonged stress that 'the organisation' put me through over the years caused the cancer I now battle with as the year's progress.

After such a period of time elapsing since I left the prison service, I'm sure the people who made my life a misery and whom I whistle blew against are in far higher positions now. Maybe they have left and are receiving their pensions, but it makes me mad as hell that they have their ill-gotten gains built into their increments through corruption between themselves. And when I told certain people, they ignored everything and did not instigate an investigation to cover up wrongdoing. They have literally got away with it because I guess they were in, or are in, positions of higher authority and power.

What has worried me is the way that the prison and police services have acted, including the court process in the Ministry of Justice. It feels like the whole lot of them are afraid that uncovering problems like fraud and corruption by senior managers with evidence to back that up means they will openly have to deal with the cliques, but by doing what they did to me meant they remained safe to carry on with their nefarious activities in their careers because if it came out, then the whole rotten pack of cards would fall. How do these high up people get themselves into such powerful positions?

The thing about the civil service is they will use all their resources and processes at their disposal against you to break you. They are using our taxpayers' money against people like me and others who try to show how corrupt things are and how they try to cover it up. I am of the mind that when staff complain about those sorts of managers, they cannot access public resources to fight their corner. They must do it themselves. It would mean the whole bullying system would come crashing down around them because they would have to defend their actions with their own money and not what is, in effect, public money. How many people do you think would do that when you have solid evidence against what they did? We are a caring and resilient country with strong people. Over time, a lot of us have been let down by those in high positions abusing us, but things must change for the better and for the benefit of all citizens. It's up to us all to make sure it happens, so we 'care about each other' to deliver for everyone, not just the corrupt, bullying few at the top!

SOURCE:

Appeal No. UKEAT/XXXX/XX/DXA EMPLOYMENT APPEAL TRIBUNAL FLEETBANK HOUSE, 2-6 SALISBURY SQUARE, LONDON EC4Y 8AE At the Tribunal On 10 July 2015 Before THE HONOURABLE MR JUSTICE X* (PRESIDENT) MRS E* BARONESS MR M RILEY APPELLANT SECRETARY OF STATE FOR JUSTICE AND OTHERS RESPONDENTS.

*Names and case numbers have been replaced.

DETAILS OF MY APPEAL CASE

SUMMARY PRACTICE AND PROCEDURE PRACTICE AND PROCEDURE - Chairman alone JURISDICTIONAL POINTS A Judge sat alone to determine an application for costs which was related to the conduct of the losing Claimant when he brought a claim that he had been discriminated against in a number of respects by the Ministry which employed him and a number of co-employees. The claim itself had been decided by a panel of three. It was held that the Judge was not entitled to sit alone in circumstances such as those of the present case. The details are available in Appendix F, page 306.

I was meant to have had this memoir written years ago. I started it after I had finished with a tribunal against the prison service after I left their employment, which I didn't win. I do believe that the stress of what people have done to me caused me to develop cancer. I have had some issues with mobility over the years due to my military service, but in 2016, after years and years of it steadily getting worse and at least fifteen operations at that point, I was referred to the Robert Jones and Agnes Hunt Hospital located in Gabowen. I had a right knee replacement, and I was discharged from hospital after five days, but as soon as it had been completed, within a couple of weeks, I started to get really bad pains in my left groin area. It was excruciatingly painful. I ended up on liquid morphine and I was referred to a hip specialist. Apparently, it's quite common after realigning a knee with a new joint because my gait had changed considerably. Things can happen to the diagonal joint, so the pain in my left groin meant I needed a left hip replacement. It took around eight months to get a slot at the hospital again. I was like a zombie after so much time on the painkiller. Thankfully, I didn't become addicted to it, and I came out of hospital after another five-day stint.

The thing about most of the operations I have had is, from a medical point of view, once you can pee and poo, they like to send you home, and that suited me just fine. The problem for me was that, as I was recuperating from the hip surgery in January, I received a letter from the NHS saying that because I had nearly reached fifty-five, I could receive a free bowel scope. I lost my mother in 2013 due to poisoning with a tablet form of chemotherapy. It killed her. My mum's death pushed me to have the scope, so in June 2017, I attended the hospital and had the procedure. I just had a painkiller, but the problem was that when the specialist was conducting it and got about halfway through, it appeared that an area was looking really inflamed and not the nice pink colour it should be. I was looking at some posters on the wall in the treatment area, and looking back at the TV screen – yes, you see at it being done! I thought to myself, "Well, whatever is inside of me looks like that in the picture."

They could not get past the obstruction, and it was causing me some discomfort, so they tried to get past the area with a smaller scope that they use on children, but the pain was still quite uncomfortable, even after the painkiller, so they stopped the process. Once I had recovered in the waiting area where patients were taken after the procedure, the doctor came to see me and said, "You either have Crohn's disease or cancer." After what I had been through, I just thought, "You must be kidding me." But as well as that, my left knee went into constant pain mode! You really can't make this up! First of all, God bless the NHS. Two days later, I was having a scan, and two days after that, I was having emergency surgery to take out about one foot of my bowel. It seems to be potluck if you end up with a colostomy bag. Thank goodness I didn't need one.

The next day, the surgeon came to see me. They told me that all the damaged tissue had been removed, along with thirty-five lymph nodes that had been sent away for testing. They recommended I have elective chemotherapy in a few months, which I agreed to. I asked the consultant how big the infected area was, and they told me it was around the size of my fist, and I have a fair sized fist. How the hell something could get that big in the intestine and not show any symptoms I'll never know. I kept up my five-day record and returned home. After a short while, the results came back from the lab confirming that I had cancer and that the disease had infiltrated into my blood channels, so that's not the best news to be hearing, as people who have gone through the process will know. I left hospital thinking, "How the hell was I going to move forward with all of this?" I am a single parent, and my son was only eleven years old. There was no way I was going to burden him with the information, so I explained it all in a way I thought a child would understand and could handle not changing the way he was as a person.

It was vitally important to me that he was not affected by my problems because he was so young and doing well at school. I did explain to him by saying, "Imagine the internal veins in a body are like a motorway, and some cars were breaking down in certain parts of it. Well, they had to take away the cars and then clean up inside by using liquids to brush up any mess that was left, leaving things nice and tidy." I have to say, I have never had any symptoms relating to cancer, but the chemotherapy made me feel ill. The number of tablets and liquids they give to offset the side effects of the treatment are needed because it can be quite debilitating.

I received twelve sessions of chemo, and the scans I was having every three months said things looked okay in my body. I was having scans from the thorax right down to the pelvic area with a contrast to pick up any issues. The consultant who had replaced my right knee had to wait around six weeks for the effects of the chemo to disperse out of my body. Once that had elapsed, I went back into hospital again for my next joint replacement, making three in total. Once again, I was out in five days and determined to get back to a level of fitness I was used to. It was a bit of a slog, but I managed to get going again, but there was no way I could ever get back to how I used to be, ever. I was hoping after four major operations, I was going to move forward. I moved forward alright. I had a scan in 2019, and the oncology consultant basically told me there were now some grey areas on my liver and a nodule on my peritoneal lining, which keeps things in place in the lower abdomen, and I would need referring to a specialist to see how I could progress.

At this point, I had a cry in the consultant's office, not because of what was happening to me but because of what would happen to my boy if I died. I saw a consultant who dealt with liver surgery, and I was informed that because I had blood in the channels that had lymph nodes, that was probably the reason why cancer was likely in the areas specified now. The country was just going into COVID lockdown, and we all know how that took off, and hospitals were inundated with poorly people. My surgery would be difficult because of what the pandemic was doing in the country and so many people ending up in hospital on ventilators, and I would need to be placed in an induced coma for two to three days after the surgery in an intensive care unit (ICU).

Once again, I needed to face up to things, but because of COVID, I had to have more elective chemotherapy, which was designed to shrink the suspected cancer on my liver. I was given a date for the surgery to take place, and I was told that three surgeons would be needed to complete the operation. Can you imagine during COVID how difficult it would be to get three surgeons together to perform it. The procedure would also take around eight to ten hours to complete, and I would be in hospital for two to three weeks! The good news was that having the chemo meant the pieces identified on my liver were shrinking, but the side effects from the chemo were chronically bad. The whole of my face, ears, neck, head, top half of my chest and back were completely covered in what can only be described as boils and blisters - the worst acne you could imagine. Trying to cope with the isolation was difficult because of the state I was in. My son was doing a lot of his schooling over the internet, and I have to say, he seemed to thrive on it better than he did in a classroom full of children.

I must have looked really bad to him, but I always put on a happy face and a positive attitude in front of him. On my own, sometimes I would have a few drinks and just cry. It was the only way I could deal with everything, but I would always drive forward. I wasn't going to be beaten by this shit. Even though I felt sick a lot of the time, I tried to use a static exercise bike to help my mind wander elsewhere.

One of my friends gave me some good advice, and psychologically, it helped me by squeezing that cancer down into the tiniest box I could fit it in and locking it away in the back of my mind. The other thing that really helped and allowed me to deal with all the various things was writing about them on my Facebook page, informing people what was happening, and putting pictures up. It was part of my way of dealing with it, getting it out there so it wasn't swirling around my noggin. It helped me a lot to put it down on paper, so to speak, and a lot of people were sending me encouraging replies, and I thank everyone for that. God bless you. Those positive vibes gave me the energy to take things day by day, week by week, month by month, and year by year!

Time moved on, and in 2020 I was given a date for surgery. I had finished chemo, so my date was set for April. Then, around three days before the procedure, I received a call saying it had been cancelled. It looked like things were in such a dire way in the country, with so many people dying of COVID and people like me also dying, awaiting elective surgery for things like cancer because they could not have their planned procedures. I was sent back to the chemotherapy unit and put back on the poison, but I just kept driving forward in my mind and my life, supporting my son as best I could. The chemo medication was destroying the nerves in my fingers and feet to such an extent that I ended up in lots of pain, which was then diagnosed as peripheral neuropathy. The gel that surrounds the nerve endings had been destroyed, but at least I was still alive. The consultant said it was likely to be permanent, and it is, but I'm trying to live with it. They had to stop the chemo, but a few months later I received a call saying that COVID numbers were stabilising, so there may be a two-month window of opportunity for me to have my procedure between September and October. I was going to be sent to a private hospital, and the surgeons were going to take 40% of my liver, which meant the one smaller lobe section of the two in my body, the peritoneal lining, my appendix, and my gall bladder would also disappear, and maybe the spleen as well, for good measure. I kept the spleen.

I would also be having something called a hyperthermic intraperitoneal chemotherapy (HIPEC) procedure after the main surgery had taken place, where liquid chemotherapy is pumped through a pipe into the abdominal cavity and then another pipe sucks it all out. They temporarily sew up the wound they have opened from the chest down to the pelvis (yes, it's quite a big slice, gutted like a fish!) to conduct the operation. The idea is that it kills off any microscopic cancer cells that may be in that area. In the back of my mind, I thought about the last cancellation, but this time I was lucky; they managed to get all the different surgeons together.

The hardest part about going into hospital was not being able to have my son come in with me because of COVID. I was dreading one of the surgeons picking up COVID. I gave him the biggest hug, knowing that one risk of the surgery was death. I kissed him, told him, "I loved him," and then I watched him being driven away from the hospital entrance. I turned around with tears in my eyes, went inside the 'Star trek Shusaku' opening doors, up in the lift to the room allocated to me, got changed and went down to the operating room for my surgery. It took all day, and the next thing I knew, I was waking up in the middle of the night and couldn't move. I was paralysed, and a nurse was with me. It seems that I must have done well in my body's recovery from surgery because they had woken me up from the induced coma. It was a weird feeling as they were asking me if I could feel ice being rubbed on my body, which I couldn't, but when they got near my collarbone, I could feel the sensation of coldness against my skin. I was dead thirsty and at least I could sip water. What they had to do was slowly withdraw the medication they were giving me. I wasn't in any pain at all as the hours ticked slowly by, they just kept doing the ice test. By the middle of the next day, I started to get the feeling back in various parts of my body, and with that, I could start to move my limbs, but the whole experience I will remember for the rest of my life. Later that day, they said I could be moved back up to a private room. I was feeling good, so I said, "I won't be here for two to three weeks."

The next day I was up and about, and the only thing they wanted me to do before I could go home was pass some stools. It appears that I was the five-day king with all the different operations I had been through, so after five days, I was out again! Anyway, I would much rather be at home recuperating than stuck in a hospital. Consultants followed things up with telephone calls, but I felt really good, so it was back to my normal CT scans with contrast and blood tests every three months.

Everything was okay for around six months, and then the consultant said a nodule had appeared in my left lung, on a lower lobe. I was referred to a consultant in Stoke on Trent and I was required to undertake some breathing tests. They came back indicating that, for my age, I was in the top percentile of people who had very good lung capacity. I was booked in for something called a PET scan, which looked at the whole of my body, and the nodule had not grown, remaining the same size as before, so the consultant lung surgeon decided just to monitor what was going on. Things were fine for another six months, then in 2022, a follow up scan indicated that the nodule had started growing, so it was back off to see the consultant who said we needed to deal with it now and resection the lung.

Two weeks later, I travelled to Stoke on Trent for the surgery, but this time I was determined to get discharged from hospital in the shortest time possible. As with most surgical procedures, they go through the risks and problems that may occur, and they always have 'death' as one option. It's a psychological thing seeing that on any documentation and signing your approval for elective surgery. Anyway, within two weeks I was having a part of my lung removed, and as you can imagine after having a number of major operations, I now look like one of Frankenstein's offspring with the number of scars I have on my body. This time, there were three entry points to remove part of my lung. I'm starting to feel like a dot-to-dot puzzle.

After they had taken a small wedge section out of my lung, I was woken up to start my recuperation almost immediately. It felt uncomfortable trying to do regular coughing exercises. There was a fair bit of blood coming up, so it was important to get it all up from inside my lung, as it could be lumpy and may clot inside there, which could be a bad thing. I don't know what was happening with the drain that had been inserted in my chest cavity. My son was with me, but all of a sudden, I could almost see an exploding flash in front of my eyes, and then I couldn't breathe properly. I kind of gasped out that I was in a lot of pain and couldn't breathe, so people were calling for help. As it happened, a nurse and the consultant who had conducted the surgery were on the ward conducting their rounds and came immediately when they heard the commotion. They knew straight away that my lung had collapsed, and they knew the pain would be quite severe. I really don't know what the nurse was doing with the draining pipe, but I could feel it being manipulated around inside me, and the consultant said everything would be better in twenty to thirty minutes. As time went on, the pain started to drift away, and my breathing got easier as my lung started re-inflating. So I now know what a collapsed lung feels like as well! It didn't stop me from getting up, and I wasn't in any surgical pain; however, I couldn't pass any urine.

Anaesthesia can do funny things to the body. I was dying for a wee, but I couldn't actually pass any urine. I tend to drink a lot of water after surgery, and this had happened to me previously after having my liver resection. I knew I would need a catheter put in to open the bladder, but what I didn't expect was what was going to happen next. There were four nurses in the room. One was performing the procedure on me, whilst the other three were watching how it was done as an on the job learning session. After applying some numbing agent, the nurse must slide a tube through the end of the penis, and then it must be pushed all the way through to the bladder. I should have charged the other nurses for a cinema entry ticket to watch the spectacle unfolding in front of them! It was a little unnerving, but as they were sliding the tube through, my penis started to grow at a fast pace. Two of the nurses left the room, whilst the other one just looked on. The nurse conducting the procedure then started to inflate the small balloon in the bladder that allows the urine to empty into a bag, and there was nothing I could do but blurt out, "Well, at least it works!" They just laughed. A tube rubbing against a prostate gland can have a funny effect on a person!

The consultant came in to see me the next morning, and he said, "It appears you have an enlarged prostate," and we both just burst out laughing. It appears the nurses were having a joke about the episode of the catheter and the rising penis in the staff rest room. It was funny though. It reminded me of the old 'Carry on' movies from years ago. I asked the consultant if I could go home, and he said I had to pass stools again. Luckily, that happened the next day. I was working hard on the physiotherapy exercises to get rid of the blood in my left lung, and as far as they were concerned, I was doing well, so I was signed off, and the next day I returned home. It took me two days to get everything done and out of hospital. Not bad going, and I beat my five-day records, especially as they had said I would probably be in hospital for five to ten days. It turns out I was the perfect patient except for the lung collapsing and the you know what! The consultant phoned me up two weeks later at home and said I had done really well and that I was being discharged back to my oncologist. We are now in 2023. My last scan was in June, which showed that the lung was healing well and my breathing was back to normal. My oncologist said everything was looking good.

I am back in September this year for another scan, but as with everything else, I keep driving forward. If anything else crops up, I will just get on with it and live life. My son is a lot older now. When I went through the lung cancer, I told him everything in a straightforward way. He is old enough to understand what it is all about now, and anyway, he's my best mate.

In relation to the evidence I still have, I decided that because the prison service had ignored my whistleblowing, and subsequently, because of that, in my opinion, they are complicit in supporting corruption, I decided to take all the information to West Mercia police, so they could investigate the information I gave them and in the public interest, take any necessary action. I raised the fact that it was fraud and corruption to ensure it was investigated properly. I dropped off the first lot of information over at Shrewsbury police station.

A month passed by, and I heard nothing, so I asked them what was going on. It would appear the information had been lost. Great data protection advert for the police, that one! Luckily for them, I had kept other copies and personally took another set over. And this time I made sure I handed it over to someone and got a name!

After a few weeks, I was asked to attend the police station to provide a witness statement. I was then told that because the alleged offence had occurred in another police area, they had to send it down to Warwickshire for them to investigate my allegations. It took a while, but when it came back, the police service down there had messed the whole investigation up - the whole bloody investigation. I was none too pleased with the outcome. The information contained within it was wrong and even contained misinformation, so I sent a letter to the police indicating that a lot of the things they had put in were not factual and they needed to make sure the information was correct. I have previously investigated things in my prison service career, and it just appeared to me that they were not serious about investigating my concerns or really interested in getting to the bottom of the fraud and corruption that had taken place, so the public could see how high up in the prison, civil, and government service it went.

I received a letter back from someone fairly high up in the police saying they would not be doing anything more in relation to the investigation process, even though their officers had messed things up. It felt like they were just sticking two fingers up at me, the public, and justice. Maybe they are part of the same shadowy clique that operates in the higher echelons of the public sector. In my opinion, they were protecting those people who were corrupt. They did not want to open a can of worms for themselves and more importantly, bring everything out in the open so the taxpayer could see. So, again, in my opinion, there were serious issues that needed to be addressed and dealt with against senior managers in the prison, civil, and government services. It does feel like the whole system that is supposed to be there to help and support you is being abused by those higher up in top positions of power. The problem is when those people in positions of high authority are caught out, who run the system, and then use it to absolve themselves of all their responsibilities under it. They close ranks to thwart justice against those who operate within it for their own and their friends' nefarious gains!

Fraud and corruption are two related but distinct concepts that involve deceiving others or abusing power for personal gain. Fraud is any intentional act or omission designed to deceive others, resulting in the victim suffering a loss and/or the perpetrator achieving a gain. Corruption is the abuse of entrusted power for private gain, including bribery. Corruption can also involve favouritism, nepotism, and aiding suppliers to commit fraud.

They are dishonest activities that cause financial or reputational harm to individuals, organisations, or societies.

I now know that everything to do with politicians and the civil service needs to be double-checked. In my opinion, you can never take things at face value anymore. What a fucked-up CORRUPT system we have operating in our country - narcissists damaging our citizens by what they do in power, who should know better, but we know people like that are incapable of learning or changing. The Lord Nolan Principles (*Appendix D*) are a set of rules that civil servants should be working to. It makes me wonder who some of the real criminals really are out there. I will leave it to the reader to decide whether they think there is, in the public interest, a case to answer. What I do know is, remaining silent about corruption within the prison, civil, and government services, instead of tackling it, shines a bright light on those in positions of authority. It shows me that our country needs proper reform from the top down.

What really concerns me is the way that the prison and police services acted and the way the court process operated in the Ministry of Justice. It feels like the whole lot of them are afraid that uncovering problems like fraud and corruption in the senior ranks, with evidence to back that up, means they will openly have to deal with it. The question I ask myself is, "Why didn't they want to do that?" Because, in my opinion, me exposing what they did and them not wanting to tackle it under whistleblowing means they remain safe, so they can carry on with their corrupt nefarious practises and stay in lucrative positions, ripping off the taxpayers of our country, and keep getting promoted higher up in the civil service and government. If it all came out, then the whole rotten pack of cards would come crashing down. How do these people get so high up and into such powerful positions in the first place? It's not what you know; it's who you know, maybe? One thing's for sure: They look down on us all with contempt! Is it the same schools and universities they attend where those friendships last for life and the clique is born and nurtured in the civil service by family generations that follow each other into it?

Do you remember when I told you at the start of the book about me commencing duty at HMP Shrewsbury as a prison officer and noticing the board that had the names of prisoners hanged there? Eight prisoners were executed in total over the years, but a fair while after I had left the prison service, I was told the last person to die, and one of those hanged was a man called George Riley, age twenty-one. It turned out he was my father's brother, and the information had been kept from us. My father left my mother in 1962 when I was six months old, and as I grew up, nothing was ever mentioned about it. To say I was shocked when I was informed who it was is an understatement. My mother had informed my half-sister about it, but to this day, I don't know when they were told. They thought I knew all about it, but I didn't, and it really was a shock to the system, especially as I had commenced my prison service career there. My mother never said a word and never spoke about it to me, and I have never been back to HMP Shrewsbury since. I may have done if I had been given the deputy governor's job instead of becoming a deputy controller, and I may have possibly then thought about one of the names a bit more on the hanging board who had the same surname as me. HMP Shrewsbury has closed down now as an operational prison, but I do wonder whether the name board is still there! I know there has been a lot of speculation about whether George committed the offence or not, which would see him executed at 08.00hrs on 9th February 1961, just under 12 months before I was born. I recently visited The Dana to see if I could possibly have a book launch in the old place and they agreed to a date, 16th December 2023. I later decided to postpone the date to coincide with the anniversary of George's execution, to the 9th February 2024.

Executioner's Bedroom

The executioner would arrive at the prison the day before the execution was due to take place. On arrival they would use the prisoner's height, weight and build to calculate the length of the drop, prepare the rope and test the equipment using a weighted sack. The sack would be left to hang on the rope overnight to ensure the rope was stretched and it would be re-adjusted in the morning if necessary.

There were times when the executioner may have stayed in a hotel if the prison was within a town, but they would usually stay within the jail so that there would be no delay to proceedings.

On the day of the execution, the executioner and his assistant would enter the condemned persons cell at 8am, the assistant would secure the prisoner's arms behind their back using a leather strap and they would be walked to a marked spot on the drop (trapdoor). A white hood would be placed over the prisoner's head and a noose around his neck. The metal eye through which the rope was looped was placed under the left jawbone which, when the prisoner dropped, forced the head back and broke the spine. The executioner pushed a large lever, releasing the trapdoor. This would take a maximum of 12 seconds. Following the execution, executioners were also responsible for cutting the prisoner down, cleaning the body and covering them in a shroud ready for an autopsy.

There have been many executioners and assistant executioners over the years, the last serving executioner in Britain was Harry Allen but the most notable are probably the Pierrepoints. Henry, his brother Thomas and son Albert all became head executioners. It was the Pierrepoints who improved the accuracy of the execution method. By taking consideration the prisoner's height, weight and build into consideration they could ensure that the most appropriate length of rope was used to make the execution as accurate, efficient and humane as possible.

Albert Pierrepoint was well known for his professionalism and precision. It was found that the neck was broken in almost exactly the same position in each of his hangings. His fastest execution on record was 7 seconds, from getting the prisoner from his cell and through the drop. He later became a voice speaking out against capital punishment.

Condemned Man's Cell

This room was once the cell in which the condemned man would spend his final nights before his execution. From the Court, the prisoner would have been brought directly to this cell; he would have no contact with other prisoners.

The prisoner is unlikely to have realised that on the other side of the door is where his execution would take place. On the morning of the execution, officers would move a bookshelf revealing a secret door leading to the execution room itself.

In England, all standard executions would be carried out within 3 Sundays of their sentence, traditionally at 8:00am.

The cell would have been larger than an ordinary prison cell, typically the size of two or three cells combined. Some had minimal facilities but there were some prisons that made the cell more comfortable including features like a fireplace. The

Newgate Prison, Condemned Mans Cell, 1800s

condemned prisoner would have access to reading material, games such as chess board, dominoes or a pack of playing cards, writing materials in the cell and tobacco.

Two prison officers would be in the room with the prisoner at all times. This would prevent the condemned prisoner from committing suicide. It was thought that suicide prior to the execution would prevent the prisoner's sentence from being able to be carried out. These officers would also provide the condemned man with some company, they would look after the prisoner, playing games like chess with them to pass the time.

The prison chaplain would also visit the condemned prisoner prior to his execution.

In the past, prisoners had often been offered alcohol just before execution. This was partly a compassionate gesture, but also to calm an inmate's nerves in their final moments and make them more co-operative.

By the end of World War II improved transport facilities rendered it unnecessary for every county to have an execution facility. Just 17 prisons retained their execution facilities. Shrewsbury Prison was one of the 17.

The last condemned prisoner to be executed at this prison was George Riley in 1961.

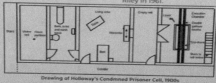

Drawing of Holloway's Condmned Prisoner Cell, 1900s

PUBLIC DOCUMENT ON SHREWSBURY BBC ARCHIVE.

Victim or villain? Did George Riley deserve to hang?

A crowd gathered outside the Dana prison as Riley died

In 1961 21-year-old George Riley was the last man to be hanged at the Dana prison in Shrewsbury.

The trainee butcher had been found guilty of the murder of a 62-year-old widow, who lived opposite his family.

He was executed, despite the efforts of his family and MPs to secure a reprieve.

Some people thought he was innocent of the crime and others did not believe he should have been executed even if he had been guilty of the killing.

The crime

Adeline Mary Smith was a 62-year-old widow who lived in Westlands Road in Shrewsbury, almost opposite the house where George Riley lived with his parents and two brothers, David and Terrance. The eldest brother Edward was away in the army.

On the night of Friday, 7 October 1960, George Riley and his friend set out for a night on the town and by closing time he had drunk 10 pints of beer. The pair went on to a dance at the local Rolls Royce canteen, where George Riley was involved in a scuffle with another man and the police were called.

By the time they called it a night, George Riley had drunk around nine whiskies on top of the beer. He later said he had never been so drunk in his life.

His friend dropped him off outside his home at 1.30am. Half an hour later, Mrs Smith's next door

George Riley was hanged at 8am on 9 February at Shrewsbury's Dana prison

neighbour heard a piercing scream, but it was not until 10am that her battered body was found on the floor of her bedroom.

The arrest

Gordon Riley (no relation) was a reporter for the Wolverhampton Express and Star based in Shrewsbury. He recalls the day of the murder clearly. "I'd been away with Shrewsbury Town Football Club covering their away game and I got back home to find my wife in great excitement.

"There had been many many calls telling her that I'd got to cover a murder story at Copthorne, where an elderly, frail lady had been battered to death in her bedroom."

Mr Riley said the address of the incident came as a surprise: "I had a strange experience, because I knew a young fellow that lived opposite where the lady was found dead in her bedroom and strangely enough, the next thing was he had been arrested. It was George Riley."

George Riley was taken to the police station at Shrewsbury where he was questioned by two officers, Detective Inspector William Brumpton and Detective Sergeant Phillips. By 6.55pm that same day he had written and signed a statement confessing to the murder.

The Express and Star report on Thursday, 9 January 1961

He had also admitted that his motive for breaking into the house was to obtain money. It later transpired nothing had been taken and Mrs Smith's purse containing less than four shillings (20p) was found untouched in her bedside drawer.

The evidence

During his trial before Mr Justice Barry at Stafford Assizes, George Riley withdrew his confession and pleaded not guilty.

However, he was convicted and sentenced to hang. Changes to the different categories of murder enshrined in the 1957 Homicide Act meant that because of the element of "murder committed in the

> **❝** On the basis of the evidence I have always felt and still feel that George wasn't the bloke who did the murder. **❞**
>
> Gordon Riley

course or furtherance of theft" capital punishment was inevitable.

Gordon Riley believes the outcome of the trial depended almost entirely on the confession: "It was without what would be called 'proper corroboration' these days."

Despite the fact that the young man had a criminal record Mr Riley believed he was innocent of murder: "On the basis of the evidence, I have always felt and I still feel that George wasn't the bloke who did the murder.

"You had to have seen the blood stains on the wall in the bedroom, virtually a silhouette of a figure, a human figure.

"No one who did the battering could have escaped without a bloodstain on their clothing and the only bloodstain they found on George's possessions was on his shaving towel where he'd cut himself."

No reprieve

George Riley's family also firmly believed in his innocence and Gordon Riley worked with them to try and obtain a reprieve: "George's father was a wonderful man. He was the cadet force instructor at Shrewsbury School. A very straight up and down, straight as a die man. A lovely man to talk to."

The MP for Nelson and Colne, Samuel Silverman who was opposed to the death penalty submitted a question in the House of Commons asking for an inquiry to see whether a miscarriage of justice had occurred, but it was ruled inadmissible on 7 February 1961.

George Riley was hanged at 8am on 9 February.

" I am satisfied there has been no miscarriage of justice and that there is no ground for an inquiry. "

RA (Rab) Butler

On 2 March Hansard records the reply of the home secretary to a request for an inquiry into George Riley's case.

RA (Rab) Butler replied: "Before reaching my decision I gave the fullest consideration to the representations made to me by the hon. Member and others, as well as to all the information available to me from many sources.

"I am satisfied that there has been no miscarriage of justice and that there is no ground for an inquiry."

Guilty as charged.

The case of George Riley was controversial and views on the rights and wrongs of his death were mixed.

One man who wrote at length about it in his book Reprieve (The study of a system) was the respected barrister, author and newspaper columnist, the late Fenton Bresler.

He visited George Riley's family and examined the evidence carefully, particularly the disputed confession and came to the conclusion that the young man was guilty of murdering Mrs Smith.

He defended the home secretary's refusal to grant a reprieve: "There were no extenuating circumstances. This was not a first conviction. It was a dastardly crime. What else could Mr Butler do?"

The execution

In his book Fenton Bresler described the final visit to the condemned man by his father and later, three brothers. His mother was too ill to go.

As he left, George's eldest brother, Edward, asked; "George, did you do it or

The Dana prison where George Riley was hanged.

not?" and the young man replied: "No I didn't."

That night, the prisoners staged what the Express and Star described as a "horrifying demonstration" against the execution. They whistled shouted and screeched and kept up a constant chanting of "Don't hang George. Let Riley go free."

Gordon Riley was one of the reporters standing outside the jail: "Just as the clock struck eight o'clock, two doves flew out from behind the bust of Howard, the prison reformer, which is over the main gate of the prison and the door opened."

The inquest

Mr Riley was elected as the journalist to attend the inquest after the execution: "I think there was an element of grief about it at that time. Having known the lad as he was growing up and knowing his parents... I'd just become the father of a daughter... I was shocked, frankly, shocked by the experience."

Journalist Gordon Riley reported the murder in the local paper

The jury declined to view the body of the deceased and the prison medical officer told the coroner, Major R W E Crawford Clarke, that death had been instantaneous.

He said he had mixed views about capital punishment: "I suppose I've got almost a biblical attitude, although I'm not religious. I'm a semi-detached Christian in many ways. I feel that probably the old world had the right idea and if you did something wrong you had to pay for it."

In the case of George Riley, he felt there had been a miscarriage of justice: "In a fair world, you have a fair trial and nowadays I think the trial system is fairer than I ever knew it in many years of sitting on hard benches."

I may never know the truth about whether my uncle George committed the crime he was found guilty of or not. However, he was found guilty by a jury of his peers. Capital punishment is no longer served by the death penalty, but I can't help thinking back and comparing it to the prisoner who was released after spending so long in prison. They were released from custody after spending so long incarcerated, as justice demanded, because they too were initially found guilty by a jury of their peers. If capital punishment was still around back then, well they would have possibly shared the same fate as my uncle George.

We see a lot of crime in the world these days, and in particular, terrorism, where people are willing to sacrifice their own lives as well as those of innocent people to further their cause. Maybe there is a case for a referendum for the death penalty to be reintroduced in our country for certain offences, as it appears that some in humanity have no respect or regard for democracy and the rule of law and order in our country. My biggest concern would be that we must make sure that we are one hundred percent sure that if it was reintroduced again, that the perpetrator is one hundred and twenty percent guilty of the offence before they are executed.

No doves flew out from behind the statue of Howard when I took this photograph.

My last thoughts of George today are, if you were guilty in the eyes of God of murder, then your place in hell is secured, if you were innocent, then you will be in God's safe keeping forever, and if you didn't kill the person, who did? His life was extinguished by Harry Allen, who was one of the government executioners of the day.

It seems to have taken me a long time to get my words down on paper, but when I actually see what I have been through, it's not surprising, and it seems to me rather ironic that it is sixty-two years to the day that George Riley was executed, and I will be sixty-two next February.

EPILOGUE

I still have contacts in the prison service. Maybe you won't be surprised to hear that I am not the only one who has examples that support what some others have experienced in the prison service, which link into the closed shop of the clique. They don't want bad press getting out from the prison service or the Ministry of Justice. When things do get out as far as the media, those at the top place gagging orders on them by way of a D-Notice, which effectively means the press cannot publish it!

In my opinion, the clique abuses their authority by controlling the narrative through corruption based on their own definition of a D-Notice or Defence and Security Media Advisory Notice (DSMA-Notice) rather than what they are supposed to measure it by. A British government instruction preventing particular information from being made public in order to protect the country. You decide whether a gagging order is appropriate for the following information that has been provided by people.

Some information has been provided to me, and I have no reason to doubt its authenticity. In the 1990's up until the early 2000's, a prison called HMP Stoke Heath was the setting for quite a few things that were allegedly going on. The prison was having money thrown at it as it was part of the youth justice board and young offenders' estate. I have been told that a number of different things were going on at the prison. One such thing was the trading of prison goods by the senior management team there. I was informed that perishable goods were being delivered to the establishment when they were needed, but a shop had been rented in a small town called Market Drayton. Cars were being driven into the establishment on nights when the prison was at its quietest, so they could be stocked up with goods, which were then driven to the shop to be sold off to the general public. I'm told the racket occurred over a ten-year period!

The same people were also buying in materials to build up flat pack horse stables, which were allegedly being sent out to the local prison doctor, who owned a field with their own animals. However, when the corruption came to light, these were eventually returned to the prison and are apparently now being used as storage containers at Stoke Heath. Along with the stables mentioned, lorry loads of straw were also being delivered to the establishment and then immediately sent out as well.

Most establishments have prison cars that staff use for official business, and it has been said that the most senior manager used the cars for their daughter's wedding as they were identical white ones. The prison also employed a tailor, and they were told to change some official prison barathea number ones, or dress jackets as they are known, which were repurposed so two OSGs could be chauffeurs for the day, so the senior manager could put on a good show for guests who attended the wedding.

The governors also purchased blazers that were not standard staff issue clothes and had the tailor attach a mixture of real gold and silver braided badges to them, and at considerable cost for the items. They were also purchasing expensive suits using prison funds and getting the tailor to alter them, so they fitted properly. If it's true, I'm sure the tailor would not have known what they should or should not do in relation to their work if governor grades told them to do it.

They mentioned that all five governor grades also used expenses to fly first class to America, stopping in New York using the Waldorf Astoria Hotel. The trip lasted for three weeks.

There was another story about connections to the Ministry of Defence (MOD) who were apparently selling off houses at a place called Tern Hill in Shropshire. One of the governors who knew someone there was offered an ex-officer's house at a highly reduced rate, well below its true market value compared to others that were purchased there at the time. The corruption was eventually uncovered, and apparently, the governing governor was asked to take early retirement! Work that one out. What do you think should have happened if it's true?

A more recent example is at a new prison called HMP Berwyn, which was built near Wrexham not long ago. I'm told that a very senior operational manager who was there had been using their prison expenses card to hire a hotel room to have carnal pleasures with a female prison officer, and apparently the officer was promoted in situ in the establishment. But rather than an investigation taking place for inappropriate use of an expense card, the prison service in headquarters decided no investigation should take place. The senior manager was apparently removed from the prison and sent down south somewhere on promotion to work. Does that sound familiar from some of the things I have raised in my memoir? Rewarding failure again with promotion reminds me of the Whitemoor days.

Another recent example is linked to HMP Drake Hall, where I used to work, and I'm told that recently, staff linked to some senior managers there may be getting promoted based on their relationships rather than on their ability. Corruption linked to that sort of thing means that impartial promotion boards need to take place, so everyone can see it is a transparent process.

I really don't know whether the information is true or not, but what I am trying to convey to the public is that things get covered up with prison service senior governors and civil servants. Corruption and covering up appear to be alive and well in the prison service, and it needs to be exposed for what it is. I would tell anyone who uncovers it not to be afraid of whistleblowing. I know I wasn't protected like the regulations promised I should have been, and I left the prison service because of the fallout from that, but if enough people who work in establishments, headquarters, area offices or shared services in Newport call it out, things can and will change.

I would encourage all those who know or suspect that things are wrong out there to contact me so things can be brought out into the open and those who abuse the system are dealt with appropriately and linked to some possible solutions I have highlighted next.

PRISON, PROBATION SERVICE AND DEPARTMENT OF WORK CONCLUSIONS & RECOMMENDATIONS.

1. A full review of sentencing guidelines for the Ministry of Justice, which reflect the problems our country now faces.

Prison sentences set by courts no longer reflect the expectations of our communities in terms of deterrence and punishment. A prison sentence needs to truly reflect the crime and support the victims far better than it does now.

2. Covering up of damaging news to the prison and probation service, which should warrant an investigation around sound policy and procedures, is being ignored. They are being covered up by inappropriate use of D-Notices. You decide yes or no

whether a gagging order is appropriate to the examples given in the epilogue.

I do wonder where the D-Notices fit in with the clique who abuse their authority, controlling the narrative through corruption based on their own definition of a D-Notice or Defence and Security Media Advisory Notice (DSMA-Notice) rather than what they are supposed to measure it by. Failure under a D-Notice breach should be carefully linked to whether it is indeed a breach based on the meaning set out by government or whether its system is being abused by civil servants to protect their own interests rather than those of the public, and by its proper use raise the level of transparency, integrity, and accountability within the civil service, media and the country!

3. Invest in new infrastructure to build four new establishments that can hold up to 5,000 prisoners.

If a drug offence warrants a twenty-year sentence, then that should be the starting point for any court, rather than going to prison for twenty years and being released in ten. Prisons are dangerous places. Security and safety must come first and then work towards rehabilitation. Those prisoners who wish to spend their whole time 'fighting' the system will be allocated to Cat B plus prisons. All those prisoners probably fall into the 20% of offenders who commit 80% of the crimes in our country. Invest in infrastructure to build 4 new 'Category B plus' prisons, each holding up to 5,000 prisoners, including foreign nationals, possibly in HS2 purchased plots in the countryside that are not going to be used and use telephone blocking systems so businesses cannot be run by prisoners from inside establishments and don't affect civilian usage in the community. (There could be a negotiation to house FNs in their own country or elsewhere, depending on cost.) I had suggested to a policy group I am in touch with doing this with Albania some time ago, and it looks like it is happening now in government, but it could be expanded at a cheaper cost than it is currently within UK prisons. We need to identify trends in drug mules coming to the UK and pay for better technology at foreign exit points to identify the problems before the mules leave their home countries and arrive here. Old inner city prisons could be repurposed and renovated for other use in the community.

4. The prison and possibly the probationary service currently operate a three-tiered management structure.

Abolish (second-tier) prison service area offices and all staff, cutting out the middle part of the prison management service, so headquarters has direct management over prisons in England and Wales. (I see an issue with this because this is where they move people who mess up instead of dismissing them, but the quality of the service needs to improve.) Review probationary services in line with the prison service in terms of management structure.

Move most of the prison and probationary service headquarters out of London to the Midlands. (Leave a small team to deal with ministers, permanent secretaries, etc.) Possibly move to Newbold Revel training centre for prison staff. There would be a cost to this, but there would be savings from the move of services, especially with staff London waiting allowances.

5. The prison and possibly the probation service operate

an in-house investigatory process controlled by its leadership to protect itself from scrutiny and poor performance generally.

An independent investigatory body should be set up to take over that process to break down barriers and target cliques that operate in all areas, particularly the higher echelons of the civil service. Link to the Independent Office for Police Conduct (IOPC). An audit of current hours used within such services would be extrapolated from their workforces to pay for the new group. This would not mean that the staff from those organisations would follow. (Natural wastage or current staff shortages pay for the new department.) A totally new group would be set up to take over and improve current systems and would be impartial to ensure transparency and accountability to the public and ministers, improving the corruption perception score of our country. This could be rolled out across all areas of the civil service and linked to the investigatory body for the prison and probation service, possibly linked to the IOPC.

Where complaints of corruption, fraud, incompetence, and bullying are raised in the workplace, proper use of procedural policy orders must be used to investigate the alleged complaint against the alleged perpetrator. Local managers cannot decide to overrule number 5.

6. Abuse of the annual appraisal system which can be manipulated for the benefit of its staff at all levels.

All appraisals will have the Lord Nolan principles set as the starting point of any discussion linked to targets and performance, which can also link into the investigatory process, which would ensure proper and transparent incremental scale increases based on sound judgement against targets, providing the public with assurances that the system is not being corrupted by staff at any level. Explore better use of AI technology to support prisons in annual appraisals to cut out fraud and corruption and link to other areas, i.e. expense claim forms.

7. No proper link between prison, probation service and the department of work that operates in a meaningful way to counteract British companies from using a criminal record to automatically disbar someone from the process of attending interviews, even if they have the skills and experience needed.

Employers will currently have people who do not admit they have committed an offence and are working in companies across the UK because they knew they would be excluded at the interview stage. Build solid foundations in the prison, probation and work services during and after release that allow those that have been found guilty of offences and incarcerated (first time offenders) the opportunity to apply for jobs, but depending on the type of work required, have a barring process depending on the offence that has been committed (link into disclosure and barring service DBS checks), which allows for better competition for employment and helps stop the revolving door process of people reoffending (serious recidivist offenders would have specialist intense community intervention to break the cycle of reoffending and it would link into the investigations process).

8. Some foreign nationals are committing offences when they are in the UK. There are approximately 11,000 offenders in gaols in England and Wales.

Foreign nationals will sign a contract on entry to the UK
that waives their rights to stay in the country if they break
certain laws or become recidivist offenders.

9. Employers use different methods to recruit
   employees.

Standardise an employer's human resource system of
recruitment in society in relation to ex-offenders who are
subject to first time imprisonment and rehabilitation.

10. Civil service policies and procedures need to reflect
    supporting the victim.

Where complaints of corruption, fraud, incompetence
and bullying are raised in the workplace, proper use of
procedural policy orders must be used to investigate the
alleged complaint against the alleged perpetrator. Local
managers cannot decide to overrule number 5.

11. Armed forces personnel need better support to move
    from a protected environment back into civilian life.
    Too many are homeless and incarcerated in our
    prisons.

A direct entry system from the armed forces into key work
areas in civilian life.

A recent justice led survey has shown that thousands of
prison officers 'want out'. It flags safety and pay concerns
as the key issues. The Justice Committee chair dubs large-
scale research findings 'shocking' as prison service battles
staff shortages. This is a problem of the clique's own
making by not risk assessing the impact of its decisions in
terms of safety and sustainability of its ideas against the

workforce, both in its real term skills and experience, to the point where the prison service is imploding and criminality is taking over. This, in my opinion, means prisons are even more dangerous places to operate in now than they ever were. Safety and security come first and are paramount to anything else that happens in a prison environment. If it is not in place, then everything else goes to rat shit whether they like it or not. The whole damn thing needs radical reform before it's too late. Everything needs re-evaluating so staff and prisoners in individual public and private sector establishments feel they can go about their business without being intimidated by the gangs that operate in different areas of HMP today and link into our local communities and further afield! A separate investigatory body with a term of reference for the prison and probation services is dovetailed with the Independent Office for Police Conduct IOPC.

Remember, Courage is a choice to do the right thing, even if we are afraid.

APPENDICES:

APPENDIX A:

20TH CENTURY HANGINGS AND THE PRISONS
THEY WERE CARRIED OUT IN

England & Wales		
Prison	**Total hanged**	**Last execution**
London - Newgate	9	06/05/02
London - Pentonville	105 (plus 7 PoW's 6 spies & 2 traitors)	06/07/61
London - Wandsworth	106 (plus 10 spies & 2 traitors)	08/09/61
London - Holloway	5 (female)	13/07/55
Manchester - (Strangeways)	71	13/08/64
Leeds - Armley	68	29/06/61
Durham	54	17/12/58
Liverpool - Walton	53	13/08/64
Birmingham - Winson Green	36	20/11/62
Bedford	7	04/04/62
Bodmin	2	20/07/09
Bristol	13	17/12/63

Cambridge	2	04/11/13
Cardiff	19	03/09/52
Caernarfon	1	15/02/10
Chelmsford	9	04/11/14
Derby	4	16/0707
Devizes	1	17/11/03
Dorchester	2	24/06/41
Exeter	11	06/04/43
Gloucester	7	07/06/39
Hereford	1	15/12/03
Hull	10	19/12/34
Ipswich	3	27/11/24
Knutsford	4	19/03/12
Lancaster	1	15/11/10
Leicester	8	17/11/53
Lewes	4	11/08/14
Lincoln	17	27/01/61
Maidstone	11	08/04/30
Newcastle	8	26/11/19
Northampton	3	10/11/14
Norwich	11	19/07/51
Nottingham	8	10/04/28
Oxford	8	12/08/52
Reading	3	04/02/13
Ruthin	1	17/02/03
Shepton Mallet	4 (plus 18 US military executions)	02/03/26 (Last civilian)

Shrewsbury	8	09/02/61
St. Albans	2	23/12/14
Stafford	8	10/03/14
Swansea	9	06/05/58
Usk	4	23/03/22
Wakefield	10	29/12/15
Warwick	4	15/12/08
Winchester	16	17/12/63
Worcester	4	03/12/19

Scotland

Prison	Total hanged	Last execution
Aberdeen (Craiginches)	1	15/08/1963
Edinburgh (Calton)	3	30/10/1923
Edinburgh (Saughton)	4	23/06/1954
Inverness	1	05/03/1908
Perth	3	02/10/1913
Glasgow (Duke Street)	11 men & 1 woman	03/08/1928
Glasgow (Barlinnie)	10	22/12/1960

Northern Ireland & Channel Islands

Prison	Total hanged	Last execution
Armagh	1	22/12/1904
Londonderry	3	08/02/1923
Belfast (Crumlin Road)	12	20/12/1961
Jersey - St. Hellier	2	09/10/1959

Appendix B:
Information on prisoner security categories

What are the male security categories?

There are four different types of male security categories. Each male prisoner will be allocated a category that represents the level of security required to keep that person/prisoner safe, secure their wellbeing, protect other prisoners and staff, and most importantly, protect the public. The following gives you an idea of where a prisoner fits into the prison system in England and Wales. Scotland and Northern Ireland have their own systems, but they will not be dissimilar.

Security categories for male prisoners:

Category A

This is given to male prisoners whose escape would be extremely dangerous to the general public, the police and national security. The aim of such a high level of security is to make escape from that prison impossible.

Category B

This is given to prisoners who do not require the highest level of security but need a high level to make any chance of escape from prison extremely difficult.

Category C

This is given to prisoners who cannot be trusted in open prison conditions, but will not necessarily have the intention, the will or the determination to make any real attempt of escape from a prison.

Category D

This is given to male prisoners who pose a low risk in

relation to security and protection of the public and who can be trusted in open prison conditions.

Male prisoners will be categorised accordingly to the likelihood of them trying to escape, planning an escape and actual attempts to escape and the risk the prisoner would pose to others if they were to be successful in an escape.

Initial Category A

Most prisoners who fall into this group will have been reported as potential Category A following reception to a remand prison and will have been held as provisional Category A leading up to their sentence. Category A prisoners are defined as "those whose escape would be highly dangerous to the public or national security." Category A prisoners are further separated into standard risk, high risk, and exceptional risk, depending on how likely they are to try to escape.

The offences that may result in consideration for Category A include:

- Murder.
- Attempted murder.
- Manslaughter.
- Wounding with intent.
- Rape.
- Indecent assault.
- Robbery or conspiracy to rob (with firearms).
- Firearms offences.
- Importing or supplying Class A controlled drug.

- Possessing or supplying explosives.
- Offences connected with terrorism.
- Offences under the Official Secrets Act.

Initial Category B

If any of the following apply to a male prisoner, they will be initially categorised as security Category B:

- Serving a current prison sentence of ten years or more.
- Serving an indeterminate sentence of at least five years or more.
- Any other indeterminate sentence.
- During a previous prison sentence, the male prisoner was considered as Category A.
- They have committed current or previous terrorist offences.
- While the prisoner was on remand, he was considered a potential or provisional Category A prisoner.
- He has served a previous sentence of ten years or more.
- The prisoner has previously escaped from a closed prison, police or escort.
- The prisoner is currently serving a sentence for an offence involving violence or a threat to life, threat of arson, firearms offences, robbery, drugs and sexual offences.

Initial Category C

A male prisoner will be given a security Category C if any of these following criteria apply:

- A previous sentence of twelve months or more for violence, threat of violence, arson, sex offences, drug dealing or importation.

- Serving a current sentence of twelve months or more for violence, threat of violence, arson, sex offences, drug dealing or importation.
- A history of absconding, failing to surrender or breaching a bail condition.
- The prisoner has an outstanding confiscation order or further charges.

Initial Category D

If none of the above conditions apply to the male prisoner, then they will be initially considered suitable for Category D open conditions.

All initial categories will be subject to further risk assessments. If during this assessment higher levels of security are indicated, then the prisoner's security category will change accordingly.

Category reviews

Where a prisoner is serving a determinate sentence, their first security category review must take place no later than twelve months after sentence was passed. The first review of a Category A prisoner will take place within two years of sentencing.

Category B and C prisoners, who are serving a sentence of more than twelve months, but less than four years, will be reviewed every six months.

Category B and C prisoners serving more than four years will be considered for a review once a year.

APPEALING A CATEGORY DECISION

If a prisoner is not happy with a decision on categorisation after a review, he can appeal that decision. There is no overall scheme for such an appeal, although prisons will have local procedures that support such an appeal. If there is no such procedure, then all appeals will be directed via the prison complaints system.

To help prisoners get the best result from any appeal, they should request full disclosure of all reasons for such a categorisation from the establishment. The prison has a duty of care to provide full reasons for any categorisation decision and the prisoner should receive this in writing.

Category A prisoners need to direct their appeal to the DHS (Directorate of High Security) for a response.

Since 2011, prisons must keep a record of the number of request and complaints relating to the decisions of categorisation, and all decisions from appeals must be carefully logged.

If following an appeal, a prisoner is still not satisfied with the results of the categorisation, they can further appeal to the Prisons and Probation Ombudsman.

It is possible to have a decision of an appeal judicially reviewed; however, this is not commonly used and would be considered a last resort through the legal process.

PRISON LAW: GENERAL

- Transferring prisons
  https://www.inbrief.co.uk/prison-law/transferring-prisons/
- Recall to prison
  https://www.inbrief.co.uk/prison-law/recall-to-prison/
- Prisoner release on license
  https://www.inbrief.co.uk/prison-law/release-on-license/

- Home detention curfews
  https://www.inbrief.co.uk/prison-law/home-detention-curfews/
- Prisoner property
  https://www.inbrief.co.uk/prison-law/prisoner-property/
- Lost property claims
  https://www.inbrief.co.uk/prison-law/lost-property-claims/
- Prisoner complaints
  https://www.inbrief.co.uk/prison-law/prisoner-complaints/
- Racism in prison
  https://www.inbrief.co.uk/prison-law/racism-in-prison/
- Prison visits
  https://www.inbrief.co.uk/prison-law/prison-visits/
- Categories of male prisoners
  https://www.inbrief.co.uk/prison-law/male-prisoner-categories/
- Categories of female prisoners
  https://www.inbrief.co.uk/prison-law/female-prisoner-categories/
- Charges against prisoners
  https://www.inbrief.co.uk/prison-law/charges-against-prisoners/

SECURITY CATEGORIES FOR FEMALE PRISONERS:

Female prisoners have four security categories, but they are not strictly the same as those used for male prisoners. Women may be held in one of four following security categories:

Category A

Prisoners whose escape would be highly dangerous to the public, police, or the security of the state and for whom escape is impossible.

Restricted Status

Any female, young person or young adult prisoner convicted, or on remand whose escape would present a serious risk to the public and who are required to be held in designated secure accommodation.

Closed Conditions

Prisoners for whom the very highest conditions of security are not necessary but who present too high a risk for open conditions or for whom open conditions are not appropriate.

Open conditions

Prisoners who present a low risk and can reasonably be trusted in open conditions and for those whom open conditions are more appropriate.

It is very rare for a female prisoner to meet the criteria for category A, and so the category in day-to-day use is normally the restricted category. The information provided for different security arrangements for male and female are for guidelines and should not be taken as gospel. Government websites will be able to help further if you are interested in learning more, but I have provided information as a background to the types of prisons I have worked at.

One other interesting point, sometimes in the prison system a gaol can function between categories, one prison I worked at was both a closed and semi-open establishment.

APPENDIX C:
SOME TYPES OF HOMEMADE WEAPONS YOU MAY FIND IN PRISONS

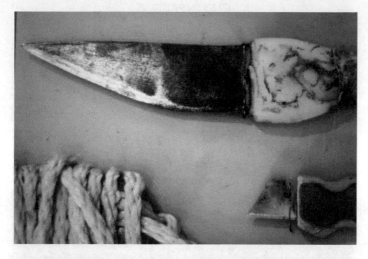

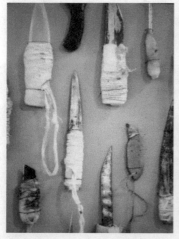
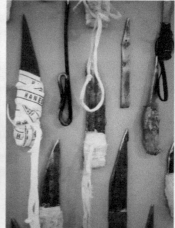

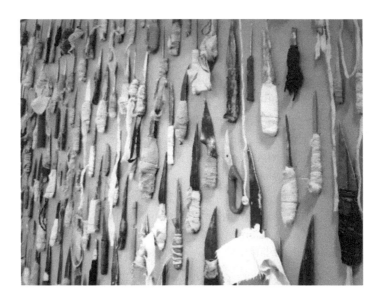

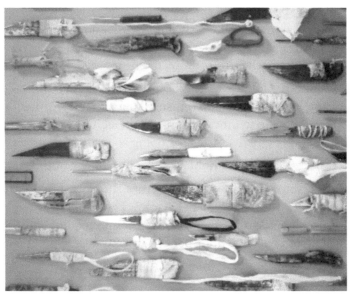

APPENDIX D:
LORD NOLAN SEVEN PRINCIPLES

Selflessness: Holders of public office should act solely in terms of the public interest.

Integrity: Holders of public office must avoid placing themselves under any obligation to people or organisations that might try inappropriately to influence them in their work.

They should not act or take decisions in order to gain financial or other material benefits for themselves, their family, or their friends. They must declare and resolve any interests and relationships.

Objectivity: Holders of public office must act and take decisions impartially, fairly and on merit, using the best evidence and without discrimination or bias.

Accountability: Holders of public office are accountable to the public for their decisions and actions and must submit themselves to scrutiny to ensure this.

Openness. Holders of public office should act and take decisions in an open and transparent manner. Information should not be withheld from the public unless there are clear and lawful decisions for doing so.

Honesty: Holders of public office should be truthful.

Leadership: Holders of public office should exhibit these principles in their own behaviour. They should actively promote and robustly support the principles and be willing to challenge poor behaviour wherever it occurs.

Appendix E:
The phonetic alphabet used on
the prison radio net

A = Alpha	N = November
B = Bravo	O = Oscar
C = Charlie	P = Papa
D = Delta	Q = Quebec
E = Echo	R = Romeo
F = Foxtrot	S = Sierra
G = Golf	T = Tango
H = Hotel	U = Uniform
I = India	V = Victor
J = Juliet	W = Whiskey
K = Kilo	X = Xray
L = Lima	Y = Yankee
M = Mike	Z = Zulu

Appendix F:
THE HONOURABLE MR JUSTICE X*
(PRESIDENT) Costs hearing

*Names have been replaced.

1. Employment Judge X, Mrs A and Mr B as a Tribunal of three decided at Stoke-on-Trent, for Reasons given on 30 May 2013, that the Claimant's claims that he had been victimised and unfairly dismissed should be rejected. On an earlier occasion Employment Judge Y, sitting alone, at a Preliminary Hearing had dismissed other claims that the Claimant had been discriminated against on the grounds of sex, age and disability. That was on 24 August 2012.

2. The Claimant had brought his claims against 11 Respondents. Following the Decision of the Tribunal the Respondent, which had succeeded on every issue, applied for costs. The decision in respect of costs was given in a Reserved Judgment on 24 February 2014 by Judge Y sitting alone.

3. Of the various grounds of appeal which were initially proposed by the Claimant, only two, both covering the same general territory, have survived to this Full Hearing of the Appeal Tribunal, all others having been rejected at the sift and Preliminary Hearing stages. Those two grounds relate to whether the Judge was entitled to hear the claim for costs sitting on his own as opposed to sitting together with Mrs A and Mr B, as he had when he determined the substantive claims.

4. The argument raised the two grounds contained in the amended grounds of appeal. The first was that the Tribunal which sat on 27 November 2013 and 8 January 2014 (that is, Judge Y sitting on his own) to determine the Respondent's costs application was not constituted in accordance within Schedule 1 of the Employment

Tribunals (Constitution and Rules of UKEAT/XXXX/ XX/DXA -2- Procedure) Regulations 2013, Rules 74 to 78 in that the Tribunal sat as Judge alone. The second ground was that: "The Employment Judge failed to seek the parties' representations before exercising any power or discretion it [sic] may have had to sit alone to determine the costs application."

5. It was suggested that no appellate authority could help determine this particular issue. Accordingly Mr Cs submissions on behalf of the Claimant relied upon general points to the effect that it was inappropriate to allow a Judge alone to make decisions on costs when he was being asked to determine issues of reasonableness in relation to the conduct at the hearing. Rule 76 of the Tribunal Rules prescribes the circumstances in which a costs order may be made. It reads: "(1) A Tribunal may make a costs order or a preparation time order, and shall consider whether to do so, where it considers that - (a) a party (or that party's representative) has acted vexatiously, abusively, disruptively or otherwise unreasonably in either the bringing of the proceedings (or part) or the way that the proceedings (or part) have been conducted; or (b) any claim or response had no reasonable prospect of success."

6. Mr Cs argument envisaged the difficulties which might arise if lay members of a Tribunal who had sat through a hearing in respect of it was later said that the conduct had fallen within the description in Rule 76 took a different view of that conduct from that taken by the Employment Judge. For the Judge to sit alone was to rule out relevant decision-makers who had participated in the decision thus far. If that were wrong, it would at least be appropriate for the Judge to be invited to consider whether he should sit alone or whether he would be assisted by the lay members.

7. The skeleton, which said little more than we have

quoted, was amplified in oral argument. The submissions ultimately made were that the Tribunal had no power within statute or rule to sit as a panel of one since the appropriate provisions required a panel of three. The UKEAT/XXXX/XX/DXA -3- argument to the contrary was advanced by Mr D, who had the advantage over Mr C of having been at the Tribunal itself. He sought to argue that there was an implied power which permitted a Judge in circumstances such as the present to sit alone when determining a costs application consequential upon a hearing. He argued this in two parts, first what he advertised as dealing with the case by way of analogy and, secondly, by reference to case-law.

8. As to analogy, he sought to argue that a Judge must, sensibly, have the power to sit alone to determine a costs application consequential on a concluded hearing. That is because there is no provision within the Rules relating to costs contained in the Employment Tribunal Rules 2013, which expressly gives a power to a Tribunal to sit as a panel of three, or for that matter a panel of one. But a very similar power is capable of being exercised by a Judge under Rule 37, from which Mr D sought to draw his analogy. Rule 37 relates to striking out. The material parts for the purposes of this argument are as follows: "(1) At any stage of the proceedings, either on its own initiative or on the application of a party, a Tribunal may strike out all or part of a claim or response on any of the following grounds - (a) that it is scandalous or vexatious or has no reasonable prospect of success; (b) that the manner in which the proceedings have been conducted by or on behalf of the claimant or the respondent (as the case may be) has been scandalous, unreasonable, or vexatious; (c) for non-compliance with any of these Rules or with an order of the Tribunal; (d) that it has not been actively pursued; (e) that the Tribunal considers that it is no longer

possible to have a fair hearing in respect of the claim or response (or the part to be struck out)." The argument has to acknowledge that (c), (d) and (e) have no reflection in the provisions in Rule 76, which we have quoted, but it emphasises that there is a great degree of overlap between 76(1)(a) and (b) and the reference to "scandalous", "vexatious" and "no reasonable prospect of success" in Rule 37. Even here, however, the correspondence is not exact, for in Rule 76 there is the addition of the words "abusively" and "disruptively".

9. If, Mr D argues, a Judge is capable at any stage of hearing a strike-out application, as he is within the Rules, then, taking the structure of the Rules as a whole, the effect is to imply a power which a Judge may exercise to sit in respect of an application made on similar grounds to those applying to a strike-out, albeit in respect of costs. There are good reasons why that power should be exercised. The overriding objective includes at Rule 2(d) "avoiding delay, so far as compatible with proper consideration of the issues" and (e) "saving expense". It is plainly a matter of convenience for the Tribunal and the parties if, when there has to be separate consideration of an application for costs and it does not immediately follow the hearing before the Tribunal, that should be conducted by the judicial member sitting on the Judge's own.

10. Prior to the hearing we invited the parties to have regard to three authorities which, despite the parties' best researches, had not come for their consideration. Two ploughed the same furrow: the decision of Peter Simper and Co Ltd v Cooke (No 1) [1984] ICR 6, a decision of this Tribunal presided over by Browne-Wilkinson J, and that of West LG AG London Branch v Mr Pan again a decision of this Tribunal, on this occasion HHJ Richardson, sitting alone, UKEAT/XXXX/XX (19 July

2011). In Pan the Employment Judge on her own ordered a fresh panel to be convened to continue the hearing of a case which had begun with her sitting with members. That was one of the grounds of challenge to her decision. As to that Judge Z said: "30. Secondly, she decided the application on her own without her members. In the circumstances of this case I see no justification for her doing so. I appreciate that some administrative inconvenience might have been involved; it might even have been necessary to hear the application on the first day of the resumed hearing, unsatisfactory though that might have been. She does not seem to have considered whether the members should have been involved. Although I appreciate that she was dealing urgently with an application which UKEAT/XXXX/XX/DXA -5- should have been made some time earlier, if at all, I think she ought to have involved the members. 31. Thirdly, her decision gives no real weight to the considerations set out in Ansar and in Peter Simper (No 1)…"

11. "Ansar" was a reference to Ansar v Lloyds TSB Bank [2006] ICR 1565 and "Peter Simper" to Peter Simper and Co Ltd v Cooke (No 1) [1984] ICR 6, to which we have already referred. As to that, Judge Z drew particular assistance from the words of Browne-Wilkinson J at page 10, between G and H: "… An industrial tribunal, at the hearing, essentially consists of three people, each with an equal voice. The chairman is, in no sense, in a dominant position. Accordingly, if an application is made to abort a hearing before a tribunal of three, in our judgment a decision whether or not to put an end to the existing hearing and to direct a rehearing is one which must essentially be taken by every member of the tribunal and not by one alone."

12. In that particular case the Appeal Tribunal had already

decided that the Judge did have a general power which could, in appropriate circumstances, have been exercised on his own to adjourn a hearing. It took the view, however, that the circumstances were such that they precluded the exercise of that jurisdiction, which had to be exercised judicially.

13. The third authority deals with a slightly different point. Whereas the decisions in Pan and in Peter Simper related to the exercise of the discretion to adjourn, the question in Birring v Rogers and Moore t/a Charity Link [2015] ICR 1001 related to the entitlement of an Employment Judge to decide to sit alone in circumstances in which statute required that, for one of the two claims which he was considering, one under the Trade Union (Labour Relations) Consolidation Act in respect of suffering a detriment for trade union activity, he could only sit as a member of a panel of three. This was combined with a claim of unfair dismissal which statute provided that he should hear alone unless he exercised his discretion not to do so. He had not considered exercising that discretion. UKEAT/XXXX/XX/DXA -6-.

14. In paragraph 18 is said: "18. … The statute provides for a discretion. The principles in Gladwell [that was a reference to Gladwell v Secretary of State for Trade and Industry [2007] ICR 264 (Elias J)] recognise that the discretion is not only to be exercised initially, though it may be negatively exercised, in effect, but also kept under review. I would add to Elias J's statement of law that the decision should be expressly and actively considered in any case in which there are combined jurisdictions, one of which requires a full Tribunal, one of which usually does not. Then the Judge will have to decide whether there should be a split hearing, one part of the claim to be heard by a full Tribunal, the other part or parts to be heard by a

Judge alone. This so obviously requires good reason for it (since it will interact with the obligations of the Tribunal to apply the overriding objective) that in my view it demands specific consideration. ..." (The Judgment then deals with the application of those principles to the particular circumstances of that case.)

15. Neither the decision of Peter Simper nor that of Pan nor that of Birring deals specifically with a decision on the question of costs. Each, however, deals with a situation in which the Tribunal Judge had a discretion which in each case it was held the Judge had failed to exercise but should have done. Discussion.

16. Although much of the argument before us was in general terms as to the desirability, on the one hand, of the Judge sitting with members, and on the other, sitting alone, in a statutory jurisdiction the first port of call to resolve an issue such as this must be statute. The statutory framework begins, relevantly, with section 4 of the Employment Tribunals Act 1996. That provides, by subsection (1), that "proceedings before an employment tribunal shall be heard by ..." It then provides, in effect, for an Employment Judge alone (4(1)(a)) and, at 4(1)(b): "... two other members, or (with the consent of the parties) one other member, selected as the other members (or member) in accordance with regulations so made."

17. There is a list in section 4(3) of those proceedings which are to be heard by a Judge alone unless a Judge should exercise his discretion otherwise. At section 4(6) the statute reads: UKEAT/XXXX/XX/DXA -7- "(6) Where (in accordance with the following provisions of this Part) the Secretary of State makes employment tribunal procedure regulations, the regulations may provide that any act which is required or authorised by the regulations to be done by an employment tribunal and is

of a description specified by the regulations for the purposes of this subsection may be done by the person mentioned in subsection (1)(a) alone or alone by any Employment Judge who, in accordance with regulations made under section 1(1), is a member of the tribunal. (6A) Subsection (6) in particular enables employment tribunal procedure regulations to provide that - ... (b) the carrying-out of pre-hearing reviews in accordance with regulations under subsection (1) of section 9 (including the exercise of powers in connection with such reviews in accordance with regulations under paragraph (b) of that subsection), or (c) the hearing and determination of a preliminary issue in accordance with regulations under section 9(4) ... may be done by the person mentioned in subsection 1(a) alone ..." In short, the Act specifically provides that, despite what is said as to the composition of a Tribunal at section 4(1) and (2), Regulations may empower an Employment Judge to sit alone at a Preliminary Hearing. It is open within the statute for such Regulations to make a provision for an Employment Judge to sit alone to make other decisions or determinations. The Rules of 2013 are scheduled to the Regulations to which we have already referred. We consider that the starting point is thus to recognise that, unless the Rules make provision for a Judge to sit alone to hear any particular category of matter, the Tribunal must sit as constituted in accordance with section 4(1), (2) and (3) of the 1996 Act. In the present circumstances, therefore, the starting point is that unless there is specific power to do otherwise a Tribunal must, in determining any matter which comes within the jurisdiction provided for by section 4(1), (2) and (3), sit as a panel of three. The approach of Mr D is, therefore, entirely right in seeking to see if the Rules make any provision expressly to confer the right to sit alone in respect of a costs application made after the determination of a substantive hearing. They do not. There is no such specific power in them. Mr D's argument would seek to imply one.

18. As to that, we note that within the Rules it is clear that the draftsman is careful to draw a distinction between the Tribunal, which is a description of course apt to include either a UKEAT/XXXX/XX/DXA -8- Tribunal, sitting as two or three members or a Tribunal constituted only by the Employment Judge, and the Employment Judge. For example, in that part of the Rules which immediately precedes the costs provisions there are four Rules which relate to the reconsideration of Judgments. They provide for the Tribunal to make a reconsideration (see Rules 70 and 73) but when dealing with the process (see Rule 72(1)) provide that an Employment Judge shall consider an application made under Rule 71 (that is, for reconsideration). The distinction is thus drawn between the Tribunal, however constituted, and the Employment Judge. The costs Rules run from Rule 74 to Rule 84. There is no comparable provision referring just to the Employment Judge. The expression always used is "Tribunal".

19. The analogy which Mr D seeks to draw, upon which he bases his argument for it to be implied that there is nonetheless the power for an Employment Judge to sit alone in circumstances such as the present, cannot, in our view, stand. There is an express provision under those parts of the Rules which relate to Preliminary Hearings (Rule 53 to Rule 56), which provides (53(1)) that a Preliminary Hearing is a hearing at which the Tribunal "may do one or more of the following" and amongst them is (c) "consider whether a claim or response, or any part, shall be struck out under rule 37". Rule 55, however, is expressly headed "Constitution of tribunal for preliminary

hearings". It provides: "Preliminary Hearings shall be conducted by an Employment Judge alone…"

20. There is then a possible exception to that, where an Employment Judge decides it will be desirable to do otherwise in the circumstances specified. There is no commensurate provision dealing with costs. We do not think that it can be sensibly argued as an analogy from a provision which requires, and has, a specific rule relating to constitution to the conclusion that there should be a similar rule implied but not expressed in respect of the costs provisions. UKEAT/XXXX/XX/DXA -9- Accordingly, as it seems to us, once it is established, as it was in this case, that the Tribunal would only properly be constituted as three without at least the consent of the parties otherwise, there would need to be a provision which permitted it to consist of one when making any relevant decision. There is no such provision which can be derived by analogy from other provisions. Nor does it come from within the Rules relating to costs.

21. Accordingly the statute and the Rules are to be construed as not permitting any power to the Tribunal to sit other than statute requires. Nor do we consider that the overriding objective has anything to add to this discussion despite Mr D's argument to the contrary. It is true that it talks about avoiding delay but the rule is to give effect to the overriding objective "in interpreting, or exercising any power given to it by, these Rules." Where there is no power there is no question of interpretation.

22. The argument was floated in the skeleton argument for the Respondent that the power to make a costs order was a case management order or closely analogous thereto. Though in Rule 62, headed "Reasons", there is a provision requiring a Tribunal to give reasons for its decision on any disputed issue, "whether substantive or

procedural (including any decision on an application for reconsideration or for orders for costs, preparation time or wasted costs)", we have had no developed argument that the part in parenthesis helps to define what is procedural. The description given to it by Mr C as an explanatory note is, we think, appropriate. It makes it clear to the parties that within the scope of "substantive or procedural" is to be included those matters which might have been thought to take place after a decision had been reached or, for that matter, ancillary to it.

But the matter, it seems to us, is put beyond doubt in any event because that which is a case management order is defined in Rule 1. Rule 1(3) provides, so far as material: UKEAT/XXXX/XX/DXA -10- "(3) An order or other decision of the Tribunal is either - (a) a "case management order", being an order or decision of any kind in relation to the conduct of proceedings, not including the determination of any issue which would be the subject of a judgment ..." A judgment is defined (Rule 1(3)(b)) as: "... a decision, made at any stage of the proceedings ... which finally determines - (i) a claim, or part of a claim, as regards liability, remedy or costs (including preparation time and wasted costs) ..." The one thing, therefore, which a decision on costs is not, is a case management order.

23. Part of Mr D's argument sought to draw comfort from the Presidential Guidance given by the President of Employment Tribunals (then His Honour Judge David Latham) on 13 March 2014. It is guidance on general case management. At paragraph 15 of that guidance the text reads, "These are examples of Case Management situations"; a number are given. Relevant to the present discussion are 15.4, disability; 15.5, remedy; 15.6, costs; and 15.7, timetabling. The gentle suggestion was made in

the Respondent's skeleton argument that, although this is guidance and therefore not itself statutory, it showed that it was recognised that a decision as to costs was on a par, at any rate, with case management decisions which one would expect generally to be taken by a Judge alone and which would not involve or necessarily involve the decision of a Tribunal as a whole. We think this is an unfortunate misreading of that which Judge Latham plainly meant to say. In describing a case management situation as "remedy" he could not sensibly be suggesting that a decision on remedy was a matter of case management. The words would have to be inserted, "making case management orders or giving directions as to the hearing in respect of" remedy. Exactly the same words it would be necessary to add in front of the word "costs" and for that matter probably the word "disability". Part of the confusion may be because they are followed by matters such as UKEAT/XXXX/XX/DXA -11-timetabling which, on any showing, is always likely to be a question of case management even though it may have serious implications for the cases of either party.

24. We do not therefore think that that, relating to case management proper (we may term it that), has anything to add to the discussion of the principles which must apply to the case before us. We acknowledge that, if at the Preliminary Hearing in the present case there had then been an application for costs, the Tribunal Judge would have been within his entitlement then and there to determine it. He would have been the Tribunal which is referred to in the costs Rules. He would have been the Tribunal because he was entitled to sit and exercise his jurisdiction in respect of the Preliminary Hearing by reason of the Rules we have already quoted.

If the application in the present case for costs had turned

entirely upon matters which related to that Preliminary Hearing, then we could see that there might be an argument that the Judge could, albeit after the hearing in respect of the substantive issues had been determined, have been considered to have jurisdiction to determine that application. It would then relate not to the substantive hearing which had occurred but rather to the matter of the Preliminary Hearing which he had determined himself, when alone constituting the Tribunal. However, whatever may be the position in respect of a case such as that, it is not the case before us. We have considered the basis for the application for costs here. It related in part to what had happened before the hearing was held before the panel constituted as three. But it also, and to a considerable extent, appears to us to relate to what happened in front of that panel.

25. Taking the view we do of the underlying law and the absence of any power in the Judge in such a case to sit on his own, we have concluded that the Judge should not have taken the decision on his own and the appeal must succeed. UKEAT/XXXX/XX/DXA -12- Discretion.

26. If we were wrong on that conclusion, then we would in any event have considered that the Judge here should have considered exercising his discretion. If we were wrong, he would have a discretion whether to sit on his own or with two others. Relevant to the exercise of that discretion would be whether, for instance, the claims for costs related to matters which all three members of the panel had witnessed and upon which each would have had their own individual views that may well have coincided. The authorities of Peter Simper v Cooke, Pan, and Birring here come into play. Where there is a discretion it is in general terms to be exercised as in the Peter Simper and Pan cases it was recognised the circumstances might

demand. Though the nature of the discretion is that a Judge might, rightly, decide to take either course open to him for good and proper reason, as best he considered met the fairness of the case, he must first consider whether to exercise that discretion. This is not one of those circumstances in which it can be said that he is entitled to assume from the silence of the parties that there is no challenge to what might seem to be an obvious course. The lay members sitting with me are keen to emphasise that this case is, if anything, the reverse. Lay litigants, having heard a case determined adversely to them by a panel of three, would be surprised to find that a subsequent claim against them was to be heard only by one of those three. This is capable in their view of giving rise to a real sense of injustice.

27. There is nothing, in short, in the circumstances which suggest that the Judge here could take it for granted that he should sit as one. For my part I would think that, if anything, the circumstances would suggest the opposite and at least that he should have made enquiry as to whether there was consent (if consent could give him the jurisdiction, which may be questionable) as to whether he should sit on his own. It should be added that there are three aspects to a decision in respect of costs. The first is whether or not the conduct of the party UKEAT/XXXX/XX/DXA -13- meets the standard set out in Rule 76(1).

The second is whether, assuming that standard to have been met, the Tribunal in any event would think it right that there should be an order for costs. The third relates to the amount in which the costs will be ordered. On the latter point, in the present case, the Judge considered at paragraphs 29 and 30 whether the evidence which he had in respect of means was such that the request for £20,000 of costs which he ordered to be paid was one which he should order in full. There is a sense that the Judge felt that he had insufficient evidence of the financial position of the Claimant. This in part may involve an assessment of the general reliability of that which the Claimant was saying and of its nature is an assessment which is often best made by the differing perspectives of those who constitute a panel of three.

28. Accordingly we have come to the conclusion that where, at any rate, a concluded decision as to liability is reached by a panel of three and thereafter a costs application is made which relates, in sufficient part at any rate, to the conduct of that hearing, there is no jurisdiction for that application to be considered other than by a panel of three, that being the panel so far as it may be assembled as heard the substantive question. And, if that were wrong, then in any event the Judge would, under the applicable statutory provisions, have a discretion which he should, in these circumstances, have exercised. There is no material to show that he turned his mind to it. The inference in the present circumstances is that he did not. Accordingly, on both grounds of appeal, though they are alternative, this appeal would succeed. Consequence

29. The parties are agreed that if we came to that conclusion, the matter should be remitted to the same Tribunal, constituted as three, for it to make a determination. We so order.

After the appeal hearing, I received a letter from the prison service via the treasury solicitors saying that they were no longer going to pursue costs.

GLOSSARY

Back door bandit: Male prisoner who sells their body to other prisoners so they can have anal sex with them.

Bacon: Paedophile.

Bagged and tagged: Evidence placed in a continuity evidence bag for the prison, police and courts.

Bang up: Used in a time of emergency or when prisoners are expected to be behind their cell doors in state A patrol. Normally used for shift change overs by staff to run an effective prison 24/7. There is normally a ten-minute call over a loud Tannoy system for normal lock up, so prisoners can get hot water and finish off their association.

Beasting: to give someone a hard time.

Beef: An argumentative problem that occurs between prisoners or with a member of staff.

Behind your door: Time to get locked in cell for some reason.

Blagger: Armed robber.

Block: Incarcerated in a segregation unit away from the main prison.

Blood clot: A derogatory term used against staff, meaning you are a mother's after birth because they threw the baby away.

Bubble, or centre: Wing staff office, which controls the operational core regime day for prisoners.

Burn: Any form of tobacco for normal smoking.

Canteen: A form which prisoners fill in to purchase items from a prison shop.

Care bear: Someone who wants to help rehabilitate prisoners.

Cat A swagger: A prisoner who thinks they are hard and walks in an unusual way.

Cell spin: Staff performing a cell search on a prisoner's accommodation.

Claret: Blood.

Cowboy: A new officer. Cowboy spelt backwards, is yobwoc, or a "young, obnoxious bastard we often con."

Crim: A person who has broken the law.

Daddy: A prisoner normally at the top of the pecking order, this could be a gangster, drug dealer, cleaner on a landing or wing, etc

Doing your bird (in a cage): Someone who is serving a sentence and is incarcerated in HM Prison for any length of time.

Doolally: Bonkers, or mad.

Grollies: Underwear.

Guv, Guvner or Boss: Used by prisoners to call operational staff who work in a prison, normally from officer, all the way up to the governing governor.

Grass, snitch, or rat: Someone passing information to staff or police.

Kit: Prisoners cell contents.

Lifer: A prisoner who has been given a life sentence by the courts.

Line: A long piece of string or thin strip of sheet to attach items to so they can be moved from one cell to another during lock up.

Nick: Prison or placing a prisoner on report.

Nonce: A prisoner who has committed a sexual or other crime in society which does not fit in with what prisoners accept as normal offending and is considered a low life and a target for mainstream prisoners to hurt.

Pad thief: Someone who goes into another prisoner's cell and steals belongings.

Patches: Normally a striped boiler suit worn by prisoners who are potential Category A, or one that has tried to escape from lawful custody.

Pit: Prisoners bed.

Plug: Secrete something inside one's bodily orifice.

Pot them: Urine and faeces mixed up to throw over somebody.

Porridge: Going to prison and serving a sentence.

Quack: Doctor/Dentist/Healthcare.

Savvy: A member of staff who has good communication skills and judgement.

Scran: Any sort of food cooked by the catering department.

Shank: Consisting of a handle with either a cutting tool or a sharp pointed piece of metal attached to it.

Shoot the bolt: Unlocking a prisoner's cell.

Skins: Tobacco paper.

Slop out: Getting rid of human waste after a night locked up in a prison with no cell sanitation.

Soft touch: Someone who gives in to prisoner demands.

SSU: Special Secure Unit.

Stiff: Someone who is dead or has died in prison.

Stripe: Using a bladed weapon normally used to slash someone's face or body.

Take out: Removal of a prisoner by staff.

Tooled up: A weapon that someone has on their person to inflict harm on someone else.

Apologies if I have forgotten any. I'm sure some of my ex-prison service colleagues will remind me!

GOVERNORS' ADJUDICATION

Prison Rule PR (adult) and young offender institution (YOI) report numbers, possible offences against establishment rules listed below. The rules would also apply to female prisoners.

PR 51 (1), YOI 55 (1) commits any assault.

PR 51 (1A), YOI 55 (2) commits any racially aggravated assault.

PR 51 (2), YOI R 55 (3) detains any person against his will.

PR 51 (3), YOI R 55 (4) denies access to any part of the prison / young offender institution to any officer or any person (other than a prisoner / inmate) who is at the prison / young offender institution for the purpose of working there.

PR 51 (4), YOI R 55 (5) fights with any person,

PR 51 (5), YOI R 55 (6) intentionally endangers the health or personal safety of others or, by his conduct, is reckless whether such health or personal safety is endangered.

PR 51 (6), YOI R 55 (7) intentionally obstructs an officer in the execution of his duty, or any person (other than a prisoner / inmate) who is at the prison / young offender institution for the purpose of working there, in the performance of his work.

PR 51 (7), YOI R 55 (8) escapes or absconds from prison / a young offender institution or from legal custody.

PR 51 (8), YOI R 55 (9) fails to comply with any condition upon which he is / was temporarily released under rule 9 / rule 5 of these rules.

PR 51 (9), YOI R 55 (10) is found with any substance in his urine which demonstrates that a controlled drug, pharmacy medication, prescription only medicine, psychoactive substance or specified substance has, whether in prison or while on temporary release under rule 9 / 5, been administered to him by himself or by another person (but subject to rules 52 / 56).

PR 51 (10), YOI R 55 (11) is intoxicated as a consequence of consuming any alcoholic beverage (but subject to rules 52A / 56A).

PR 51 (11), YOI R 55 (12) consumes any alcoholic beverage whether or not provided to him by another person (but subject to rules 52A / 56A

PR 51 (12) / YOI R (13) has in his possession (a) any unauthorised article; or (b) a greater quantity of any article than he is authorised to have.

PR 51 (13) / YOI R 55 (14) sells or delivers to any person any unauthorised article.

PR 51 (14) / YOI R 55 (15) sells or, without permission, delivers to any person any article which he is allowed to have only for his own use.

PR 51 (15) / YOI R 55 (16) takes improperly any article belonging to another person or to a prison / young offender institution.

PR 51 (16) / YOI R 55 (17) intentionally or recklessly sets fire to any part of a prison / young offender institution or any other property, whether or not his own.

PR 51 (17) / YOI R 55 (18) destroys or damages any part of a prison / young offender institution or any other property, other than his own.

PR 51 (17A) / YOI R 55 (19) causes racially aggravated damage to, or destruction of, any part of a prison / young offender institution or any other property, other than his own.

PR 51 (18) /YOI R 55 (20) absents himself from any place

(where) he is required to be or is present at any place where he is not authorised to be.

PR 51 (19) / YOI R 55 (21) is disrespectful to any officer, or any person (other than a prisoner / an inmate) who is at the prison / young offender institution for the purpose of working there, or any person visiting a prison / young offender institution.

PR 51 (20) / YOI R 55 (22) uses threatening, abusive or insulting words or behaviour.

PR 51 (20A) / YOI R 55 (23) uses threatening, abusive or insulting racist words or behaviour.

PR 51 (21) / YOI 55 (24) intentionally fails to work properly or, being required to work, refuses to do so.

PR 51 (22) / YOI R 55 (25) disobeys any lawful order.

PR 51 (23) / YOI R 55 (26) disobeys or fails to comply with any rule or regulation applying to him.

PR 51 (24) / YOI R 55 (27) receives any controlled drug, pharmacy medicine, prescription only medicine, psychoactive substance or specified substance or, without the consent of an officer, any other article, during the course of a visit (not being an interview such as is mentioned in PR 38 /YOI R 16).

PR 51 (24A) / YOI R 55 (28) displays, attaches or draws on any part of a prison / young offender institution, or on any other property, threatening, abusive or insulting racist words, drawings, symbols or other material.

PR 51 (25) / YOI R 55 (29) (a) attempts to commit, (b) incites another prisoner / inmate to commit, or (c) assists another prisoner / inmate to commit or to attempt to commit, any of the foregoing offences.

GOVERNORS' PUNISHMENT OR PUNISHMENT ANOTHER
QUALIFIED PERSON CAN AWARD

Caution PR 55 (1) (a) and (2) / YOI R 60 (1) (a) and (3) A caution will be appropriate when a warning to the prisoner seems sufficient to recognise the offence and discourage its repetition.

Forfeiture for a period not exceeding 42 / 21 days of any of the privileges under rules 8 / 6 – PR 55 (1)(b) / YOI R 60 (1)(b) This means loss of privileges granted under the local incentives scheme, (or the YJB's rewards and sanctions).

Exclusion from associated work for a period not exceeding 21 days PR 55 (1) (c) This punishment only applies to adults. It is different to forfeiture of the privilege of time out of cell for association under the previous rule.

Removal for a period not exceeding 21 days from any particular activity or activities of the young offender institution other than education, training courses, work and physical education in accordance with rules 37, 38, 39, 40 and 41 – YOI R 60 (1) (c) This punishment only applies to young offenders.

Extra work outside the normal working week for a period not exceeding 21 days and for not more than two hours on any day – YOI R 60 (1) (d) Another punishment only applicable to young offenders, which again explains itself.

Stoppage of, or deduction from earnings for a period not exceeding 84 / 42 days PR 55 (10 (d) / YOI R 60 (1) (e) The adjudicator will specify the percentage of earnings to be lost, up to 100% (less the cost of postage stamps and PIN phone credits.

Cellular confinement for a period not exceeding 21 days PR 55 (1) (e) and (3) In the case of an offence against discipline committed by an inmate who was aged 18 or over at the time of commission of the offence, other than an inmate who is serving the period of detention and training under a detention and training order pursuant to section 100 of the Powers of Criminal Courts (Sentencing) Act 2000, confinement to a cell or room for a period not exceeding ten days – YOI R 60 (1) (f) and (2) 2.14 The Prison Rule means an adult prisoner may be given cellular confinement for up to 21 days for a single offence or consecutive punishments adding up to 21 days for a number of offences arising from a single incident. The YO Rule means that if the inmate was 18 or above at the time of the offence and is not serving a DTO, a punishment of cellular confinement or confinement to a room for up to ten days for a single offence or consecutive punishments adding up to ten days for a few offences arising from a single incident may be given.

In the case of a prisoner otherwise entitled to them, forfeiture for any period of the right, under rule 43 (1), to have the articles there mentioned PR 55 (1) (g) This punishment only applies to unconvicted prisoners who, under PR 43 (1) may pay to be supplied with and keep in possession books, newspapers, writing materials, and other means of occupation other than any that the IMB or Governor object to. They may be punished by forfeiting these items for any period the adjudicator may decide.

Removal from his wing or living unit for a period of 28 / 21 days PR 55 (1) (h) / YOI R 60 (1) (g) Removal from wing or unit means that the prisoner or young offender (including people under 18) is relocated to other accommodation within the establishment (i.e., away from friends and familiar surroundings), but otherwise continues to participate, as far as possible, in normal regime activities in association with other prisoners or inmates.

Procedure for the recovery of monies for damage caused by prisoners to prisons and prison property General Principles. The main aim is to recover the cost for the destruction of or damage to a prison or prison property. It is not used as a punishment but as a way of compensating HMPPS for the loss. The intention is that the prisoner is required to "put right" the damage caused (such as replacement of the item or paying for the damage to be repaired) and there is no punitive element to the amount the prisoner is required to pay back. A requirement to pay compensation can be made for up to 100% of the damage caused, including labour costs (see paragraph 1.12 for further details) but the maximum cannot exceed the value of the damage caused or, in any event, exceed £2000.

Rule 45 Forty-five. — **(1)** Where it appears desirable, for the maintenance of good order or discipline or in his own interests, that a prisoner should not associate with other prisoners, either generally or for particular purposes, the governor may arrange for the prisoner's removal from association accordingly.

REFERENCES

Retrowow 2023, *How much did things cost in 1973?*, accessed 4 September 2023, https://www.retrowow.co.uk/social_history/70s/cost_1973.php#google_vignette

BV - #0021 - 290124 - C0 - 203/127/19 - PB - 9781914151828 - Gloss Lamination